Conun

Conundrums

A Critique of Contemporary Psychoanalysis

JON MILLS

Routledge
Taylor & Francis Group
New York   London

Routledge
Taylor & Francis Group
711 Third Avenue
New York, NY 10017

Routledge
Taylor & Francis Group
27 Church Road
Hove, East Sussex BN3 2FA

Printed in the United States of America on acid-free paper
Version Date: 20110627

International Standard Book Number: 978-0-415-89884-3 (Hardback) 978-0-415-89885-0 (Paperback)

Library of Congress Cataloging-in-Publication Data

Mills, Jon, 1964-
    Conundrums : a critique of contemporary psychoanalysis / Jon Mills.
        p. cm.
    Includes bibliographical references and index.
    ISBN 978-0-415-89884-3 (hbk. : alk. paper) -- ISBN 978-0-415-89885-0 (pbk. :
    alk. paper) -- ISBN 978-0-203-14819-8 (e-book)
    1. Psychoanalysis--United States. 2. Psychoanalysis. I. Title.

BF173.M5272 2012
150.19'5--dc23   2011025340

Visit the Taylor & Francis Web site at
http://www.taylorandfrancis.com

and the Routledge Web site at
http://www.routledgementalhealth.com

In memory of Merton Gill

Contents

Preface

This is a controversial book because it attempts to highlight the merits and shortcomings of contemporary psychoanalytic theory and practice. For this reason alone, those overly identified with contemporary paradigms will likely find it an unwelcome trespass. It is controversial in the nonordinary sense in that it critiques contemporary models from "the inside out," so to speak, not from "the outside in." What I mean by this is that I am not a typical critic of psychoanalysis, that is, one who is usually an outsider from another field or discipline often trained in different theoretic traditions, methodologies, and modes of discourse who then attempts to question, dissemble, abnegate, or deconstruct psychoanalysis from the bleachers, as if it were a spectator's sport. Rather, I am a practicing psychoanalyst who is also an academically trained philosopher. More specifically, I am an analyst identified with many contemporary points of view in how I practice therapeutically, the technical principles of which are also the subject matter of my critique.

Unlike Frederick Crews, the Berkeley English professor and popular Freud basher who purportedly had a so-called lousy analysis and took his revenge on the field, or Adolf Grünbaum, the philosopher of science and positivist who was presumably never analyzed, I am sympathetic to the profession yet believe it continues to foster a guild mentality based on reinforcing a climate of unquestionable dogma. As a result, what becomes most dangerous to psychoanalysis is that it remains insular from self-critique. A profession that historically preaches to an unreflective choir is not advancing its value. For this reason, I feel compelled to offer my reflections on a discipline rife with controversy, yet one that is so promising if a certain consilient attitude is adopted by the psychoanalytic community as a whole. Whether this is realizable, I cannot say.

This is the first book of its kind that offers a sustained critique of the current domain of psychoanalytic thought favoring relational, postmodern, and intersubjective perspectives, which have gained prominence in North America over the past three decades. In fact, the appeal of the relational turn in psychoanalysis has steadily spread in attractiveness and popularity throughout the world. But with the proliferation of this new movement, psychoanalysis today has largely devolved into a psychology of consciousness: post- and neo-Freudians form a marginalized community within North America in comparison to contemporary relational and intersubjective theorists, who emphasize the phenomenology of lived conscious experience, dyadic attachments, affective attunement, social construction, and mutual recognition over the role of insight and interpretation. Despite the rich historical terrain of theoretical variation and advance, many contemporary approaches have displaced the primacy of the unconscious. Notwithstanding the theoretical hair-splitting that historically occurs across the psychoanalytic domain, we are beginning to see with increasing force and clarity what Mitchell and Aron (1999) referred to as the emergence of a new tradition, namely, relational psychoanalysis. Having its edifice in early object relations theory, the British middle school, American interpersonal traditions, and self psychology, relationality is billed as "a distinctly new tradition" (Mitchell & Aron, 1999, p. x). What is being labeled as the

American middle group of psychoanalysis (Spezzano, 1997), relational and intersubjective systems theories have taken center stage. It may be argued, however, that contemporary relational, postmodern, and intersubjective perspectives have failed to be properly critiqued from within their own school of discourse.

The scope of this book is largely preoccupied with tracing the (a) philosophical underpinnings of contemporary theory, (b) its theoretical relation to traditional psychoanalytic thought, (c) clinical implications for therapeutic practice, (d) political and ethical ramifications of contemporary praxis, and (e) its intersection with points of consilience that emerge from these traditions. Central arguments and criticisms advanced throughout this project focus on operationally defining the key tenets of contemporary perspectives, the seduction and ambiguity of postmodernism, the question of selfhood and agency, illegitimate attacks on classical psychoanalysis, the role of therapeutic excess, contemporary psychoanalytic politics, and the question of consilience between psychoanalysis as a science and psychoanalysis as a part of the humanities.

My critique is an attempt to give some form, coherency, and voice to a plurality of ideas and approaches that have been identified in some fashion with contemporary thought, especially the relational turn. Of course, any broad critique is bound to have partial success at best, because everyone's contributions to that literature base cannot be sufficiently addressed in the scope of this circumscribed project. Supporters of the relational movement may charge me with being unfairly harsh in denuding the weak points in contemporary theory and in exposing various conundrums; however, such an analysis becomes a necessary undertaking if psychoanalysis is to continue to advance in theoretical vigor and sophistication.

Some readers may also object to my attempt to find a unifying strand in the relational tradition because contemporary perspectives vary widely in scope and emphasis and come out of many different schools and historical backdrops. As Philip Bromberg

(2009) rightfully noted, despite the fact that human development, pathology, and therapeutic growth are relationally configured, it does not mean that the relational viewpoint adheres to "one given set of ideas" (p. 348). Of course, it does not. Although it is possible I may be accused of conflating or lumping many different writers into one category we call *relational*, from my point of view, anyone who privileges the notions of the interpersonal, intersubjective, dialogical exchange, coparticipant interaction, or dyadic dynamics within a field-systems approach is referring to the primacy of relational principles despite the existence of theoretical divergences and secularity that characterize contemporary points of view. Although it is important to observe such distinctions and specificity of differences, if the main premise of the "new-view" theorists is that relationships are at the heart of the human psyche and forge the ontogenesis of personality, psychopathology, and the analytic encounter, then it would not be entirely remiss to refer broadly to these contemporary perspectives as relational. This is especially relevant when contemporary thought reexcavates and coalesces within old paradigms such as attachment theory, which has formed the empirical basis of infant observation research today, and a variety of early object relations venues (many elements of which are collectively represented by the middle school)—from Ferenczi's exploration of offering affectionate technique and mutual analysis to Winnicott's holding environment, which prefigures technical advances in contemporary clinical theory and praxis. However, the critical question becomes, What differentiates new thinking from old paradigms? Is there a common trend in contemporary thought that favors philosophical undercurrents to theory, interpersonal approaches to practice, and professional worldviews that challenge the scientific *Weltanschauung*? A brief perusal through the leading contemporary psychoanalytic journals suggests there is.

Edgar Levenson (2010) highlighted our current "climate of ecumenism" (p. 8) despite the trenchant orthodoxies that saturate the political landscape of psychoanalytic plurality today (Cooper,

2008). Nersessian (2010) believed that psychoanalysis has become a cacophony of disjointed opinions, where there are opposing positions on how we construct and understand psychoanalytic theory, clinical process, and therapeutic action. Perhaps, less contentiously, it is more of a matter of emphasis. It may be more accurate to say that contemporary psychoanalysis is mainly a response to—if not a revolt against—constricting prescriptive technique foisted upon us by previous generations. Although there are discrepancies between clinical theory and the process of therapeutic action between past and current analytic models, each successive historical paradigm within psychoanalysis has had to confront the problems of extension and synthesis. It still remains irresolute.

Today, classical and contemporary perspectives appear to be mired in dichotomization, where there exists "a passionate disagreement between participants who talk past each other for a number of reasons that can be enumerated more readily than they can be resolved" (Friedman, 2010, p. 142). I believe that this is due, in part, to inevitability. Contemporary analysts are reacting to the paternal indoctrination of classical training and what it *symbolizes*. This is an important point to emphasize, because what is symbolically experienced is what propels us to think and act. In turn, the contemporary analyst symbolizes the freedom fighter against officious ideology inculcated by authoritarian psychoanalytic culture. In this way, the contemporary psychoanalytic scene may be analogous to an organized microrevolution over an oppressive paternity promulgating submission and lack of independent thought. We should not relegate this tendency to oedipal acting out. It is not. Contemporary movements are naturally in response to the need for technical and political reform in the service of developing a robust, critical value system discontent with its inherited intellectual bondage. The relational movement in particular is inevitable, for who wants a cold, stern judgmental object, when one can have a warm, nurturing permissive subject? Although the reader may be tempted to reduce this analogy to an oedipal struggle, I wish to stay focused on the question of natural rebellion, theoretical evolution, technical improvement, and the therapeutic pursuit of gratifying developmental needs for human relatedness, which I believe have been a large part of the success contemporary analysts have enjoyed over their classical counterparts. They certainly have an appeal to the current marketplace. People no longer want to be simply analyzed; they want to feel the presence of a human being who feels along with them in their existential journeys and provides them with emotional ingredients that are far more important than mere interpretations or insight.

Throughout this project I refer to the term *contemporary psychoanalysis* as largely encompassing relational, intersubjective, and postmodern discourse that largely define American psychoanalysis today. The term *contemporary* is also frequently adopted and used to denote "new" psychoanalytic training institutes largely started by psychoanalytic psychologists within many major cities in North America (e.g., from Los Angles to Toronto), which stand in relation to the "old guard" these training centers wish to distinguish themselves from. Although there are concomitant movements within the current psychoanalytic landscape, including empirical studies in infant attachment, cognitive neuroscience, traumatology, affect theory, defense mechanisms, psychopathology, and psychotherapy process research, I will largely stay focused on a critical analysis of the philosophical tenets that underlie the relational tradition, broadly conceived. Readers who expect a survey of contemporaneous movements in post-Freudian and Kleinian thought, object relations theory, Lacanian studies, modern Spotnitzian circles, self psychology, empirical psychoanalytic psychology, and neuropsychoanalysis will be disappointed. This is not the intention of this book.

One self-identified criticism of this project lies in the periodic nature of my ambivalence and obfuscation, at times quite intentional, which I also feel compelled to impose on the reader. In a Derridean fashion, there is at certain times a preferred style of juxtaposing binary oppositions, then undermining each side by negating its own position, thus leaving an aura of undecidability. This may confuse or frustrate some readers because it appears that in certain places I do not take a stand, or when I do, it may then appear that I set out to undo my previous commitments. Some critics may even say that this is particularly evident when I meander through arguments for and against psychoanalysis as a science *and* hermeneutics, thus potentially destabilizing the strengths and weaknesses of both discourses, when in the end I may be viewed to champion a union or consilience between each respective discipline despite having favored particular hermeneutic critiques all along, which is what the book's central methodology employs—an appeal to interpretation through a phenomeno(logical) deconstruction of the text. Such oscillation may build a dialectical tension for the reader, but it leaves the subject pondering the paradox of ambiguity. Here I can harbor no regrets for seeking a seamless synthesis despite the fact that none is to be found.

Although I do try to avoid polemics, this project is bound to be interpreted as polemical simply because it involves critique. Analysts often have little patience for criticism, especially when one's theoretical orientation or clinical philosophy is intimately tied with one's professional and/or personal self-identity. But what sets this critique apart from others before me is that it offers a sustained series of arguments that attempt to systematically evaluate the *philosophical premises* that justify contemporary analytic theory and clinical practice. Like others before me, at times I can't help but analyze the analysts and their (unconscious) motives. Anyone interested in psychoanalytic gossip will surely perk up with enthusiasm *or* contempt when I take the liberty of examining indiscretions in what might not be inappropriately called a nihilistic hermeneutic critique, but one that, I believe for the most part, is even-handed. I will consider myself successful if the reader concludes that I at least attempt to remain neutral when assessing the merits and limitations of each position without showing dogmatic loyalties or partisanship.

I offer no apologies or caveats for this critique other than I wish no one ill will or malice. I am interested in advancing psychoanalysis as an intellectual discipline, and to do so we must be willing to subject ourselves to disciplined criticism. In my attempt to provide a duality or double reading of each problematic I identify, I hope to convey a commitment to the pursuit of reflexive truth with multiple shades of meaning. The fate of advancing psychoanalysis rests on our ability to embrace critique rather than repudiate it.

About the Author

Jon Mills, Psy.D., Ph.D., ABPP is a philosopher, psychologist, and psychoanalyst in private practice and runs a mental health corporation in Ontario, Canada. He is a Diplomate in Psychoanalysis and Clinical Psychology with the American Board of Professional Psychology, Fellow of the American Academy of Clinical Psychology, Fellow of the Academy of Psychoanalysis, and is Past-President and Fellow of the Section on Psychoanalytic and Psychodynamic Psychology of the Canadian Psychological Association. He received his Ph.D. in philosophy from Vanderbilt University, his Psy.D. in clinical psychology from the Illinois School of Professional Psychology, Chicago, and was a Fulbright scholar at the University of Toronto and York University. He is Professor of Psychology & Psychoanalysis at the Adler Graduate Professional School in Toronto, is editor of two book series in the philosophy of psychoanalysis, and is on the editorial board of *Psychoanalytic Psychology*. He is the author of many works in psychoanalysis and philosophy, including eleven books, among which are *Origins: On the Genesis of Psychic Reality*; *Treating Attachment Pathology*; *The Unconscious Abyss: Hegel's Anticipation of Psychoanalysis*;

and an existential novel, *When God Wept*. He received a Gradiva Award in 2006 for his scholarship, and again in 2011 for *Origins*, presented by the National Association for the Advancement of Psychoanalysis in New York City.

1

Philosophical Presuppositions of Relational Psychoanalysis

Relational psychoanalysis is an American phenomenon, with a politically powerful and advantageous group of members advocating for conceptual and technical reform. Relational trends are not so prevalent in other parts of the world, where one can readily observe the strong presence of Freud throughout Europe and abroad, Klein in England and South America, Lacan in France and Argentina, Jung in Switzerland, the Independents in Britain, Kohut in the midwestern United States, and the Interpersonalists in the East, among others. Despite such secularity and pluralism, relational thinking is slowly gaining mainstream ascendency. Perhaps this is due in part to the following factors: (a) In the United States there is an increasing volume of psychoanalytically trained psychologists who graduate from and teach at many progressive contemporary training institutes and postdoctoral programs, thus exerting a powerful conceptual influence on the next generation of analysts who are psychologically rather than medically trained;* (b) there has been a magnitude of books that have embraced the relational turn and are financially supported

---

* Note that most identified relational analysts are psychologists, as are the founding professionals associated with initiating the relational movement, including Mitchell, Greenberg, Stolorow, Aron, Davies, Hoffman, and Stern, just to name a few.

by independent publishing houses that lie beyond the confines of academe, thus wielding strong political identifications; (c) there has been a proliferation of articles and periodicals that have emerged from the relational tradition and hence favor relational concepts in theory and practice; and (d) several identified relational analysts or those friendly to relational concepts are on the editorial boards of practically every respectable peer-refereed psychoanalytic journal in the world, thus ensuring a presence and a voice. Politics aside, it becomes easy to appreciate the force, value, and loci of the relational turn:

1. Relational psychoanalysis has opened a permissible space for comparative psychoanalysis by challenging fortified traditions ossified in dogma, such as orthodox conceptions of the classical frame, neutrality, abstinence, resistance, transference, and the admonition against analyst self-disclosure.

2. Relational perspectives have had a profound impact on the way we have come to conceptualize the therapeutic encounter and specifically the role of the analyst in technique and practice. The relational turn has forged a clearing for honest discourse on what we actually do, think, and feel in our analytic work, thus breaking the silence and secrecy of what actually transpires in the consulting room. Relational approaches advocate for a more natural, humane, and genuine manner of how the analyst engages the patient rather than cultivate a distant intellectual attitude or clinical methodology whereby the analyst is sometimes reputed to appear as a cold, staid, antiseptic, or emotionless machine. Relational analysts are more revelatory, interactive, and inclined to disclose accounts of their own experience in professional space (e.g., in session, publications, and conference presentations); enlist and solicit perceptions from the patient about their own subjective comportment; and generally acknowledge how

a patient's responsiveness and demeanor is triggered by the purported attitudes, sensibility, and behavior of the analyst. The direct and candid reflections on counter-transference reactions, therapeutic impasse, the role of affect, intimacy, and the patient's experience of the analyst are revolutionary ideas that have redirected the compass of therapeutic progress away from the uniform goals of interpretation and insight to a proper holistic focus on psychoanalysis as process.

3. The relational turn has displaced traditional epistemological views of the analyst's authority and unadulterated access to knowledge, as well as the objectivist principles they rest upon. By closely examining the dialogic interactions and meaning constructions that emerge within the consulting room, relational psychoanalysis has largely embraced the hermeneutic postmodern tradition of questioning the validity of absolute truth claims to knowledge, objective certainty, and positivist science. Meaning, insight, and conventions of interpretation are largely seen as materializing from within the unique contexts and contingencies of interpersonal participation in social events, dialogical discourse, dialectical interaction, mutual negotiation, dyadic creativity, and reciprocally generated co-constructions anchored in an intersubjective process. This redirective shift from uncritically accepting metaphysical realism and independent, objective truth claims to reclaiming the centrality of subjectivity within the parameters of relational exchange has allowed for a reconceptualization of psychoanalytic doctrine and the therapeutic encounter.

No small feat indeed. But with so many relational publications that largely dominate the American psychoanalytic scene, we have yet to see relational psychoanalysis undergo a proper conceptual critique from within its own frame of reference. With the exception of Jay Greenberg (2001), who has turned a critical eye toward some of the technical practices conducted within the relational community today, most of the criticism comes from those outside the relational movement (see Eagle, 2003; Eagle, Wolitzky, & Wakefield, 2001; Frank, 1998a, 1998b; Josephs, 2001; Lothane, 2003; Masling, 2003; Silverman, 2000). For any discipline to prosper and advance, it becomes important for it to evaluate its theoretical and methodological propositions from within its own evolving framework rather than insulate itself from criticism because of threat or cherished group loyalties. It is in the spirit of advance that I offer this critique as a psychoanalyst and academically trained philosopher who works clinically as a relational analyst.

Because the relational movement has become such a progressive and indispensable presence within the history of the psychoanalytic terrain, it deserves our serious attention, along with a rigorous evaluation of the philosophical foundations on which it stands. I do not want to polemically abrogate or undermine the value of relationality in theory and practice but want only to draw increasing concern to specific theoretical conundrums that may be ameliorated without abandoning the spirit of critical, constructive dialogue necessary for psychoanalysis to continue to thrive and sophisticate its conceptual practices. Admittedly, I may ruffle some feathers of those overly identified with the relational movement. But it is my hope that through such crucial dialogue, psychoanalysis can avail itself to further understanding.

KEY TENETS OF THE RELATIONAL MODEL

I should warn the reader up front that I am not attempting to critique every theorist who is identified with the relational turn or contemporary perspectives in general, which is neither desirable nor practical for our purposes, a subject matter that could easily fill entire volumes. Instead, I hope to approximate many key tenets of relational thinking that could be reasonably said to represent many analysts' views on what relationality represents to the field. To prepare our discussion, we need to form a working definition of precisely what constitutes the relational platform. This potentially becomes problematic given that each analyst identified with this movement privileges certain conceptual and technical assumptions over those of others, a phenomenon all analysts are not likely to dispute. However, despite specific contentions or divergences, relational analysts maintain a shared overarching emphasis on the centrality of relatedness. This shared emphasis on therapeutic relatedness has become the centerpiece of contemporary psychoanalysis to the point that some relationalists boast to have achieved a "paradigm shift" in the field.* On the face of things, this claim may sound palpably odd to some analysts, because the relational tradition hardly has a unified theory let alone a consensual body of knowledge properly attributed to a paradigm. Nevertheless, for our purposes, it becomes important to delineate and clarify what most relational analysts typically agree upon. Where points of difference, disagreement, and controversy exist, they tend not to cancel out certain fundamental theoretical assumptions governing relational discourse. Let us examine three main philosophical tenets of the relational school.

The Primacy of Relatedness

When Greenberg and Mitchell (1983) inaugurated the relational turn by privileging relatedness with other human beings as the central motive behind mental life, they displaced Freud's drive model in one stroke of the pen. Although Greenberg (1991) later tried to fashion a theoretical bridge between drive theory and a relational model, he still remained largely critical. Mitchell (1988, 2000), however, had continued to steadfastly position relationality in antithetical juxtaposition to Freud's metapsychology until his untimely death. From his early work, Mitchell (1988) states that

---

* In fact, Mitchell (1988), in his introduction to *Relational Concepts in Psychoanalysis*, coins his and Greenberg's newly formed relational model as a "paradigmatic framework" by referring to Kuhn's description of the nature of scientific revolutions, a point he emphatically reinstates in the preface of *Relationality* (2000, p. xiii).

the relational model is "an alternative perspective which considers relations with others, *not drives*, as the basic stuff of mental life" (p. 2, emphasis added), thus declaring the cardinal premise of all relational theorists. He clearly wants to advocate for a "purely" relational model that is opposed to drive theory when he declares that "the concept of drive, as Freud intended it, has been omitted" (p. 60) from the relational perspective. Greenberg (1991) makes this point more forcefully: The relational model is "based on the *radical rejection of drive* in favor of a view that *all motivation* unfolds from our personal experience of exchanges with others" (p. vii, emphasis added). Echoing Mitchell, Greenberg makes a universal proclamation attributed to all relational theorists when he states, "Analysts operating within the relational model of the mind are united in their claim that it is misguided to begin theorizing with drive" (p. 69).

The centrality of interactions with others, the formation of relationships, interpersonally mediated experience, human attachment, the impact of others on psychic development, reciprocal dyadic communication, contextually based social influence, and the recognition of competing subjectivities seem to be universal theoretical postulates underscoring the relational viewpoint. These are very reasonable and sound assertions, and we would be hard-pressed to find anyone prepared to discredit these elemental facts. The main issue here is that these propositions are nothing new: Relational theory is merely stating the obvious. These are simple reflections on the inherent needs, strivings, developmental trajectories, and behavioral tendencies propelling human motivation, a point that Freud made explicit throughout his theoretical corpus, which became further emphasized more significantly by early object relations theorists through to contemporary self psychologists. Every aspect of conscious life is predicated on human relatedness by the simple fact that we are thrown into a social ontology as evinced by our participation in family interaction, communal living, social custom, ethnic affiliation, local and state politics, national governance, and common linguistic practices that by definition cannot be refuted or annulled by virtue of our embodied and cultural facticity, a thesis thoroughly advanced by Heidegger (1927/1962) yet originally dating back to antiquity. But what is unique to the relational turn is a philosophy based on antithesis and refutation, namely, the abnegation of the drives.

Intersubjective Ontology

Relational psychoanalysis privileges intersubjectivity over subjectivity and objectivity, although most theorists would generally concede that their position does not refute the existence of individual subjects or the external objective world. Yet this is still a topic of considerable debate among philosophy let alone the field of psychoanalysis, which remains relatively naive to formal metaphysics. It is unclear at best what *intersubjectivity* may mean to general psychoanalytic audiences because of the broad usage of the term and despite its having very specific and diversified meanings. Among many contemporaneous thinkers, *intersubjectivity* is used anywhere from denoting a specific interpersonal process of recognizing the individual needs and subjective experiences of others to referring to a very generic condition of interpersonal interaction.

It may be helpful to identify two forms of intersubjectivity in the analytic literature: a *developmental* view and a *systems* view, each of which may be operative at different parallel process levels. Robert Stolorow and his colleagues, as well as Jessica Benjamin, are often identified as introducing intersubjective thinking to psychoanalysis, although this concept has a 200-year history dating back to German Idealism. Intersubjectivity was most prominently elaborated by Hegel (1807/1977) as the laborious developmental attainment of ethical self-consciousness through the rational emergence of *Geist* in the history of the human race. This emergent process describes the unequal power distributions between servitude and lordship culminating in a developmental, historical, and ethical transformation of recognizing the subjectivity of the other, a complex concept Benjamin (1988) has selectively reap-propriated within the context of the psychoanalytic situation as the ideal striving for mutual recognition.

Like Hegel, Stern (1985), Benjamin (1988), and Mitchell (2000) view intersubjectivity as a developmental achievement of coming to acknowledge the existence and value of the internalized other, a dynamic that readily applies to the maternal–infant dyad and the therapeutic encounter. Daniel Stern (1985) has focused repeatedly on the internal experience of the infant's burgeoning sense of self as an agentic organization of somatic, perceptual, affective, and linguistic processes that unfold within the interpersonal presence of dyadic interactions with the mother. In his view, intersubjectiv-ity is like Hegel's view of it: There is a gradual recognition of the subjectivity of the m/other as an independent entity with simi-lar and competing needs of its own. In Fonagy's (2000, 2001) and his colleagues' (Fonagy, Gergely, Jurist, & Target, 2002) contribu-tions, he describes this process as the development of "mentaliza-tion," or the capacity to form reflective judgments on recognizing and anticipating the mental states of self and others. Stern's work dovetails nicely with the developments in attachment theory (Cassidy & Shaver, 1999; Hesse & Main, 2000; Main, 2000; Mills, 2005c; Solomon & George, 1999) and reciprocal dyadic systems theories derived from infant observation research.

Following Stern's developmental observation research, Beebe, Lachmann, and their colleagues (Beebe, Jaffe, & Lachmann, 1992; Beebe & Lachmann, 1998) have also focused on the primacy of maternal–infant interactions and, thus following the relational turn, have shifted away from the locus of inner processes to rela-tional ones (Beebe & Lachmann, 2003). Beebe and Lachmann's dyadic systems theory is predicated on intersubjectivity and the mutuality of dyadic interactions, whereby each partner within the relational matrix affects each other, thus giving rise to a dynamic systems view of self-regulation based on bidirectional, coordi-nated interactional attunement and cybernetic interpersonal assimilations, resulting in mutual modifications made from within the system.

Stolorow, Atwood, and their colleagues (Stolorow & Atwood, 1992; Stolorow, Brandchaft, & Atwood, 1987; Orange, Atwood, & Stolorow, 1997) cast intersubjectivity as a more basic, ontological category of interdependent, intertwining subjectivities that give rise to a "field" or "world," similar to general references to an intersubjective "system" or an "analytic third" (Ogden, 1994). Stolorow and his collaborators are often misunderstood as saying that intersubjective constellations annul intrapsychic life and a patient's developmental history prior to therapeutic engagement (see Frank, 1998b), but Stolorow et al. specifically contextualize intrapsychic experience within the greater parameters of the intersubjective process (Orange et al., 1997, pp. 67–68). Yet it becomes easy to see why Stolorow invites misinterpretation. Intersubjectivity is ontologically constituted: "experience is *always* embedded in a constitutive intersubjective context" (Stolorow & Atwood, 1992, p. 24, emphasis added). Elsewhere he states that the intersubjective system is the "constitutive role of relatedness in the making of *all* experience" (Stolorow, 2001a, p. xiii, emphasis added). Even in a more recently published interview, Stolorow (2010) affirms that "all … forms of unconsciousness are constituted in relational contexts" for " 'unconscious organizing principles' are intersubjectively constituted" (p. 7). Notice here that he states that *any* form of unconscious process is intersubjectively—hence relationally—constituted. This implies that even unconscious drives, which are part of our embodied biological constitutions, are enacted and composed by relational elements; therefore, drives are originally derived from conscious experience.

These absolutist overstatements lend themselves to decentering intrapsychic activity over relational interaction and draw into question the separateness of the self, the preexistent developmental history of the patient prior to treatment, the prehistory of unconscious processes independent of one's relatedness to others, and *a priori* mental organizations that precede engagement with the social world.* These statements appear to replace psychoanalysis as a science of the unconscious with an intersubjective ontology that gives priority to conscious experience.† To privilege consciousness over unconsciousness appears, to me, to subordinate the value of psychoanalysis as an original contribution to understanding human experience. Even if we as analysts are divided by competing theoretical identifications, it seems difficult at best to relegate the primordial nature of unconscious dynamics

---

* Although Stolorow, Atwood, and Orange have defended their positions quite well in response to their critics, often correcting them on facets of their writings most readers— let alone sophisticated researchers—would not be reasonably aware of without going to the effort of reading their entire collected body of combined works, one lacuna they cannot defend in their intersubjectivity theory is accounting for *a priori* unconscious processes prior to the emergence of consciousness, subject matter I thoroughly address elsewhere (see Mills, 2002a, 2002b). Although having attempted to address the role of organizing principles and the unconscious (Stolorow & Atwood, 1992), because they designate intersubjectivity to be the heart of *all* human experience, they commit themselves to a philosophy of consciousness that by definition fails to adequately account for an unconscious ontology, which I argue is the necessary precondition for consciousness and intersubjective life to emerge (Mills, 2010).

In their criticism of my assessment of their philosophy, Stolorow et al. (2006) claim that because I do not adequately situate the context of their writings when quoting or interpreting their work, I "annul" the notion of the unconscious in their combined theories, which they uphold. But this is not accurate. Although they account for the notion of the unconscious, it becomes decentered, not annulled. They do not deny the significance of the unconscious, they simply privilege conscious experience, to which they give priority because of the primacy of intersubjectivity. Although I readily concede that the authors object to being equated with other relationalists who do not adequately address the nature and being of the unconscious in contemporary discourse, Stolorow et al. still bear the onus of explaining their own textual contradictions. Stolorow (2007) describes what he calls the "ontological unconscious," which he defines as "a loss of one's sense of being" (p. 26), in relation to his own professed trauma of finding his wife dead in bed after succumbing to cancer. Although he has my sympathy, it is important to note that he is describing the emotional aftereffects of how conscious experience deeply affects our psychic structure, therefore privileging a theory of consciousness that is superimposed on our unconscious mental processes. His choice of the word *ontological* is also puzzling to me, because ontology implies being and presence rather than loss and absence. Perhaps a better descriptor would be the term *ontological abjection* in order to denote the phenomenology he is attempting to articulate.

† Freud (1925) ultimately defined psychoanalysis as "the science of unconscious mental processes" (p. 70).

to a trivialized backseat position that is implicit in much of the relational literature. For Freud (1900), the "unconscious is the true psychical reality" (p. 613), which by definition is the necessary condition for intersubjectivity to materialize and thrive.

Although there are many contemporary analysts who are still sensitive to unconscious processes in their writings and clinical work, including Donnel Stern, Philip Bromberg, Thomas Ogden, Darlene Bregman Ehrenberg, and Jody Messler Davies, among others, hence making broad generalizations unwarranted, it nevertheless appears that on the surface, for many relational analysts, the unconscious has become an antiquated category. While Stolorow, Atwood, and Orange have certainly advocated for revisionist interpretations of unconscious processes, Stolorow (2001a) in particular specifically relates a theoretical sentiment that is common among many relationalists: "In place of the Freudian unconscious … we envision a multiply contextualized experimental world, an organized totality of lived personal experience, *more or less conscious*. … In this view, psychoanalytic therapy is no longer an archeological excavation of deeper layers of an isolated unconscious mind" (pp. xii–xiii, emphasis added).

To be fair to Stolorow, in this above passage he does emphasize various phrases that point toward unconscious processes, such as subjective defenses that "exclude whatever feels unacceptable, intolerable, or too dangerous in a particular intersubjective context" (2001a, pp. xii–xiii). But this statement could imply a defense model of dissociation that does not necessarily require a dynamic unconscious based on repression theory, a point that Freud attempted to distinguish from contemporaries such as Morton Prince, Charcot, and Janet. Moreover, Stolorow (2001a) uses the term *prereflective* in his text (p. xiii), which he later qualifies as being equivalent with unconsciousness (see Stolorow et al., 2006, p. 185). But this equivalence does not necessarily follow, or at least it is not transparent to me. It would be helpful for Stolorow to define his terms in language that is customary to a certain readership and not simply invoke language that means different things to different philosophers that come from different philosophical traditions.*

Stolorow (2010) attempts to assign a substantial role to the unconscious when he refers to "unconscious organizing principles"; however, it becomes rather dubious whether such organizing principles precede human interaction, namely, are they structurally operative *a priori* processes, or are they the result of relational interaction with others? He states, "Developmentally, recurring patterns of intersubjective transaction within the developmental system give rise to principles that unconsciously organize subsequent emotional and relational experiences. Such unconscious organizing principles are the basic building blocks of personality" (p. 6). Here I believe he is saying, and most analysts would agree, that conscious experiences with others and the world are encoded and laid down within the mnemonic systems that govern unconscious life and are subjected to various internal processes *as* organizations that lend order to such experiences. However, he does not specify whether there are any organizing

---

* The notion of prereflectiveness is associated with several continental philosophers dating back to Hegel and Fichte, but it is most notably associated with Sartre, who, inspired by Brentano's notion of intentional versus nonpositional states of consciousness, disavows Freud's dynamic unconscious for a model of self-deception (*mauvaise foi*) based on prereflective consciousness. Given that Stolorow has often identified himself with the phenomenological tradition (see Stolorow, 2004b), this could easily confuse any reader familiar with the history of the concept of prereflexivity. For example, Sartre's (1943/1956) magnum opus, *Being and Nothingness*, was a phenomenological project on ontology. Given that Stolorow is now a graduate of philosophy, he is enamored—and rightfully so—with the many diversified, albeit competing and contradictory, philosophical theories that challenge traditional psychoanalytic concepts. And here we are likely to be in frank agreement on many subjects. I particularly see a commonality between our attempt to account for the phenomenology of lived experience, developmental trauma, intrapsychic organization, personal meaning and metaphor, and unconscious structure. But our main point of difference, as far as I can tell, is that I am fundamentally a psychoanalytic ontologist and that Stolorow is a psychoanalytic phenomenologist. He privileges consciousness over unconsciousness, whereas I have argued extensively (Mills, 1996, 2002b) that conscious experience, hence the realm of phenomenology, must be necessarily prepared *a priori* by an unconscious ground (*Ungrund*). Therefore, my main point here is to situate Stolorow et al. (2006) in the same camp as other relationalists who privilege consciousness over unconscious process, especially given that they concede that they have "challenged its prioricity" (p. 186).

principles operative *prior* to intersubjective transactions. He furthermore does not explain with any clarity or precision how these organizing principles operate, let alone delineate the processes or mechanisms by which they transpire. They are merely a presumptive given. Yet these details are important to explicate when one is postulating unconscious orienting principles.

Stolorow goes on to say, "'Unconscious organizing principles' *are* the intersubjectively constituted thematic structures *that account for* the recurrent patterning of one's psychological life" (p. 7, emphasis added). Notice that here he assigns causal determinism to the intersubjective system, what he refers to as manifesting "world horizons," a term he takes from Binswanger and Gadamer, which he explains "determine what can or must be experienced and what must not be experienced" (p. 7). This statement could be interpreted as tantamount to dissociative enactments that do not require a dynamic unconscious to organize anything. He further tells us, "The very boundary between conscious and unconscious (the repression barrier) is seen, not as a fixed intrapsychic structure within an isolated mind, but as a *property* of ongoing dynamic intersubjective systems" (p. 7, emphasis added).

Notice that he refers to the "boundary" between consciousness and unconsciousness as a "property" of intersubjective systems. Because a property is emergent from within the interactive "systems" of the two or more subjects involved, it therefore emanates from such interactions and does not possess any causal determination of its own. It is merely relegated to the status of an epiphenomenon.* By definition, it becomes devoid of agency. Furthermore, it does not emanate from a dynamic unconscious agency Freud was so careful to articulate. From Stolorow's

---

* In philosophy of mind, epiphenomenalism is associated with brain–mind dependence. Much of empirical science would contend that any brain state can be causally explained by appealing to other physical states or structural processes. Philosophers typically qualify this explanation by saying that physical states cause mental events but mental states do not have causal efficacy over anything, a point William James first made when he coined the term *epiphenomena* to account for phenomena that lacked causal determinism.

account, anything that is unconscious becomes forged or created by conscious relational dynamics, such as dissociative processes, and therefore the so-called unconscious becomes ancillary rather than primary in instituting such organizing principles.

Stolorow (2010) tries to demonstrate the viability of a dynamic unconscious when he refers to the "prereflective unconscious," which he attributes to "the system of organizing principles that structure an experiential world. … Their unconsciousness derives from the fact that ordinarily we just experience our emotional experiences, without reflecting on the thematic structures or meanings that organize them" (p. 8). But the "system of organizing principles" is never explained. Unconsciousness is equated with a lack of reflection, what has become typically referred to as "implicit" by the vogue standards employed by contemporary psychoanalysis today. On the one hand, Stolorow wants to explain the notion that "prereflective organizing principles are not contents of experience; they are structures that organize experience" (p. 8), but he does not expatiate on *what* structures are or *how* structures are structured. They are just posited to exist implicitly within the mind. But because the mind is constituted via intersubjective relations, the structures themselves must also be, by logical extension, a construction of consciousness. Yet Stolorow states that prereflective unconsciousness is attributed to "affective-relational experiences occurring in a non-linguistic, sensorimotor form" (p. 8). Here I agree with him and, more important, feel that through this line of thinking, Stolorow's speculations on a prereflective unconscious can fit compatibly within a dynamic theory of the unconscious where the role of agentic organizing principles become the locus of mental life (see Mills, 2010). However, as it stands, his contradictory theoretical positions and convoluted style of writing reinforce these problematics and foreclose clarity for the reader.

Other points of scholarly misunderstanding stem from Stolorow's use of the term *experience*, a word almost exclusively used by phenomenologists. With the exception of Alfred North

Whitehead (1929/1978), who speaks of the cosmos as "throbs" or "drops of experience," which I have articulated in the context of a wider unconscious ontology (Mills, 2003b; Stolorow et al. 2002, p. 48), the only other author I am aware of in the relational literature who systematically invokes the notion of "unconscious experience" is Donnel Stern (1997) who, from my reading, prefaces his thesis on postmodern principles that privilege language and linguistic social structures, hence a conscious enterprise, over a dynamic unconscious that prepares such processes to emerge in the first place. In their quoted passage (Stolorow, Atwood, & Orange, 2002, p. 48), they attempt to distinguish two forms of unconsciousness, each of which emerges from conscious experience. They attempt to describe that which is repressed, although this could be interpreted as merely being dissociated, as well as that which was "not to be allowed to come into full being" or that which was "never able to become articulated." To me, Stolorow et al. appear to be saying the same thing Don Stern describes as "unformulated experience." The question still remains whether the unconscious precedes or is forged through conscious experience. If intersubjectivity is privileged as a totalistic category of experience, then we are reasonably led to speculate that the unconscious is created by conscious (linguistic) experience, hence becoming a repository for shapes of lost or dissociated consciousness—thus subordinated in its causal efficacy, agentic functions, and dynamic teleology—or it is dispensed with altogether. Here relational authors should attend to these conundrums more carefully rather than merely use the word *unconscious* and assume we all understand its meaning when these theoretical revisions challenge its very existence, purpose, and function.

For Stolorow and many other relational thinkers, psychoanalysis tacitly favors a theory of consciousness. But despite my concerns with his work as just demonstrated, in all fairness to Stolorow, he and his colleagues have cogently embraced the primacy of contextual complexity situated within intersubjective relations, an observation most would find difficult to refute.

What is clearly privileged in the relational platform above the unique internal experiences and contingencies of the individual's intrapsychic configurations is the intersubjective field or dyadic system that interlocks, emerges, and becomes contextually organized as a distinct entity of its own. The primary focus here is not on the *object*, as in relatedness to others (object relations) or the objective (natural) world, or on the *subject*, as in the individual's lived phenomenal experience, but rather on the *system* itself. The terms *intersubjective system, field, territory, domain, realm, world, network, horizon, matrix*—or whatever words we wish to use to characterize the indissoluble intersection and interactional enactment between two or more human beings—evoke a spatial metaphor, hence they imply presence or being, the traditional subject matter of metaphysical inquiry. Following key propositions from the relational literature, the intersubjective system must *exist* for it is predicated on being, hence on actuality; therefore we may assume it encompasses its own attributes, properties, and spatiotemporal dialectical processes. This can certainly be inferred from the way in which relational analysts use these terms even if they don't intend to imply this as such, thus making the system into an actively organized (not static or fixed) entity of its own. Ogden (1994) makes this point most explicitly: "The analytic process reflects the interplay of three subjectivities: that of the analyst, of the analysand, and of the analytic third" (p. 3). In fact, the intersubjective system is a process-oriented entity that derives from the interactional union of two concretely existing subjective entities, thus making it an *emergent property* of the multiple (often bidirectional) interactions that form the intersubjective field. This ontological commitment immediately introduces the problem of agency, a topic I will repeatedly address throughout this critique.

How can a system acquire an agency of its own? How can the interpersonal field (i.e., the analytic third) become its own autonomous agent? What happens to the agency of the individual subjects that constitute the system? How can a "third" agency materialize and have determinate choice and action over the separately existing human beings that constitute the field to begin with? What becomes of individual freedom, independence, and personal identity with competing needs, intentions, wishes, and agendas that define individuality if the "system" regulates individual thought, affect, and behavior? What happens to the system if one participant decides to no longer participate? Does the system die, is it suspended, does it reconstitute later? What becomes of the system if one participant exerts more will or power over that of the other subject? Is not the system merely a temporal play of events rather than an entity? And if these experiences were possible, it would render the system impotent, acausal, and nonregulatory, which directly opposes the relational view that the intersubjective field, dyadic system, relational matrix, or analytic third has causal influence and supremacy over the individual autonomy of its constituents. The system would merely be an epiphenomenon, thus completely lacking determinate freedom or influence, hence merely relegated and deferred to the individual subjects that constitute the field. So how can the intersubjective system be granted such an exalted status by the relational movement? What becomes of the individually constituted and constitutive self? These questions are indeed difficult to sustain because they imply that the intersubjective system has no causal power, autonomy, or deference to individually mediated events that compose the system to begin with. These conundrums have led Peter Giovacchini (2005) to conclude that for the intersubjectivists, the individual mind becomes this ephemeral ether that evaporates the moment one enters into dialogue or social relations with anyone. Although intersubjectivists do not claim that the individual mind vanishes, they do unequivocally concede that it becomes subordinated to the intersubjective system or relational matrix that regulates it.

Psychoanalytic Hermeneutics

The relational turn has largely embraced a constructivist epistemology and method of interpretation, what Hoffman (1998) refers to as "critical" or "dialectical" constructivism based on "mutual influence and constructed meaning" (p. xii) in the analytic encounter. Many relational authors generically refer to "co-constructed" experience that is sensitive to the contextually derived elements of the interpersonal encounter subject to each person's unique perspective and interpretation but ultimately shaped by mutually negotiated meaning that is always susceptible to a fallibilistic epistemology (Orange, 1995). As Stolorow (1998) puts it, "the analyst has no privileged access" to the patient's mind or what truly transpires between the analyst and the analysand, for "objective reality is unknowable by the psychoanalytic method" (p. 425). Drawing on Kant's Idealism, whereby claiming that we cannot have true knowledge of things in themselves, these epistemological positions are largely gathered from postmodern sensibilities that loosely fall under the umbrella of what may not be inappropriately called psychoanalytic hermeneutics, namely, methods of interpretation derived from subjective experience and participation in social relations that constitute meaning and knowledge.

Constructivist positions, and there are many kinds—social, ethical, feminist, empirical, mathematical—hold a variety of views with points of similarity and divergence depending upon their agenda or mode of inquiry. Generally we may say that many relational analysts have adopted a variant of social constructivism by claiming that knowledge is the product of our linguistic practices and social institutions that are specifically instantiated in the interactions and negotiations between others. This readily applies to the consulting room, where knowledge emerges from dialogic relational involvement wedded to context. This is why Hoffman and others rightfully state that meaning is not only discovered but also created, including the therapeutic encounter and the way we come to understand and view our lives. In fact, analysis is a creative self-discovery and process of becoming. Mild versions of constructivism hold that social participation and semantic factors lend interpretation to the world, whereas extreme forms go so far as to claim that the world, or some significant portion of it, is constituted via our linguistic, political, and institutional practices. Despite the generic use of the terms *construction* and *co-construction*, relational analysts have largely avoided specifically delineating their methodology.

With the exception of Donnel Stern (1997), who largely aligns with Gadamer's hermeneutic displacement of scientific conceptions of truth and method;* Donna Orange's (1995) perspectival epistemology, which is a version of James's and Peirce's pragmatic theories of truth; and Hoffman's brand of dialectical constructivism—the term *dialectic* lacking any clear definition or methodological employment—relational psychoanalysis lacks a solid philosophical foundation, one it claims to use to justify its theories and practices. Perhaps with the exception of Stolorow and his collaborators' numerous attempts, none of the relational analysts I've mentioned provide their own detailed theoretical system that guides analytic method, hence falling short of offering a formal framework based on systematically elaborated, logical rigor we would properly expect from philosophical paradigms. Of course, psychoanalysis can claim that it is not philosophy, so placing such demands on the field is illegitimate, but contemporary frameworks are basing their purported innovations on justifications that derive from established philosophical traditions. Therefore, it is incumbent upon these "new view" theorists (Eagle et al., 2001) to precisely define their positions. Without doing so, relational analysts will continue to invite misinterpretation. Moreover, the

---

* It should be noted that Gadamer's hermeneutics is an analysis of the text, not the human subject. Despite this qualification, he does, in my estimate, develop a dialogical model of interpretation as though the text were treated as a "thou," hence a human being we find ourselves in conversation with, and this undoubtedly had special significance for why Stern gravitated toward Gadamer's hermeneutics. It may be argued, however, that Ricoeur has an equally appealing approach because he insisted that philosophical hermeneutics was more fundamentally reflective than the methods used in the behavioral sciences for the simple fact that it does not alienate itself from its subject matter, unlike the behavioral sciences that view people as objects rather than as subjects of inquiry. Ricoeur further believed that hermeneutics must serve an epistemological function by incorporating its own critical practices within its mode of discourse, which is not unlike many relational theorists today who criticize how previously held theories and objectivist assumptions have the potential to distort our methods of knowledge and interpretation, thus championing the role of the analyst's participation in analytic space.

psychoanalytic community may continue to misinterpret their frequent use of employing arcane and abstruse philosophical language culled from a very specific body of demarcated vocabulary that is reappropriated within the analytic context, to such a degree that the reader is either confused or sufficiently impressed, because on the face of things, it may seem profound. The obfuscating use of philosophical buzzwords may give the appearance of profundity, but they may be quite inaccurate when they are dislocated from the tradition in which they originally emerged.

Take, for example, Hoffman's use of the term *dialectical*. This word imports a whole host of different meanings in the history of Western philosophy. Is he merely invoking the interplay of opposition? Does this imply difference only or also similarity? How about the role of symmetry, continuity, measure, force, unity, and/or synthesis? Is there a certain function to the dialectic, a movement, a process, or an emergence? If so, how does it transpire? Does it follow formal causal laws or logical operations, or is it merely acausal, amorphous, accidental, invariant, undecidable, spontaneous? Is it universal or merely contingent? Is it a necessary and/or sufficient condition of interaction, or perhaps just superfluous? Is his approach Socratic? Does he engage the impact of Kant, Fichte, Schelling, Hegel, or Marx on his view of the dialectic? He does not say. Hoffman (1998) emphasizes "ambiguity and construction of meaning." While I do not dispute this aspect to the dialectic, I am left pining for more explanation. Is there a teleology to the dialectic, or is everything "unspecified and indeterminate" (p. xvii), what he tends to emphasize in a move from "symbolically" well-defined experience, to "underdeveloped, ambiguous" features of mental activity or the lived encounter, to "totally untapped potentials" (p. 22)? Here Hoffman seems to be equating dialectics with construction *qua* construction. We might ask, Constructed from what? Are we to assume the intersubjective system is the culprit? Cursory definitions are given, such as the implication of "an interactive dynamic between opposites" (p. 200, fn2), but he ultimately defers to Ogden (1986):

"A dialectic is a process in which each of two opposing concepts creates, informs, preserves, and negates the other, each standing in a dynamic (ever changing) relationship with the other" (p. 208). This definition emphasizes dichotomy, polarity, and change but lacks articulation on how opposition brings about change, let alone what kind (e.g., progressive or regressive, given that change annuls the concept of stasis) or whether this process is subject to any formal laws, pressures, trajectories, or developmental hierarchies. Nor does he explain how opposition emerges to begin with. Is the dialectic presumed to be the force behind all construction? And if so, why? In all fairness to Hoffman, he does concede to the "givens" of reality and appreciates the historicity, causal efficacy, and presence of the past on influencing the present, including all modes of relatedness, and in shaping future possibilities. While I am admittedly using Hoffman here in a somewhat caviling manner, my point is to show how omission and theoretical obscurity in progressive psychoanalytic writing leaves the attentive reader with unabated questions.*

A coherent framework of psychoanalytic hermeneutics has not been attempted since Ricoeur's (1970) critique of Freud's metapsychology, and there has been nothing written to my knowledge that hermeneutically critiques contemporary theory. What appears

---

* I have advocated for a dialectical psychoanalysis for the past decade (Mills, 1996, 2000a, 2002a) and more recently offered a systematic psychoanalytic metaphysics that relies on a revisionist view of Hegel's ontology of the dialectic (Mills, 2010). Hegel refers to the unrest of *Aufhebung*—customarily translated as "sublation," a continual dialectical process entering into opposition within its own determinations and thus raising this opposition to a higher unity, which remains at once annulled, preserved, and transmuted. Hegel's use of *Aufhebung*, a term he borrowed from Schiller but also an ordinary German word, is to be distinguished from its purely negative function, whereby there is a complete canceling or drowning of the lower relation in the higher, to also encompass a preservative aspect. Therefore, the term *aufheben* has a threefold meaning: (a) to suspend or cancel, (b) to surpass or transcend, and (c) to preserve. In the *Encyclopaedia Logic*, Hegel (1817a/1991) makes this clear: "On the one hand, we understand it to mean 'clear away' or 'cancel,' and in that sense we say that a law or regulation is canceled (*aufgehoben*). But the word also means 'to preserve'" (*EL* § 96, *Zusatz*). Unlike Fichte's (1794/1993) meaning of the verb *aufheben*, defined as to eliminate, annihilate, abolish, or destroy, Hegel's designation signifies a threefold activity by which mental operations at once cancel or annul opposition, preserve or retain it, and surpass or elevate its previous shape to a higher structure.

is a pluralistic mosaic—perhaps even a cacophony—of different amalgamated postmodern, hermeneutic traditions derived from constructivism, critical theory, poststructuralism, feminist philosophy, sociology, linguistics, narrative literary criticism, deconstructionism, and—believe it or not—analytic philosophy that have shared visions and collective identifications but with misaligned projects and competing agendas. For these reasons alone, I doubt we will ever see one coherent comparative-integrative contemporary psychoanalytic paradigm. These disparate groups of theories exist because human knowledge and explanation radically resist being reduced to a common denominator, and here the relationalist position is well taken. There is too much diversity, complexity, difference, particularity, and plurality to warrant such an onerous undertaking. Although I have emphasized the recent upsurge of attention on constructivist epistemology in relational circles, it may be said that a consensus exists for most practicing analysts that absolute truth, knowledge, and certainty does not rest on the crown of the analyst's epistemic authority and that insight, meaning, and explanation are an ongoing, emerging developmental aspect of any analytic work subject to the unique intersubjective contingencies of the analytic dyad.

Having sufficiently prepared our discussion, I now wish to turn our attention to what may perhaps be the most controversial theoretical debate between the relational traditions and previous analytic schools, namely, the subject–object divide. Contemporary relational psychoanalysis claims to have transcended the theoretical ailments that plague classical analysis by emphasizing the irreducible subjectivity of the analyst (Renik, 1993) over objective certainty, the fallacy of the analyst's epistemological authority, the primacy of context and perspective over universality and essentialism, and the adoption of a "two-person psychology" that is thoroughly intersubjective. But these premises are not without problems. Does the analyst's subjectivity foreclose the question of objectivity? Does epistemically limited access to knowledge necessarily delimit our understanding of truth and reality? Does particularity and pluralism negate the notion of universals and collectivity? Does a nominalist view of subjectivity necessarily annul the notion of essence?* And does a two-person model of intersubjectivity minimize or cancel the force and value of intrapsychic reality and lived individual experience? These are but some of the philosophical quandaries that arise from the relational literature. But with a few exceptions, it may be said that contemporary psychoanalytic theory is premised on reappropriating old paradigms under the veil of popular garb. Here enters postmodernism.

---

* It has become fashionable for contemporary analysts to abrogate the notion of "essence" within relational discourse (e.g., see Dimen, 1991; Teicholz, 1999; Young-Bruehl, 1996). These views are largely in response to medieval interpretations of Aristotle's notion of substance as a fixed universal category. However, it is important to note that there are many divergent perspectives on essence that do not adhere to a substance ontology with fixed, immutable, or static properties that adhere in an object or thing. Hegel's (1807/1977, 1812/1831/1969) dialectic, for example, is necessarily (hence universally) predicated on process, which constitutes its structural ontology. From this account, essence does not suggest a fixed or static immutable property belonging to a substance or a thing; rather it is dynamic, *relational*, and transformative. As a result, Hegel underscores the notion that *essence is process*, which is largely compatible with many relational viewpoints today.

2

The Problem With Postmodernism

Throughout this chapter I wish to challenge the postmodern turn in contemporary psychoanalysis for its antimodern tendencies, theoretical contradictions, and the wholesale acceptance of the primacy of language. Because postmodernism denies traditional metaphysical and epistemological paradigms, it also compromises the status of psychoanalysis as a legitimate human science by opposing the notions of objectivity, interpretation, and truth claims about reality. Relational psychoanalysis in particular has selectively adopted various features of pomocentrism that oppose the notions of selfhood, agency, essentialism, and the nature of universals. I wish to advocate for a return to a discourse on the modern tenets of universality, essence, and objectivity that properly appreciates the role of ontology and how it informs all aspects of subjectivity, contextuality, culture, and collective social experience.

Since Mitchell's (1988) and Greenberg's (1991) instantiation of the relational platform, contemporary psychoanalysis has increasingly embraced postmodern paradigms originally initiated by several key developments in 20th-century European continental philosophy. These genres include (but are not limited to) preoccupations with phenomenology, the hermeneutic tradition, and the linguistic turn. Among these postmodern assumptions are the abnegation of the Enlightenment modern notions of rationality,

objectivity, epistemic certainty, truth, universal absolutes, individuality and free will, and positivistic science, just to name a
few. What we see abundant today in the analytic literature are
constant references to relatedness in lieu of intrapsychic life, an
emphasis on intersubjectivity over internality, constructivism
versus discovery, context and perspective rather than universal
proclamations, contingencies contra absolutes, skepticism over
certainty, consensus—not truth—and conscious experience over
the primacy of unconscious mentation. In fact, if one were to
randomly peruse through any volume of the leading periodicals
representing the relational tradition, most notably *Psychoanalytic
Dialogues,* one could be led to believe that psychoanalysis was
invented 30 years ago upon Greenberg and Mitchell's (1983) inau-
guration of the relational trend. And with this new addition to the
history of psychoanalysis comes a swing of the pendulum away
from the precepts that characterize the sciences and modern philosophy and everything they stand for, namely, claims about the
nature of reality, universal laws, objective methodology, logical
coherence, epistemological standardization, and truth.

As a psychoanalyst, philosopher, and relational practitioner,
I have a great deal of respect for how relational psychoanalysis
has created a permissible space for questioning and revamping
the theoretical and technical convictions passed down from previous generations; nowhere do we see such a forceful reformation
in psychoanalytic practice since Kohut. Indeed, such rehabilita-
tive approaches in the consulting room are perhaps the greatest
accomplishments relational psychoanalysis offers our discipline
as a whole, a subject matter I will thoroughly address in a future
chapter. But regardless of these advances, on the theoretical side
of things, relational psychoanalysis at times lacks philosophical
sophistication. What I believe is fundamentally problematic in
much of the relational literature is its implicit and naive adoption
of the postmodern turn. In its efforts to justify its viability as a
behavioral science through engaging the humanities, and without having to adopt the stringent (rigid) criteria of mainstream

empirical science, contemporary psychoanalysis seems to have jumped on the postmodern bandwagon without considering the consequences. In some instances, contemporary writers use the term liberally when they often have no firm grasp of what they mean by *postmodernism* to begin with.* Postmodern sensibilities are arbitrarily applied to literature, art, politics, feminism, spirituality, gender and queer theory—even architecture—each having radically different meanings and contextual variations depending upon which discipline you consult. The same arbitrariness and slipshod propositional assertions are being made today within the contemporary psychoanalytic domain, often under the guise of scholarship passed off as legitimate philosophical justification, when the merits for such justification are suspiciously dubious to begin with.

I hope to convince the reader that relational psychoanalysis is in need of theoretical restoration if it plans to prosper and advance. Postmodernism is not the answer. In fact, postmodern principles threaten the established tradition of psychoanalysis as a legitimate behavioral science as well as a theoretically refined contribution to the humanities, and they have practical and political consequences for our discipline. Because postmodernism is a loosely assembled body of disparate theories replete with contradictions, it becomes a philosophical embarrassment when annexed by relational writers who use postmodern propositions selectively to champion their cause.

One indelible problem is the nature and meaning of universals that are flippantly disregarded by postmodern relationalists. Another is the antimetaphysical and antiepistemological frameworks that tacitly govern postmodern politics, especially promulgated by feminist revisionists, poststructuralism, social constructivists, and the vogue of deconstructionism. Moreover, the ontology of the unconscious, self-experience, freedom, will

---

* For example, see Hartman's (2005) inaccurate assessment of the role and meaning of postmodernism in contemporary psychoanalysis.

and agency, moral absolutes, and the existence of an autonomous self become eclipsed by postmodern commitments. My contention is that relational psychoanalysis has everything to gain by returning to a modern discourse on the explication of universals that allows for particularity and contextual complexity. It may do so while avoiding the pitfalls associated with postmodern proclamations that ultimately stand for categorical refutation, relativism, and nihilism under the political, contradictory guise of affirming a particularly biased agenda—itself, ironically, the very thing it wishes to negate.

THE LURE AND AMBIGUITY OF POSTMODERNISM

The word *postmodernism* is a very ambiguous term. What exactly do we mean by postmodernism? And what is its burgeoning role in psychoanalytic discourse? Within the past two decades, we have seen a resurgence of interest in philosophy among contemporary relational and intersubjective theorists who have gravitated toward key postmodern tenets that draw into question the notion of universals, absolute standards of truth and objectivity, and the problem of essence within clinical theory and practice. The lure of postmodernism is widely attractive because it explains the hitherto unacknowledged importance of the analyst's interjected experience within the analytic encounter; displaces the notion of the analyst's epistemic authority as an objective certainty; highlights contextuality and perspective over universal proclamations that apply to all situations regardless of historical contingency, culture, gender, or time; and largely embraces the linguistic, narrative turn in philosophy. Although postmodern thought has propitiously criticized the pervasive historical, gendered, and ethnocentric character of our understanding of the world, contemporary trends in psychoanalysis seem to be largely unaware of the *aporiai* postmodern propositions introduce into a coherent and justifiable theoretical system. Although postmodernism has no unified body of theory, thus making it unsystematized, one

unanimous implication is the demise of the individual subject.
Postmodernism may be generally said to be a cross-disciplinary
movement largely comprising linguistic, poststructural, constructivist, historical, narrative, deconstructivist, and feminist social
critiques that oppose most Western philosophical traditions. As
a result, postmodern doctrines are antimetaphysical, antiepistemological, and anticolonial, thus opposing realism, foundational-
ism, essentialism, neutrality, and the ideal sovereignty of reason.
In this respect, they may be most simply characterized by negation—No! Moreover, erasure—~~Know~~.

Although postmodern sensibility has rightfully challenged the
omnipresence of historically biased androcentric and logocentric
interpretations of human nature and culture, it has done so at the
expense of dislocating several key modern philosophical tenets
that celebrate the nature of subjectivity, consciousness, and the
teleology of the will. Consequently, the transcendental notions
of freedom, liberation, individuality, personal independence,
authenticity, and reflective deliberate choice that compose the
essential activities of personal agency are altogether disassembled.
What all this boils down to is the dissolution of the autonomous,
rational subject. In other words, the self is anaesthetized.

Postmodernism has become very fashionable with some relationalists because it may be used selectively to advocate for certain
contemporary positions, such as the co-construction of meaning
and the disenfranchisement of epistemic analytic authority, but
it does so at the expense of introducing antimetaphysical propositions into psychoanalytic theory that are replete with massive
contradictions and inconsistencies. For example, if meaning is
merely a social construction, and all analytic discourse that transpires within the consulting room is dialogical, then meaning and
interpretation are conditioned on linguistic social factors that
determine such meaning, hence we are the product of language
instantiated within our cultural ontology. This means that language and culture are *causally determinative*. Donnel Stern (1997)
nicely summarizes the contemporary psychoanalytic platform:

"This view of language, along with psychoanalytic constructivism itself, are outgrowths of the many streams of contemporary thought (philosophy of science, post-structuralism, pragmatism, and contemporary hermeneutics) that join together in the one great postmodern conclusion: *All experience is linguistic*" (p. 7, emphasis added). Stern is unmistakably clear: "language is the condition for experiencing" (p. 7). If all experience is linguistic, then what becomes of unconscious mental processes? How would one account for "prelinguistic" organizations that belong to the experiential world of an infant, such as sentient, sensori, and affective reverberations? If language is the ground or condition for experience, then by definition this excludes biologically based regulatory processes, such as the teleonomic and teleological pressures inherent to the drives (see Mills, 2010). Here Stern's position, by implication, apparently negates the biological sciences.

Just so there is no misunderstanding, let us examine another quote from Mitchell (1998):

> What we are struggling toward in contemporary revisions of psychoanalytic epistemology is a framework that allows us to take what we might think of as the analyst's culture into account in the process through which the analyst and the patient hold on to the facts and co-construct a new mythology about them. (p. 11)

Here Mitchell is against any objectivist stance, instead advocating for intersubjective social construction via factual invention. In fact, he goes on to say that all minds are constructed; more specifically, "mind is understood *only* through a process of interpretive construction" (p. 16, emphasis added). Here "construction" means linguistic creation as the invention of a "*new mythology.*"

Another representative of the postmodern relational position is Adrienne Harris, who, like Mitchell, canonizes language. Harris (1996) tells us,

> The other is always shadowed in any speech act. Speaking always has an addressee, an interlocutor. If speech is, therefore, always embedded in some object relationship, dialectically the object relation is buried in the speech practice. Speaking is thus the

source of self-structure and of the doubleness or multiplicity of self-structure and its registration. (p. 544)

Here Harris reifies language and identifies speaking (not the unconscious) as the "source"—hence the origin—of self-structure. Furthermore, Harris implies that being itself is predicated on language, for "the activity of being is generated in the constant slippage between self and other, [where] communication is of paramount importance" (p. 544). And because therapeutic action is necessarily conditioned by verbal exchange, language causally structures the analytic dyad, and even more to the extreme, as Mitchell (1998) proposes, it "interpretively constructs" another's mind (p. 16), which Morris Eagle (2003) argues is absurd.

The implications of these positions immediately annul metaphysical assertions to truth, objectivity, free will, and agency, among other universals. For instance, if everything boils down to language and culture, then by definition we cannot make legitimate assertions about truth claims or objective knowledge because these claims are merely constructions based upon our linguistic practices to begin with, rather than universals that exist independent of language and socialization. So, by definition, the whole concept of epistemology is merely determined by social discourse, so one cannot conclude that truth or objectivity exists. These become mythologies, fictions, narratives, and illusions regardless of whether we find social consensus. Therefore, natural science— such as the laws of physics,* mathematics, and formal logic—is merely a social invention based on semantic construction that by

---

* In a publishing hoax exposing the lack of "intellectual rigor" in postmodern studies, physics professor Alan D. Sokal (1996c) published an article called "Transgressing the Boundaries: Towards a Transformative Hermeneutics of Quantum Gravity," where he deceived the journal's editorial reviewers and readers in arguing that quantum gravity is a social and linguistic construct. In "Transgressing the Boundaries: An Afterword" published in *Dissent* (1996a) and, in slightly different form, in *Philosophy and Literature* (1996b), Sokal tells us, "Anyone who believes that the laws of physics are mere social conventions is invited to try transgressing those conventions from the windows of my apartment. I live on the twenty-first floor" (see fn3; http://www.physics.nyu.edu/sokal/afterword_v1a/afterword_v1a_singlefile.html).

definition annuls any claims to objective observations or mind independent reality. In other words, metaphysics is dead and buried—nothing exists independent of language.

These propositions problematize the whole contemporary psychoanalytic edifice. If nothing exists independent of language and the social matrix that sustains it (in essence, the relational platform), then not only is subjectivity causally determined by culture but subjectivity is dismantled altogether. When analysts use terms such as *construction*, hence invoking Foucault—whose entire philosophical project was to get rid of the subject and subjectivity—or even worse, *deconstruction*, thus exalting Derrida— the king of postmodernism, whose entire corpus is devoted to annihilating any metaphysical claims whatsoever, thus collapsing everything into undecidability, ambiguity, chaos, and chance— analysts open themselves up to misunderstanding and controversy, subsequently inviting criticism.

What perhaps appears to be the most widely shared claim in the relational tradition is the assault on the analyst's epistemological authority to objective knowledge. Stolorow (1998) tells us, "Objective reality is unknowable by the psychoanalytic method, which investigates only subjective reality … there are no neutral or objective analysts, no immaculate perceptions, no God's-eye views of anything" (p. 425). What exactly does this mean? If my patient is suicidal, and he communicates this to me, providing he is not malingering, lying, or manipulating me for some reason, does this not constitute some form of objective judgment independent of his subjective verbalizations? Do we not have some capacities to form objective appraisals (here the term *objective* being used to denote making reasonably correct judgments about objects or events outside of our unique subjective experience)? Is not Stolorow making an absolute claim despite arguing against absolutism when he says that "reality is unknowable"? Why not say that knowledge is proportional or incremental rather than totalistic, thus subject to modification, alteration, and interpretation rather than categorically negate the category of an objective epistemology?

The point I wish to emphasize is that the psychoanalytic method, which is based on phenomenal interpretations of shared (albeit separately registered or organized) experience in the analytic encounter, can indeed allow us to render reasonably correct (objective) judgments independent of others' subjective states of mind. When Stolorow (1998) tells us that "objective reality is unknowable by the psychoanalytic method" (p. 425), is he intimating that some other method can indeed have epistemic access to objective reality that is foreclosed by psychoanalytic investigation? If so, then what is it? And even if this is his claim, why would we privilege such methodological practices over our own if they also rely on the senses, reason, and subjective interpretations of observable phenomena? When making objectivist claims about reality independent of the subject's mind, all scientific disciplines interpret the natural world through the filter of human subjectivity. This does not negate the epistemic fact that we *can know* certain aspects of the natural world independent of the subject's unique subjectivity that interprets it.

I agree with Stolorow, Atwood, and Orange (2006) that contextualizing is not nullifying, it only situates or demarcates a particular object of study, subject matter, or datum for observation, theoretical reflection, or critical inquiry. Yet there is always a dilemma to context, a discussion that lies beyond the scope of this project. I fully agree with my colleagues that "phenomena ... are always and only grasped as dimensions of personal experiencing" (p. 187). What else could phenomena be grasped by? We cannot step outside of our own minds, except only in theory or fantasy, yet this of course is mediated by mind. Regardless of our irreducible subjectivity, this does not necessarily mean that "objective reality is unknowable," a debate we may leave for another time.

Although Stolorow is not trying to deny the existence of the external world, he is privileging a subjective epistemology, and this is no different from Kant's (1781/1965) view expounded in his *Critique of Pure Reason*. Ironically, this was also Freud's (1900) position in the dream book: "The unconscious is the true psychical reality; *in its innermost nature, it is as much unknown to us as the reality of the external world, and it is as incompletely presented by the data of consciousness as is the external world by the communications of our sense organs"* (p. 613). Following Kant, both Stolorow and Freud are critical realists: They accept the existence of objective reality because there must be something beyond the veil of appearance, but they can never know it directly. There is always a limit to pure knowing, a noumena—the *Ding an sich*, or the Fichtean (1794) *Anstoss*—a firm boundary, obstacle, or check. This is the hallmark of early German Idealism, which seems plausible and is defensible. But Stolorow, in collaboration with his colleagues, makes other claims that implicitly overturn his previous philosophical commitments. He reifies intersubjectivity at the expense of subjective life; subordinates the role, scope, and influence of the unconscious; and favors a relational focus in treatment rather than on the intrapsychic dynamics of the analysand. For example, take Donna Orange's extreme claim: "There is No Outside." For someone who rejects solipsism, this seems hard to believe.

Because postmodern perspectives are firmly established in antithesis to the entire history of Greek and European ontology, perspectives widely adopted by many contemporary analysts today, relational psychoanalysis has no tenable metaphysics. This begs the question of an intelligible discourse on method for the simple fact that postmodern sensibilities ultimately collapse into relativism.* Because there are no independent standards, methods, or principles subject to uniform procedures for evaluating conceptual schemas, postmodern perspectives naturally lead to relativism. Categories of knowledge, truth, objectivity, and reality are merely based on *contingencies* fashioned by language, personal experience or opinion, preference and prejudice, parallel perspectives, social

---

* Although some relationalists refuse to be labeled as relativists, James Fosshage (2003) attributed relativism to the relational tradition by highlighting a "paradigmatic change from positivistic to relativistic science, or from objectivism to constructivism" (p. 412). I would like to use the term in reference to its original historical significance dating back to pre-Socratic ancient philosophy, most notably inspired by the Greek sophist Protagoras, that generally denies the existence of universal truths or intrinsic characteristics about the world in favor of relative means of interpretation.

agreement, negotiated meaning, collective value practices that oppose other collective practices, and/or subjectively capricious conclusions. Contingency always changes and disrupts established order or causal laws; therefore there are no universals, only particulars. The relational focus on context, construction, and perspective is clearly a contingency claim. We can't know anything, but we can invent something to agree upon. This hardly should be toted under the banner of "truth," because for the postmoderns there is no truth, only truths—multiple, pluralistic, nominalistic, hence *relative* to person, place, and time. Although we may all agree that subjectivity is infused in all human experience by virtue of the fact that we can never abrogate our facticity as embodied, sentient, desirous conscious beings—hence a universal proposition that transcends history, gender, cultural specificity, and time—this does not *ipso facto* rule out the notion of objectivity or realism.

For all practical purposes, the epistemic emphasis on subjectivity that opposes objectivity is a bankrupt claim because this devolves into untenability where everything potentially becomes relative. From the epistemic (perspectival) standpoint of a floridly psychotic schizophrenic, flying apparitions really *do* exist, but this does not make it so. Relativism is incoherent and is an internally inconsistent position at best, to simply being an unsophisticated form of sophistry based on crass opinion. I once had a student who was an ardent champion of relativism until I asked him to stand up and turn around. When he did I lifted his wallet from his back pocket and said, "If everything is relative, then I think I am entitled to your wallet because the university does not pay me enough." Needless to say, he wanted it back.

Relativism collapses into contradiction, inexactitude, nihilism, and ultimately absurdity because no one person's opinion is anymore valid than another's, especially including value judgments and ethical behavior, despite qualifications that some opinions are superior to others. A further danger of embracing a "relativistic science" is that psychoanalysis really has nothing to offer over other disciplines that may negate the value of psychoanalysis to begin with (e.g., empirical academic psychology), let alone patients themselves whose own opinions may or may not carry any more weight than the analysts they seek out for expert professional help. When one takes relativism to the extreme, constructivism becomes creationism, which is simply a grandiose fantasy of omnipotence.

Mitchell's (1998) epistemological critique of metaphysical realism—hence on the knowability of the object world—in favor of linguistic interpretive construction may very well be the hallmark of relational pomocentrism. Based upon his antiobjectivist dismissal of scientific observation and analytic neutrality, from this standpoint there is no such thing as a fact. Instead, all human experience is predicated on language and interpretation, and this specifically means conscious conceptual thought. Not only does this privilege consciousness over unconsciousness, it logically displaces the presumption that unconscious mentation precedes conscious thought, for language is a socially constructed enterprise. I have grave concerns with this conceptual move in contemporary circles because psychoanalysis loses its contribution to the human sciences, which places unconscious processes at the pinnacle of mental operations. Frie (1997) has persuasively argued that although language is a necessary condition for human subjectivity, it is far from being a sufficient one—not to mention the fact that preverbal, affective, somatic, aesthetic, and extralingusitic experiences precede, exceed, and/or are operative on parallel, complementary levels of being and experiencing regardless of their conceptual mediation.

Another arena of contradictions relational postmoderns face with their antimetaphysical endorsements is that they paradoxically affirm the very thing they wish to refute. Being is that which has presence—namely, that which presents itself. By denying metaphysics one automatically affirms metaphysics by predicating negation. Negation, that is, the negation of metaphysical realism, is itself an ontological assertion instituted through speech. If anything we predicate or renounce is necessarily conditioned by language, then language is an ontological category. Language presupposes being due to its predicating presence, for predication by definition is a constitutive activity of engaging that which is posited to exist. Even the negation of existence—namely, non-being—is not devoid of ontological predication, for nothingness cannot exist unless it is in relation to being, hence its mutually implicative, dialectical complementarity.

I suppose this debate ultimately hinges on how psychoanalysts come to define *objectivity*, once again, a semantic determination. Words clarify yet they obfuscate; so do their omissions. Is this merely paradox, perhaps overdetermination, or is this a Derridean trope? One thing is for sure (in my humble opinion!): Relational and intersubjective theorists seem to have a penchant for creating false dichotomies between inner–outer, self–other, universal–particular, absolute–relative, truth–fallacy, and subject–object. For those familiar with the late modern Kantian turn through to German Idealism, phenomenology, and early continental philosophy, contemporary psychoanalysis seems to be behind the times. The subject–object divide has already been closed.*

---

* Schelling's (1800/1978) *System of Transcendental Idealism* may be said to be the first systematic philosophy that dissolved the subject–object dichotomy by making pure subjectivity and absolute objectivity identical: mind and nature are one. It can be argued, however, that it was Hegel (1807/1977, 1817) who was the first to succeed in unifying the dualism inherent in Kant's distinction between phenomenal experience and the noumenal realm of the natural world through a more rigorous form of systematic logic that meticulously shows how subjectivity and objectivity are dialectically related and mutually implicative. Relational psychoanalysis has left out one side of the equation, or at least has not adequately accounted for it. On the other hand, Hegel's process metaphysics cogently takes into account both subjective and objective life culminating in a holistic philosophy of mind (*Geist*) that takes both itself and the object world within its totality as pure self-consciousness, hence an absolute (logical) epistemological standpoint based on the dynamics of process and contingency within universality. When relational analysts return to the emphasis on subjectivity by negating the objective, they foreclose the dialectical positionality that is inherently juxtaposed and reciprocally intertwined in experience. For example, Hegel arduously shows how objectivity is the developmental, architectonic culmination of subjective life: Regardless of our own unique personal preferences and qualities, developmental histories, or individual perspectives, we as the human race live in communal relation to one another constituted by language, social customs, ethical prescriptions and prohibitions, and civil laws we have come to call culture, hence an objective facticity of human invention. Despite Hegel's opacity, here the relationalists can find not only a philosophy embracing the fullest value of subjective and intersubjective life but also one that describes the unconscious conditions that make objective judgments possible (see Mills, 2002b, for a review).

Although postmodern psychoanalytic thought is attractive for its emphasis on contextuality; linguistic, gender, and cultural specificity; political reform; postcolonial antipatriarchy; the displacement of pure reason and phallocentrism; and the epistemic refutation of positivistic science, it does so at the expense of eclipsing metaphysical inquiry, which was the basis of Freud's foray into understanding the ontology of the unconscious and establishing psychoanalysis as a science of subjectivity.

THE SEPARATENESS OF THE SELF?

One persistent criticism of relational theorizing is that it does not do justice to the notion of personal agency and the separateness of the self (Frie, 2003). Many relationalists and intersubjectivists fail to adequately account for the problem of agency, freedom, the notion of an enduring subject or self, and personal identity. It may be argued that relational thinking dissolves the centrality of the self, extracts and dislocates the subject from subjectivity, decomposes personal identity, and ignores the unique phenomenology and epistemological process of lived experience by collapsing every psychic event into a relational ontology, thus usurping the concretely existing human being while devolving the notion of contextualism into the abyss of abstraction.

Most relational analysts would not deny the existence of an independent, separate subject or self and in fact have gone to great lengths to account for individuality and authenticity within intersubjective space. A problematic is introduced, however, when a relational or intersubjective ontology is defined in opposition to separateness, singularity, distinction, and individual identity. For example, Seligman (2003) represents the relational tradition when he specifically tells us that "the analyst and patient are co-constructing a relationship in which neither of them can be seen as *distinct* from the other" (pp. 484–485, emphasis added). At face value, this is a troubling ontological assertion. Following from these premises, there is no such thing as separate human beings, which is tantamount to the claim that we are all identical because we are ontologically indistinguishable. If there is no distinction between two subjects that form the relational encounter, then only the dyadic intersubjective system can claim to have any proper identity. Relational analysts are not fully considering the impact of statements such as these when they propound that "everything is intersubjective" because by doing so it annuls individuality, distinctiveness, and otherness, which is what dialectically constitutes the intersubjective system to begin with. Clearly, we are not the same when we engage in social discourse or form relationships with others, which simply defies reason and empirical observation: Individuals always remain unique, even in social discourse. We retain a sense of self independent from the intersubjective system while participating in it. Of course, contemporary psychoanalysis uses the term *self* as if it is an autonomous, separate entity while engaging in social relations, but when it imports an undisciplined use of postmodern theory, it unwittingly nullifies its previous commitments. Jon Frederickson (2005) perspicaciously argues that despite the relational emphasis on subjectivity over objectivity, relational analysis inadvertently removes the subject from the subjective processes that constitute relational exchange to begin with, hence contradicting the very premise it seeks to uphold.

Further statements such as "There is *no* experience that is not interpersonally mediated" (Mitchell, 1992, p. 2, emphasis added) lend themselves to the social-linguistic platform and thereby deplete the notion of individuation, autonomy, choice, freedom, and teleological (purposeful) action because we are constituted, hence *caused*, by extrinsic forces that determine who we are. Not only does this displace the centrality of subjectivity—the very thing relationality wants to account for—it does not take into account other nonlinguistic or extralinguistic factors that transpire within personal lived experience such as the phenomenology of embodiment; somatic resonance states; nonconceptual, perceptive consciousness; affective life; aesthetic experience; *a priori* mental processes organized prior to the formal acquisition of language; and, most important, the unconscious. The confusional aspects to relational thinking are only magnified when theorists use terminology that align them with postmodernism on the one hand, thus eclipsing the self and extracting the subject from subjectivity, yet they then want to affirm the existence of the self as an independent agent (Hoffman, 1998). Although some relational analysts advocate for a singular, cohesive self that is subject to change yet endures over time (Fosshage, 2003; Lichtenberg, Lachmann, & Fosshage, 2002), others prefer to characterize selfhood as existing in multiplicity: Rather than one self there are "multiple selves" (Bromberg, 1994; Mitchell, 1993). But how is that possible? To envision multiple "selves" is philosophically problematic on ontological grounds, introduces a plurality of contradictory essences, obfuscates the nature of agency, and undermines the notion of freedom. Here we have the exact opposite position of indistinguishability: Multiple selves are posited to exist as separate, distinct entities that presumably have the capacity to interact and communicate with one another and the analyst. But committing to a self-multiplicity thesis rather than a psychic monism that allows for differentiated and modified self-states introduces the enigma of how competing existent entities would be able to interact given that they would have distinct essences, which would prevent them from being able to intermingle to begin with.

This brings us back to question the separateness of the self if the self is envisioned to belong to a supraordinate emergent agency that subordinates the primacy of individuality and difference. For relationalists who uphold the centrality of an intersubjective ontology, the self by definition becomes amalgamated within a relational matrix or intersubjective system. Beebe, Lachmann, and Jaffe's (Beebe, Jaffe, Lachmann, 1992; Beebe & Lachmann, 2003) relational systems or dyadic systems approach specifies that each partner's self-regulation is mutually regulated by the other and the interactions themselves that govern the system, therefore locating the source of agency within the system itself. But this is problematic. What becomes of the self in the system? Is it free from the causal efficacy of the relational encounter, or is it determined by the encounter? Does the self evaporate, or is it merely dislocated, hence demoted in ontological importance? And what about the locus of agency? How can an interactional process acquire any agency at all? Of course, Beebe and her colleagues would say that the self does not vanish, but by attributing agency to a bidirectional, coordinated "system" rather than the intersection, negotiation, and competing autonomous assertions of two individuated "agencies," they open themselves up to charges that they reify the system by turning it into an agentic entity that has the power to execute competing (reciprocal) modes of determination.

We see the same problem in Ogden (1995):

> The intersubjective third is understood as a *third subject* created by the unconscious interplay of analyst and analysand; at the same time, the analyst and analysand qua analyst and analysand *are generated* in the act of creating the analytic third. (*There is no analyst, no analysand, no analysis, aside from the process* through which the analytic third is generated). (p. 697, emphasis added)

Not only does Ogden specifically hypostatize the intersubjective system by making it an existent "subjective" entity, hence another subject—like a person—he also asserts that each subject in the dyad is "generated," presumably as a co-construction, yet this is left unexplained. But he also nebulously introduces the notion that the analytic dyad is "generated" through the process of "creating" the analytic third, hence overshadowing his previous claim that the "third" is "created" by the intersubjective dyad, a convoluted thesis that invites misinterpretation. What I believe Ogden wants to convey is that the analytic dyad is *transformed* in the act of intersubjective engagement, but this assumption is subsequently overturned when he implies that the duality creates the third yet is generated by the third, hence begging the question of what exactly constitutes agency, causality, and the analytic third. This is evinced by his irrefutable erasure of personal identity altogether by claiming that there is "no" analyst or analysand—hence a negation—independent of the "process" that brought the third subject into being to begin with, thereby collapsing his argument into a tautology or self-contradiction.

I believe the relational turn would be better served to indubitably acknowledge that the intersubjective system, field, or matrix is not an agentic subject, being (*Sein*), or entity (*ens*) but rather a "space" forged through transactional psychic temporal processes. By conceiving the relational matrix as intersubjective space instantiated through temporal dynamic mediacy generated by separate subjective agencies in dialogue, the ontological problematic of an emergent, systemically constituted (hence created) entity or analytic third is ameliorated. From my account, there is no third subjectivity or agency, only experiential space punctuated by embodied, transactional temporal processes that belong to the unique contingencies of the human beings participating in such interaction, whether this be from the developmental perspective of the mother–infant dyad to the therapeutic encounter.

To speak of a third subject or subjectivity that materializes out of the vapor of dialogical exchange is to introduce an almost impossible problematic of explaining how a noncorporeal entity could attain the status of being *qua* being (*ŏv*), let alone how such entity could claim to have agentic determination over the dyad. Here we unnecessarily introduce the notion, albeit unintentionally, of how the concept of the intersubjective system morphs into a *macroanthropos*.

But this is not to say that the intersubjective dyad does not introduce a new movement or generative element within the analytic milieu, what we may refer to as a "new presence," the presence of affective and semiotic resonance echoed within an unconscious aftermath born from the spontaneity of the lived phenomenal encounter. This is what I believe the best intentioned writers are thinking of when they speak of a *relational field theory*, not as an entity but as a complex succession of temporal processes that mutually transpire yet are asymmetrically (not equally) generated from within the intrapsychic configurations of each person's

psyche interjected and instantiated within interpersonal transactions—both transitive and mimetic yet under degrees of freedom—that are further mutually projected, filtered, incorporated,
assimilated, transfigured, and reorganized within each participant's internality. Therefore, these are temporal psychic processes
that dialectically unfold and are realized through actively constituted intersubjective space. This is not a third subject or agency,
only the product of enriched, complex interactional transmutations, partially co-constructed but ultimately conditioned on the
unique contingencies (unconscious, historical, developmental,
etc.) and teleological (purposeful) trajectories that inform each
participant's inner experience, choice, and actions within any
interpersonal encounter.*

UNCONSCIOUS EXPERIENCE, DISSOCIATION, AND THE QUESTION OF MULTIPLE SELVES

Contemporary perspectives on the unconscious vary widely in
scope and content, from displacing the dynamic unconscious
altogether, to appealing to neuroscience, to favoring postmodern sensibilities that subordinate psychical processes to language.
Donnel Stern and Philip Bromberg are two such proponents of
these redirective shifts in contemporary thought, and the force
of their ideas have arguably reshaped the way many contemporary analysts have come to conceive of mental processes. However
rich in clinical utility, these theoretical postulates are not without
serious conceptual omissions, particularly when raising the question of selfhood, agency, and unconscious enactments. In what
follows, I will attempt to offer an adumbrated meditation on the
philosophical implications of their claims with the hope that this

---

* Here it is important to reiterate the distinction between a climate, ambiance, or emergent
process we may generally refer to as a third movement within relational exchange that
may include both conscious and unconscious reverberations within each person's subjective interiority within the patient–analyst dyad, thus always in dynamic flux and subject
to retransformation, as opposed to a third subject, entity, or agency that materializes out
of the analytic encounter.

may lead to a spirited dialogue between advocates of a dissociative model of mind and those who privilege a dynamic unconscious.

Both Stern and Bromberg have enjoyed theoretical prominence within contemporary psychoanalysis by questioning the presupposed dominion of the unconscious over the puissance of consciousness and language. One cannot ignore in good faith how herculean, causally efficacious, and advantageous conscious experience, especially the role of language, has on psychological organization and development, which of course transpires within the contours of our familial attachments and cultural environs. Notwithstanding, there appears to be a predilection among some theorists to construct a false dichotomy between these categories when both stand in relation to their dialectical, hence symmetrical, counterparts. Yet for others, there is a tendency to collapse one category into the other, thereby erasing any distinction between the two realms or orders.

One such proponent is Don Stern. As I understand him (1997), unconscious experience is only that which was introduced in some fashion through consciousness yet actively interrupted, suspended, unattended to, blocked, and/or avoided, hence left unformulated, whether this be material semiotically encoded and sequestered on parallel levels of distributive processing, defensive constellations designed to protect the subject from psychic threat, the pure (formal) realm of potentiality, or as prereflective non-propositional thought lacking attention, self-conscious awareness, or mnemonic potency. In the end, Stern seems to equate unconscious experience with anything that is linguistically unarticulated and lacks "clarity and differentiation" (p. 37). This definition could equally apply to the most sophisticated forms of unconscious mental functioning or a simple act of conscious inattention.

Since Freud's early departure from a dissociative model of consciousness for a repression model of unconscious process, psychoanalysis has been tacitly led to believe that dissociation and repression are mutually exclusive categories, when they are not. Contemporary theorists seize upon this assumption when advocating for dissociation as a better theory for understanding unconscious experience (e.g., see Davies & Frawley, 1999; Howell, 2005) at the expense of retaining repression as a viable construct that aids clinical theory. The either–or false dichotomy that gets erected is that dissociation displaces the need for a repression model or that dissociation becomes subsumed or tantamount to repressive functions. Stern (1997) defines dissociation as "the avoidance of certain formulations of present experience … [which is] a channel or current along which certain meanings can flow and others cannot. To dissociate is simply to restrict the interpretations one makes of experience … [or] a restriction on the experiences we allow ourselves to have" (p. 88). Here Stern equates this phenomenon with unconscious experience, but not in any dynamic way, that is, not in a way that an unconscious agency orchestrates, executes, sustains, or harbors. Dissociation from this definition is entirely possible through the operations of consciousness. What we may infer is unconscious is really only *nonconscious* events, such as those regulatory functions belonging to our neurobiology. Here there is no need to postulate a dynamic unconscious. There is no unconscious teleology, no unconscious ego directing such mental actions, no unconscious intentionality of any kind. "Formulations" or "interpretations" that are "avoided" or barred are simply linguistic processes that are either foreclosed or "restricted." What Stern calls the unconscious is merely formed through the repudiation or absence of linguistic construction.

We also see a similar line of conceptualization in Jody Messler Davies and Mary Gail Frawley's (1999) depiction of dissociation as "an organization of mind … wherein traumatic memories are split off from associative accessibility to the remainder of conscious thought, but rather than being repressed and forgotten … they alternate in a mutually exclusive pattern with other conscious ego states" (p. 273). Davies and Frawley juxtapose dissociation as a process of splitting that relegates mnemonic content, not to an unconscious reservoir but rather to an altered state of "conscious ego states." From this definition, as with Stern, there is no need to posit a dynamic unconscious. Dissociation simply becomes a conscious phenomenon.

But this definition soon encounters problems. How can memory persist alongside other conscious ego states when by definition one cannot remember them at any given moment? If something is conscious, would it not be accessible, at least in principle, especially if the subject is primed to draw one's attention to it or to be alerted to it? In fact, if this is indeed the case, this would be tantamount to Freud's early theory of preconscious awareness, namely, the *Pcs* system. Yet this process of memorialization is not described by Davies and Frawley. How could "memories" sustain themselves without some form of unconscious preservation given that they are not "associatively accessible" to consciousness? Are we to attempt to resolve this conundrum by postulating another parallel stream of consciousness that keeps the two domains separate, which is what the early pioneers of dissociation theory proposed, especially those espoused by Janet and Charcot in France and simultaneously Morton Prince in the United States? And if so, how is contemporary relational theory any different from the old guard? Furthermore, one may ask, How can "traumatic memories" be related to "patterns" of "consciousness" when by definition they are not remembered or accessible to consciousness? Parallel or corresponding levels of consciousness become untenable unless either you advocate for alternate or multiple agencies organizing those complex mnemonic, affective, and ideational states that are kept separate from one another or you ascribe to the notion of a central agency that orchestrates and assigns the divisibility and dispersal of conscious content. Given Davies and Frawley's disavowal of a repression model in favor of a dissociative model of consciousness, by definition their position would fall under some form of parallelism or occasionalism. But if you posit this possibility, how would you reconcile the question of multiplicity and agency? And even if you were able to successfully defend a coherent theory of dissociation based solely on a model of consciousness, this would still mean an eclipse of the fundamental tenet of psychoanalysis—the primacy of unconscious mentation.

Stern's focus on dissociation as both a defensive process and a benign passivity of inattention further parallels Bromberg's work on the subject. What Stern calls "unformulated," Bromberg (1998) calls "unsymbolized." In fact, it is in the realm of "pre-symbolized experience" (p. 132) where dissociation transpires on unconscious levels of information processing that block or abort the emergence of formulated conceptual thought due to danger associated with conceptual formulations that are too cognitively intense to bear. Like Freud's repression censor, this implies an active banning or barring of consciousness, an aborting of the symbolization process altogether. Here Bromberg underscores the centrality of trauma on psychic organization. Bromberg emphasizes the defensive and adaptive transformational capacities of dissociation, as well as the pathological. He specifically points toward how dissociation leads to self-hypnoidal and amnesic mental states and how it becomes a normative and essential operation in the organization of personality. Of course, that which we are unaware of at any given moment becomes a form of unconsciousness even if our attention may be drawn to it. The question becomes how are these self-hypnoidal and amnesic states instituted if by definition we are unaware of our Self during such operations? More specifically, how is dissociation capable of lending order and organization to personality structure if by definition it is fractious and nonconsolidatible?

What is not directly discussed by Stern or Bromberg is *how* unconscious agentic processes instantiate themselves as dissociative enactments. Presumably Stern would deny the unconscious any agency—or at least this is inferred from his text—whereas Bromberg would not. But these are not questions they directly entertain. It is not enough to confirm the ontic function of dissociation without explaining how it is made possible to begin with. What I have argued elsewhere is that unconscious experience as dissociability is derived from the basic dialectical processes that govern mental life, first and foremost constituted through unconscious agency and, more specifically, the unconscious ego (Mills, 2002b). Dissociation is momentary fragmentation in self-continuity—itself a spacing—a split, fissure, or gap in being. From this standpoint, dissociation is the agentic expression and overdetermination of unconscious motivation as teleological intent.

In many ways, dissociation is a failure at representation—whether this be a failure to *re-present* visual images of events, such as traumas, affective resonance states, or somatic forces that persist as embodied unconscious memorializations. Such unconscious schemata may actively resist becoming recollected within conscious awareness when under the direction of defense and self-protective currents or evade conceptual formulation or linguistic articulation in consciousness for a variety of reasons, defensively motivated or not. Moreover, as Naso (2007) points out, dissociative content may have simply not been encoded because of adaptive and normatively benign aspects of inattention, detachment, or compartmentalization. But most important, dissociative processes must be directed by a mental agent executing such dynamic activity, and here, with the exception of Ron Naso (2010), I do not see this issue being directly addressed by many contemporary writers. Dissociability in its most elemental form is none other than the proclivity of the psyche to split or modify itself from its original simple unity as embodied apperceptive desire (Mills, 2002b), dividing itself into bits or pieces of self-experience through self-externalization, only then to *regather* and *re-cover* its self-division and externalization and incorporate itself back into its immediate self-constitution or internal structure, only to have the process repeat itself endlessly through an ongoing trajectory of dynamic pattern (see Mills, 2000b, for a review). In psychoanalysis, we have come to call this process *projective identification*.

My understanding of the unconscious is that it is process oriented, process driven, and process derived, what I have outlined in a theoretical system I have coined *dialectical psychoanalysis* or *process psychology* (Mills, 2000a, 2002a, 2010). Process psychology displaces the primacy of language over the unconscious, but it does not negate the value of signification. Instead, the unconscious institutes *and* incorporates the sign and builds a whole elaborate matrix of unconscious semiotics that conforms to its own laws and its own rules of signification fashioned by its own hands. Here we have the presence of unconscious freedom. The linguistic turn in psychoanalysis only partially accounts for unconscious dynamics, for the postmodern collapse of the subject and subjectivity in favor of the reification of language in my mind is misguided. What is fundamentally at stake is the ontological status of the unconscious.

Freud (1915b) alerts us to the fact that the unconscious declares itself as discontinuities in consciousness, what I prefer to call *spacings of the abyss*. We know them as apertures, perforations, or lapses in experience, where time is momentarily eclipsed by the presencing of absence—a hole in being. Dissociation is only one such phenomenon in our "gaps of experience," what Stern (1997) refers to as "empty space" in the "beginning of life" (p. 60). But such empty space is full of nonbeing, of nothingness, hence nothing is there, only experiential flow, appetitive pulsation—desire, a hovering over a clearing simultaneously exposed yet closed, open yet occlusive, the yawning gulf of the abyss. The abyss is never completely consolidated or unified, only discontiguous but unifying in its functions.

Although many contemporary psychoanalytic theorists remain naive to formal metaphysics, various factions have also posed divided and contradictory notions on the nature and meaning of the self. What has generally been uncontested among several predominant postmodern positions—more specifically within the genre of Foucault, Deleuze, and Derrida—is the insistence that the autonomous self is a fiction. As Lacan (1977) puts it, the ego is an illusory misrecognition (*méconnaissance*) of the Other. These convictions reify society, culture, and language, hence semiotics, which in turn define all discourse about selfhood and thus causally determine any element of personal agency that we might attribute to an individuated subject. In other words, all aspects of personal subjectivity have been conditioned by cultural signifiers that subordinate the individual to the symbolic order of language operative within one's society. From this standpoint, there is no individual, hence no self. And what we may customarily call a *self* is really nothing other than a linguistic invention based on social construction.

On the other hand, as previously noted, when discourse on the self is given attention in the relational literature, the notion of the self has been theoretically altered from a singular unity to a multiplicity of selves. Popular among some relationalists today—most notably Bromberg, Mitchell, Harris, and Davies—is the belief that there is no singular unitary self; rather there are a multiplicity of selves that exist within each subject, which in turn are ultimately governed by an intersubjective or dyadic system that determines how multiplicity is instantiated to begin within. Bromberg (1998) is clear when he says, "There is no such thing as an integrated self" (p. 186), instead there are "other" (p. 13), "many" (p. 311), or "several" (p. 256) selves. It is one thing to argue that there are multiple ego-alterations or self-states that populate intrapsychic life due to the multiple operations of psychic modification (such as through the parameters of dissociation and defense), but it is quite another thing to say that each subject contains a conglomeration of multiple selves that may or may not be in touch with one another yet exist and act as independent nominal agents within a singular mind. Although I agree that self-states may be modified elements of original instantiations as previous expressions of mental processes that have undergone internal division, differentiation, and transmogrification—which may further be experientially realized as atemporal, nonunified, incongruent, dissociated, and/or alienated aspects of mind—it is unfathomable to me how one can view a singular subject as possessing multiple selves that coalesce as extant independent entities.

Multiplicity can be legitimately explained as a unique and particularized experiential activity within the mind that has potentially

formed or acquired new organizations of self-experience and
adaptation through defensive transformations of earlier or con-
flicted archaic processes in response to real or perceived threat,
anxiety, and/or trauma; this is substantiated time and again in
clinical practice. But when you commit to the proposition of multiple entities within a singular subject, you have the messy burden
of explaining how multiple entities could possibly exist within a
singular embodied being whereby each entity inhabits the same
body, perceptual apparatus, and experiential medium regardless
of qualitative differences in desire, content, or form. The resultant
array of conundrums is unbounded: Who is the governing agent
among agencies, and how could you epistemologically justify that
there is such a governing agent to begin with? Who or what orga-
nizes or unifies the cacophony of experience if there are different
beings within one mind? Who or what is ultimately in control of
the mind? How can multiple selves share anything derived from
their own nature when by definition they are independent entities that compose different natures? Separate entities by definition cannot share or participate of the same nature because they
have separate essences by virtue of their differences. Yet discourse
on multiplicity directly assumes that separate selves within a singular mind can intuit, feel, absorb, influence, and communicate
with one another, hence they must have a shared essence in order
to do so. Therefore, multiple selves within one mind cannot exist
because they would not have any ability to converse or have contact with the other selves in any way unless they were derived
from the same essence. Some theorists seemingly confound this
issue. Separate selves eliminate the possibility that there could
be any shared psychic participation among these different selves
because they would have to have separate experiential mediums
or apparatuses that radically vary in phenomenological content
and form. What this means is that all experience would have to
be perceived and assimilated by a separate psychic register within
each self or self-state and hence organized by independent agentic
forces processing and guiding self-experience. But how could this

be so? How could two or more entities with two or more essences cohabitate and participate of each other's essence when they are ontologically distinct, thus incapable of intermingling without altering their essences, hence annulling any notion of difference to begin with? These are palpable logical contradictions that any metaphysical theory of duality or multiplicity must be able to account for in order to salvage some theoretical credibility.

From my standpoint, a multiplicity thesis is most legitimately justified by appealing to a developmental monistic ontology governing the subjective mind of each individual, thus accounting for psychic division, differentiation, and modification of content and form (viz., self-states) without generating separate psychic entities (*qua* selves), each with its own separate essence. To justify a theory of mutually exclusive, multiple essences that have the capacity to interact and intermingle would lead to some form of occasionalism, monadology, or parallelism, each with its own particular set of problems. Explanations of modified self-states, psychic realms, or experiential orders of subjectivity are quite different from multiple subjects, and this is precisely what the relationalists who avouch such a theory of multiple selves need to consider.

Elizabeth Howell (2005) conceptualizes mind as reducible to dissociative processes, and she is following in the same theoretical trend as many relational postmoderns. This view lends itself to parsimonious and possibly reductionistic accounts of the complexifications of mental functioning, not to mention it introduces a theoretical problematic for not adequately addressing the question of agency within a dissociative model. If everything we call mental or psychical is a multiplicity of self-states, how is a state organized? What processes or mechanics are operative that constitute dissociability to begin with? Does this merely devolve into neurobiology? From my account, one has to have active unconscious agentic functions executing mental activity, or this argument collapses into and privileges a materialist model of consciousness. Following this line of reasoning, the unconscious is not a necessary psychoanalytic construct let alone an ontological force in the mind. Furthermore, if you do not allow for agency directing mental activity on multiple levels of systemic psychic organization conjoined as a unifying totality that makes multiplicity possible, then you have a problem with human freedom and causality to boot. If dissociation theory is to replace a model of dynamic unconscious processes and is said to account for all normative and pathological enactments, then how are enactments executed if you cannot sufficiently account for agency? And if agency is to be attributed to consciousness, and dissociation occurs outside of conscious awareness, then are we not begging the question of what constitutes dissociation? If dissociative enactments devolve into consciousness, then this is contradictory because dissociation is presumed to transpire outside of conscious awareness. And if the answer is somewhere to be found in brain processes, then are we not committed to material reduction or a merelogical fallacy?* Not only does this not adequately answer the question and mechanics of dissociative ennactments, it subverts the philosophical question of unconscious agency.

Freud (1894) talks about how the splitting of consciousness that takes place in defense is in the service of keeping affect and ideation "detached" from one another. This ideation, however, is not

---

* Certain conclusions made by contemporary theoreticians and researchers—such as there is no dynamic unconscious or that nonconscious encoded events implicit in memory structure displace our previous understanding of unconscious activity (see Iannuzzi, 2006)—do not hold up to logical scrutiny when they fall under a category mistake or are guilty of the fallacy of simple location. Furthermore, this line of thinking, namely, that the brain is the cause of mind and all mental activity, is what Bennett and Hacker (2003) refer to as the "merelogical fallacy" in neuroscience. This is a fundamental attribution error where one ascribes the acts or characteristics of a whole to its parts. This argument is derived from Aristotle's notion of formal causality: One cannot reduce the complexity of a whole system or design (i.e., selfhood, personality) to its material substance (brain). But this is precisely what neuroscience attempts to accomplish: The human being, personhood, or mind devolves into material-efficient reductive forces. From this paradigm, mind is nothing but brain. So contra John Searle (1992), who insists on consciousness as a property of the brain, or Daniel Dennett (1991), who ascribes psychological processes to parts of the brain, these explananda are mereological errors because they do not take into account the psychical acts that constitute the person as a whole. Rather, they reduce the human being to a subsystem of parts that fracture the supraordinate nature of a complex system (Mills, 2010).

merely dissociative, where signification and thought are relegated to what is simply "unformulated," as Stern would tell us. Rather, for Freud ideas are "weakened" yet held in dynamic reserve until a "fresh impression ... succeeds in breaking through the barrier erected by the will" (p. 50). This is the beginning of Freud's theory of a dynamic unconscious that thinks, feels, and actively converts mental phenomena either by producing associative links or by creating disjunctions: The former involves assigning a semiotic to unconscious experience, the latter involves instituting a protective function. Here I believe that Freud succeeds in both accounting for dissociation within consciousness and explaining how the content of what becomes dissociated (i.e., affect, sense impressions, ideas) is organized within the abyss. This means that unconscious content has a life and a force of its own that is sustained within a dynamic underworld and creates unconscious pressure that becomes an onus for the ego to deal with. What this ultimately means is that dissociation and repression are not incompatible processes or contrary psychoanalytic theoretical models that clash with one another or cancel each other out. Unlike Stern (2010), who professes that "in most Interpersonal and Relational schemes, dissociation replaces repression" (p. 110), I believe they operate on stratified levels of psychic reality carried out and maintained by the dynamic agency that properly belongs to the unconscious ego.

Dissociative enactments must be exercised by an agentic teleological organization of mind executing the enactments, or else you have the intractable problem of multiple essences conversing, or you have the view of the mind as a biological machine that is turned on by the environment devoid of freedom and agency. This sounds like Skinner is potentially alive and well in contemporary psychoanalysis. Although I cannot do justice to this complex issue here, I do propose that an adequate solution may be found by conceiving the multiplicity of the self as a dispersal of modified and differentiated self-states or microagents that are ontologically conjoined and inseparable from a unitary self that is a *unifying unifier*, but one that is not static or unified. Rather, the self is pure process that is systemically and developmentally organized as a dynamic self-articulated complex holism. Here the inherent dichotomizing that characterizes the unitary versus multiple self debate can find resolve in a process psychology that dialectically accounts for plurality within a unifying conception of mind.

POMOCENTRISM, ANTIESSENTIALISM, AND THE QUESTION OF UNIVERSALS

Postmodern doctrines have been selectively embraced by many identified minorities or those who belong to culturally, politically, and racially disenfranchised groups, including women; people of color; ethnic, religious, and nationalist supporters; socialists; GLBT (gay-lesbian-bisexual-transgendered) advocates; and those who simply defy mainstream society or live alternative lifestyles. These groups personify difference, and it is no wonder why they vilify the status quo. Perhaps among the most avid opponents of postmodernism are feminists of various kinds, from the more virulent radicals to those who simply oppose the androcentric mind-set that has dominated Western metaphysics since the pre-Socratics, which have, in part, historically informed the subjugation and political oppression of women. A similar sentiment may be found among other disenfranchised groups as well—such as the racially or ethnically encumbered—thereby informing disparate subcultures that are based on a philosophy of antiestablishment.

Such pomocentrics—if we may call them that—have a shared common conviction: Historically established traditions simply fail to capture their inner experience, epistemology, and phenomenological view of the world, so they must be renounced. Because of this disjunction between personal feeling and the impersonal rationalism that underlies modernity and contemporary science, pomocentrics are quick to dispense with the metaphysical tradition altogether mainly because it owes its legacy to "dead European White males," a common sentiment expressed among feminists, ethnocentric academics, social critics, and the like. We want to be sensitive to the emotionality that often accompanies such reactionary motives to forsake antiquated philosophies, especially if they have contributed to personal, collective, or political prejudices that have directly or indirectly harmed an identified group, but we must be mindful that such positions are often based on subjective reactions to negative feelings that eclipse a more critical or logical examination of a given theoretical model. In fact, when pomocentrics profess to question the establishment by attacking, let's say, absolute truth claims, they themselves make absolute pronouncements that reinforce absolutism rather than refute it, thus devolving into a philosophy of contradiction. As I have previously argued, we may see this time and again by many identified postmoderns who wish to replace traditional paradigms for their own theoretical framework, which by definition should not carry any more weight than the viewpoints of those they criticize because of their implicit relativist interpretations of nature and culture. For example, take Adrienne Harris's (1996) notion of antiessentialism: "The project of postmodernism details the fracturing of social and individual perceptions of time and space as a particular hallmark of contemporary consciousness" (p. 541). This endorses the belief that universals are either nonexistent or irrelevant. If perception is merely relative, then we can make no universal, hence historical or ontological, statements about the mind, let alone accept the belief that certain structural processes of mind, including metaphysical assertions of space and time, are common to all people regardless of context or culture.

Another problem with pomocentrism is that it is firmly wed to (a) antifoundationalism—thus denying that there is any ground or formal structure to knowledge and epistemic justification—and (b) antiessentialism, which is the refutation that predication and objects have an essential versus accidental nature. These propositions are once again committed to the negation of shared common universals. This is due, in part, to the need to preserve the notion of uniqueness and particularized experience that stands in contrast to an all-encompassing universal. Here lies another series of self-contradictions: Postmodernism denies the existence of the autonomous self, but then it wants to champion the uniqueness of lived subjective experience. Not only does this underscore the primacy of perspectivism belonging to an individual, it also extends to a collection of subjects that share a collective identification with one another. When postmodernism is not extracting the subject from subjectivity, it wants to generalize the uniqueness of lived experience to a group phenomenon.

Here, not only do we see a particular applied to a universal, we also see the negation of the universal through the particularization itself. When a particularized notion is turned into a shared commonality or group identification, it at once avows universalization—by claiming that lived experience does not solely belong to an individual—as it simultaneously negates the absolutism inherent in universalization—by claiming that shared group experience opposes other group experience. But here incongruity and circularity spin on and on: When you claim one group has a different experience than another group, this is an absolutist claim, hence a *particularized* universal. If there is some *capacity* for shared identifications of particularized experience, then there must be a common ground or essence representative of any collection of subjects regardless of their own unique experiential lives or the lives of other subjects that identify with an opposing group. Although many modern philosophies attempt to explain the coexistence and unification of the individual within the collective, the subjective within the objective, and the particular within the universal, postmodernism contradicts both positions while claiming to have its cake and eat it too.

In their enthusiasm to jettison foundationalist and objectivist principles inherent to essentialism, pomocentrics fail to properly understand that essentialism does not necessarily annul uniqueness or difference but instead accounts for it within the larger parameters that define human experience. Here we may observe a confusion between phenomenology and ontology, the former being privileged and emphasized whereas the latter being displaced. But how can Being be displaced? Do we not exist? Or are we merely a figment of our imaginations—like the postmodern ego—a fiction, illusion, or social construction? Although we may surely not agree about the nature of our existence and essential characteristics, it nevertheless becomes palpably absurd to imply, let alone deny, that we exist—that we share a common ontic ground and existential structure. No sane person truly believes this, so the implications of such arguments must be motivated by ignorance or other psychological factors, such as political identifications governed by a discourse of emotion and ideology.

Contemporary psychoanalysts tend to devalue essentialism without fully understanding what it means (see Dimen, 1991; Teicholz, 1999; Young-Bruehl, 1996). This is particularly evident in psychoanalytic gender studies. Let us examine Muriel Dimen's (1991) view: "The core of gender is difference, not essence" (p. 342), thus reinforcing that "gender looks to consist not of essences but of complex and shifting relations among multiple contrasts or differences. Sometimes these contrasts remain distinct, at other times they intersect, and at still other times they fuse and exchange identities" (p. 339). Dimen seems to make a number of ontological contradictions: (a) She at once affirms difference as being "distinct," hence she inadvertently proclaims difference to be the hallmark of experience, which by definition dialectically forges separate essences or entities that are something not identical to something else (rather than saying difference logically depends on similarity); (b) then she says these separate entities, presumably gendered subjects, "intersect," which then draws into question how separate subjects can relate if they have separate natures; and (c) then she further claims that they can "exchange identities," therefore proclaiming that separate beings can alter their structural form, hence their essence. From these statements, Dimen is apparently not aware that difference, similarity, and essence are perfectly compatible categories when viewed from a holistic monistic ontology.

The bad press on essentialism may be said to derive from mediaevalist interpretations of Aristotle that ascribe necessary properties to entities, which inhere as fixed, universal, and irrevocable characteristics that define any substance, when essentialism may also be viewed as mutable processes subject to change and alterations within content and form, thus allowing for context, contingency, particularization, and difference within a generic process of activity that is common to a genus. From this standpoint, what is essential, hence necessarily universal, is process. For example, in the process philosophies of Hegel (1807/1977) and Whitehead (1929/1978), process is an agentic trajectory of dynamic pattern that bears and incorporates similarity and difference within a holistic, self-articulated, complex synthetic teleology. Here essence not only appears as difference but dialectically generates all forms of being and becoming.

Furthermore, universality as process accounts for flux, transformation, and change within a motional pattern of invariance; therefore essence may account for both the ontological features of an entity and that which propels its activity, thus accounting for its appearances or phenomenology.* These are complex philosophical arguments that have been addressed by many Western metaphysicians, but they do not concern us here.† The main point

---

* For Hegel (1807/1977), "appearance is essence" (p. 147). In Hegel's dialectical system, essence appears as its manifestations, for nothing can exist unless it is made actual. Hence, phenomenology and particularization must have an ontological ground that fuels its expressions.

† Although essentialism is an ancient theory about the sources of order, power, and organization in the world, we are beginning to see essentialist metaphysics applied to a number of current movements in the philosophy of nature (see Ellis, 2002) and process philosophy (see Mills, 2002a). The basic tenet of the new essentialism is that the laws of nature derive from and are immanent within things themselves rather than are imposed on them from an external source, such as God. Instead, activity in the universe, and here specifically within the parameters that propel human nature, is understood from within the intrinsic organizations forged through its own processes due to internal causal forces, capacities, reactions, and proclivities that are activated and arranged in relation to extrinsic events. Here essence is not what is causally determined to constitute an entity, rather it is what is constituted through the entity's own burgeoning activity. This allows for a metaphysics of freedom that is sometimes eclipsed from other forms of essentialism.

is that psychoanalytic interpretations of essence only assume a particular brand in the history of philosophy with ostensive logical limitations, yet these interpretations and their criticisms are generalized to all metaphysical systems when this is simply unwarranted. The real objection that pomocentrics hold is the possibility that we as human beings could all be composed of some identical attribute, property, or activity when the vast sea of differences tells us otherwise. Here again enters the phenomenology–ontology confound.

Is there a shared common essence that motivates all human beings? If the answer to this question is no, then there can be no universals. I take for granted that different experiences shape our individual epistemologies that in turn inform our personal identities and collective identifications, and just as we are affected by our families and society differently, we have different defenses and desires, therefore we have different psychologies. But this does not negate the notion of universals. Despite the fact that particular aspects of intrapsychic life may not be duplicated or identical to others' subjective experience or that certain groups who share a certain commonality based on thrownness, sex, gender, ethnicity, race, religion, economics, political identification, or embodiment cannot be adequately compared to others, we are more fundamentally conjoined in essence than in phenomenology. This is one reason why we as clinicians fundamentally observe universal patterns emanating from within each individual psyche regardless of historicity, gender, culture, or race. For example, what we commonly call "defense mechanisms" occur in all minds and have so since the beginning of human life. Although the content may vary from person to person, from time to time, in a geographic location, and from skin color to skin color, the form or pattern is universal. Denial is denial no matter what is being denied. This transcends particularization. In fact, defenses are *essential* to human existence, without which we would surely all be basket cases.

The same may be said for endogenous drives or biological urges (*Triebe*), as well as the phenomena of transference and repetition.

Although what is being transferred, reactivated, or dislocated from psychic territory originating in the patient's personal past onto the contingencies of the immediate analytic encounter will vary from person to person in particular content, thematic structure, and form, we would be hard-pressed to find an analyst willing to deny these universal occurrences present in all patients. The same is true for countertransference enactments. Repetition is the desire, motive, or compulsion to reexperience an earlier event within the present, albeit under different contingencies and expressed valences. Just as the organic impetus informing the need to satiate hunger and thirst is a universal process unique to living species, defense, transference, and repetition are predicated on unconscious organizations that are purported to exist within us all.

Postmodernism must be able to account for universality if it plans to prosper as a viable theory. The way postmodern perspectives are being arbitrarily annexed in contemporary psychoanalytic circles so far has led to conceptual contradictions that undermine theoretical coherency and negate the modern philosophical tenets that psychoanalysis fundamentally rests upon. This negation primarily derives its justification from the epistemological attack on the rational and scientific philosophical traditions that postmodernism seeks to displace through the linguistic turn. From this standpoint, objectivity, universality, and essentialism are misguided categories that are either simply unknowable or nonexistent. Just because we may reasonably question the epistemological grounds to knowledge, truth, and certainty and perhaps even conclude that it is not possible to attain unadulterated access to such answers, this does not mean that these universal categories do not exist in themselves, only that human consciousness is limited in its apprehension of that which exceeds our experience or observation. This is one reason why the great philosophical rationalists from Plato and Aristotle to Descartes, Kant, and Hegel all championed logic to breach the limits that empiricism, with its self-imposed confinement to observation and measurement, and phenomenology, with its sole focus on subjective conscious experience, simply could not achieve. Although Kant (1781/1965) imposed a limit to pure reason as the inability to directly know things in themselves, he nevertheless posited the existence of natural objects and systematically delineated the universal categories that make their understanding possible. Hegel (1812/1831/1969), on the other hand, argued that we can know things in themselves through pure thought by virtue of the fact that we posit them.

CONCLUDING RELATIVISTIC POSTSCRIPT

In this chapter I have attempted to introduce in a variety of ways the incoherency of many postmodern claims while acknowledging the virtue of the postmodern message, namely, respect and value for difference. But with the overzealous commitment to celebrating difference and plurality comes an underappreciation for universal aspects of meaning and existence that conjoin us all. Here contemporary psychoanalysis could profit from revisiting modernism characterized by the inherent holism that allows for the unification of difference within universality, a philosophical position that accounts for particularization within its broad metaphysical inquiry.

Postmodern discourse privileges phenomenology over ontology, which tends to overshadow all other dimensions of being and experience because we are so fundamentally attuned to uniqueness and difference, when this antipode fails to adequately account for their coexistence. We all share common elements of experience despite the fact that difference signals unique features of being that cannot be duplicated by virtue of the privitization of lived experience or qualia that by definition is singular and special and has subjective determinate priority in value. In other words, although we are at times attuned to the self-certainty of our immediate inner experiences, feelings, and thoughts, which by definition signal the primacy of our unique individuality and separateness from others, we are also conjoined as the I that is We, and the We that is I—as a collection of subjects who live, breathe, and experience in shared communal proximity, what we call society—hence composed of the norms and values that govern psychosocial life. This is why civilization stands over individuality yet comprises it, for civilized cultures are committed to an ethic that governs and protects the rights of its citizenry for the purpose or sake of upholding a shared valuation system we call humanity.

We cannot legitimately pass the false generalization that particularization cancels universality. Instead, particularization may be understood within the context of *subjective universality*—the notion that individual difference is an objective, collective experiential activity of mind that is expressed idiosyncratically yet shared by all. Self and subjectivity are objectively instantiated in culture and our social institutions through intersubjective exchange. Here the universality of subjectivity as a collection of individualized, autonomous subjects conjoined through intersubjective social engagement allows for both difference and plurality within a dynamic complex totality of universality, unification, and generality. Singularity is individuated yet belongs to the whole. Unless one is a misanthrope, disturbed, traumatized, or deranged, all people deep down want to be happy, to experience peace, to flourish or prosper, to beget or create, to have a family or be a part of what a family signifies—love, acceptance, empathy, validation, recognition—the very fabric of the relational platform. And here enters the wisdom of what relationality truly has to offer.

3

Illegitimate Attacks on Classical Psychoanalysis

What is perhaps the most salient transgression repeatedly made by relational psychoanalysis is its unrelenting misinterpretation of Freudian theory. What is so vexing to many analysts is the polemical denunciation of classical thought, which is used by many contemporary analysts to advocate for their position, arguably a politically driven ideology, at the expense of providing accurate scholarship. Masling (2003) has criticized Mitchell for setting this trend among the relational tradition, thereby leading to continued unsubstantiated claims that are overstated, provocative, confrontational, brazen, and taken out of context. Richards (1999a) argues that the relational school has constructed a false dichotomy between drive theory and relational theory, when in fact Freud's mature theoretical system clearly accounts for relational concepts (Reisner, 1992), a position Frank (1998a) cogently reveals began in Freud's early career. Furthermore, Lothane (2003) persuasively argues that Freud was an interpersonalist, whereas Roazen (1995) and Lohser and Newton (1996) show that Freud was at times quite relational in his therapeutic actions as evinced by testimonials acquired from the firsthand accounts of his patients.

I certainly do not want to categorize all relationalists by placing them in the same camp sharing unanimous convictions, nor do I wish to charge them all with denouncing Freud or casting aspersion toward classical psychoanalysis. There are many thoughtful theorists who have attempted in many ways to bridge the gaps between the intrapsychic and the interpersonal, mind and body, as well as to reconcile classical technique with contemporary sensibilities. I can appreciate differences of interpretation, explanation, scholarly distinctions, and redirecting shifts in emphasis that have informed the history of the psychoanalytic domain, and I actually think it is a good thing to promote a healthy debate of ideas. Having said that, I do not feel most representatives of the relational tradition have accurately understood Freud's mature theoretical corpus or have they fully grasped the relational aspects or implications of Freud's thought. In fact, relational psychoanalysis has made its claim to originality and popularity "based on the radical rejection of drive" (Greenberg, 1991, p. vii). Whether this was the intention of the pioneers of the relational movement, I cannot say, but regardless of their motives, they have left their legacy in print, and the implications of what they wrote are left open to interpretation. In the discussion that follows, I wish to highlight various distortions of classical thought that have given rise to this antipode and, in some cases, antipathy between the Freudians and modern conflict theorists on one side and the interpersonal and relational supporters on the other. Although I cannot do justice in capturing every nuance and perspective between these competing schools of thought, which would easily be a book in its own right, I will attempt to reasonably represent what most analysts are likely to agree to be the main theoretical differences that underlie classical versus relational views on the mind.

THE QUESTION OF DRIVE VERSUS RELATIONALITY

Let us first examine the exaggerated polarization the relational turn has created between the concepts of relation and drive, an antithesis it has capitalized on to serve as a launching pad for its "new" theory. Mitchell (1988) specifically tells us that his approach is "a purely *relational* mode perspective, unmixed with drive-model premises" (p. 54). Let us not be mistaken here. Mitchell is very clear when he advocates for a "purely" relational model. But in the same paragraph he also accuses Freud of "eschewing any role for primary relatedness in his theory and relying instead solely on drive economics" (p. 54). This last sentence unambiguously shows that either he has not read Freud carefully, hence revealing a scholarly faux pas, or he is deliberately relying "solely" on an economic interpretation of mind, a very early position Freud had posited, but one he had clearly built upon and theoretically expanded by the time he introduced his structural-tripartite-process model of the psyche (see Freud, 1923, 1932–1933). In fact, when discussing the economic or quantitative aspects of mental functioning in his final treatise, *An Outline of Psycho-Analysis*, where he is attempting to summarize his life's work, Freud (1940) plainly tells us that "this explanation is unsatisfactory" (p. 184). But here in Mitchell's (1988) early writings, he is already advocating for purity of his own relational perspective in opposition to drive psychology, which he sets up as antithetical paradigms. He unequivocally states, "The strategy adopted in this volume has been to develop an integration of the major lines of relational-model psychoanalytic theorizing into a broad, integrative perspective—from which the concept of drive, as Freud intended it, has been omitted" (p. 60). Mitchell's stated reasons for doing this are that he does not want to force an unnatural fit by introducing a mixing of the two models. Of course he offers an argument for this, but that is not the point here. What I am trying to determine is the ground and fulcrum of relational theory. In other words, what does it philosophically stand for? What are its main postulates that all relationalists would uphold or, at least in principle, what they would likely hold in consensus or theoretically espouse as a group? Greenberg (1991) speaks for a collective relational voice when he opines,

> Analysts operating within the relational model of the mind are united in their claim that it is misguided to begin theorizing with drive … relational analysts look to what can be perceived around us: We should not emphasize endogenous determi-

nants of experience; the qualities of relationships themselves are decisive. (p. 69)

The first part of Greenberg's pronouncement is to lay down a universal generalization that relational analysts are "united" in their belief that one should not begin theorizing with drive; instead relationalists "emphasize" relationships. Fair enough. But why jettison drive altogether?

What is valid is that there is a matter of difference in emphasis one places on drive determinants versus relational forces that operate on those determinants. But is that enough to spark a new theoretical tradition? My guess is that Greenberg and Mitchell needed more punch to their theory if they wanted to truly differentiate themselves from the classical school. That is likely one reason why they theoretically insisted on the militant denunciation of drive.

Relationships may be "decisive," but are they all-encompassing? In other words, do they account for all mental phenomena? Many authors, myself included, would adamantly aver that this is impossible. Decisiveness in the service of parsimony does not endear itself easily to the learned person intent on understanding and explaining the complexifications and totality of mental life. Greenberg (1991) goes on to say that it is Mitchell who "captures the central point that relational theorists want to make" (p. 70), namely,

Within the relational model, psychological meanings are not regarded as universal and inherent; bodily experiences and events are understood as evoked potentials which derive meaning from the way they become patterned in interaction with others. From this viewpoint *what is inherent is not necessarily formative*; it does not push and shape experience, but is itself shaped by the relational context. (Mitchell, 1988, p. 4)

Mitchell argues, and I agree with him here, that meaning is derived from relational patterning, but he confounds meaning with the "underlying structure of experience" (p. 4). Are there not other embodied processes that are operative within the realm of meaning construction and social relations that are not necessarily mediated by relatedness or conditioned on social interaction? For example, does desire have an inherent impetus or constitutional process that *impels* it to crave, to seek, to find—regardless of what the object, motive, or content of its desire may be? If desire is purely conditioned on relatedness (also a Lacanian claim), then what happens to drive? Mitchell (1988) wants us to keep in mind that relational psychoanalysis is premised on a "purely *relational*" (p. 54) model of psychic activity and human behavior where Freudian drive theory "has been omitted" (p. 60), what Greenberg (1991) forcefully states is theoretically "based on the radical rejection of drive" (p. vii). Despite the fact that we may object to a necessary theoretical bifurcation of the two schools, insisting instead that a mixed model or a unifying, synthetic, pluralistic, or comparative-integrative approach—even a composite theory—is not only viable but clinically useful, we must take Mitchell and Greenberg at their word. In their opinion, drive becomes an antiquated category for explanation in their theoretical system.

Mitchell (1988) in particular is making an ontological commitment when he believes that relational psychoanalysis has no place for "the metapsychological concept of drive" (p. 61). Earlier, he announces rather presumptuously, even brazenly in a haphazard generalized manner, that "the theory of instinctual drive, which is the conceptual framework housing *all* of Freud's ideas … has been, like all human intellectual creations, essentially superseded" (1986, p. 458, emphasis added). Notice he says that all of Freud's ideas essentially boil down to drive theory. Nothing could be further from the case. Drives are part of our evolutionary nature, which account for why and how we are able to form relations and relationships with others and the world around us. He also makes a category mistake by favoring an apple to an orange—the body (drives) and relatedness (social interaction) are not equivalent categories, nor are they separate processes that one must theoretically choose. They are inseparable from one another. In fact, each are embodied processes (whether we speak of biology or sociology) and must necessarily be so in order to exist. Although they are not categorically the same, they are nevertheless mutually implicative.

Greenberg (1991) also takes the relational position to the extreme: "Drive, in the view of the relational theorists, is not an unconditioned, irreducible, pre-existing force that accounts for our deepest motives and generates its own experiential categories. *There is no such force*" (p. 70, emphasis added). This is a dogmatic ontological assertion. Greenberg is resolute when he declares the "essential premise of the relational model: It is unnecessary and misleading to build theory around any concept of a pre-experiential force that brings people into relationships with others" (p. 70). These last two statements alone are clearly at loggerheads with metaphysics and science to boot.

Let us philosophically unpack these claims. First of all, there are no *a priori* organizations, according to Greenberg. He is a committed Lockean. The experiential world of the subject is brought into being by the environment, specifically human beings. Mind is initially a blank slate (*tabula rasa*) in which all forms of experience are superimposed. He would not subscribe to the Kantian or Freudian view that experience is made intelligible by structural, cognitive (ontological) categories of understanding or that the world is perceived through preexperiential forms of sensibility that allow the perceptive world to arise within consciousness to begin with. By logical extension, the unconscious for Greenberg could only be justified as being forged through relational—hence conscious—experience. He could not logically or persuasively defend the position that unconsciousness precedes consciousness, let alone that unconscious processes remain a primary "force" in the mind, given that he has disposed with the necessity of such a force having any preexperiential order or activity. In short, there are no preexisting universal cognitive structures to mind. Greenberg's propositions naturally lead to the inferential conclusion that for the relational analyst, relationships are both a necessary and a sufficient condition in which all mental phenomena can be adequately explained. Although relationships are an ontological necessity for human experience and development, as I will argue, they are hardly a sufficient condition that explains all aspects of psychological life.

Greenberg (1991) specifically tells us that he adheres to "the empiricist philosophical tradition" where one only needs to look for "what can be perceived around us" (p. 69). If perception of the world is his criteria for justifying meaning relations, then how is perception brought about to begin with? In other words, how is it constituted? Is it constituted through relationships—hence a *causal* imposition? But then how does the process or mechanism of perception arise in the first place? Do other people place the *capacity* for perception in our minds? And if so, how is that possible? These are the philosophical implications of his statement that there is no "preexisting force" that accounts for our perceptions of the world. And if these problematics are not enough, by his own presuppositions, he could not even defend (without collapsing into logical contradiction) the psychoanalytic thesis that wishes and defenses are imbued upon our experiential perceptions of the world unless he makes the qualification that all desire is ultimately the Other's desire that is mimetic in nature. And once you introduce that assumption, then there is really no place for freedom and agency within a relational paradigm.

Greenberg also aligns with "Ortega y Gassett … when he expressed what could be a manifesto for the relational model: *Man has no nature*" (p. 85). From this statement, Greenberg is clearly an antiessentialist, and within the history of philosophy, he would be labeled a nominalist for abnegating the notion that we all share a collective universal nature or essence that is a structural necessity of being human. Notice Greenberg refers to this as a relational "manifesto." This is an apparent confutation, because nominalism is tantamount to the notion that anything we name, refer to, or describe, such as *human* or *reality*, does not really refer to things, rather they are merely linguistic constructions we invent. Hence it is not necessary to even posit having relationships let alone import the ontological necessity of relationships as having a causal influence over subjective mental life, because according to a nominalist view of the mind, there are no universals. And what is furthermore contradictory is that relationalists want to claim that *relationships are essential and universal* to forging mental life. Here is another example of pomocentric thinking that leads to logical self-contradiction in terms.

Overall, Greenberg's claims have nothing to do with the fact that meaning is an interactional phenomenon; rather, they are antimetaphysical statements that fail to describe the conditions or ground that ontologically prepares or brings forth experience to begin with. In other words, Greenberg's thesis that there is no "preexisting force" to psychic activity naively dismisses the whole idealist tradition of philosophy, one that by most standards has successfully overturned the simplistic empiricism of its time, lessons that remain deeply embedded within contemporary philosophy and science today.

If there is "no force" in the mind prior to relationships, then how are mental phenomena derived? When we speak of "force," we are logically inhering a principle of internally derived activity that exists prior to any interpersonal encounter. If mental phenomena originate from others, then how were others derived in the first place? If you appeal to others before that, then you are hopelessly ensnared in an infinite regress where even the question of "What comes first: the chicken or the egg?" is lost in obfuscation. If you appeal to something outside of the mind, such as familial life, culture, language, history, and so forth, you still have the intractable problem of explaining how mind is acquired to begin with. And if you appeal to general brain events or neuroscience, then you are not committed to a "purely relational" psychoanalytic model.

Mitchell, on the other hand, clearly wants to create a fissure between his relational matrix theory and drive theory in order to advocate for why his framework is superior to Freud's, a position he reinforced throughout his entire body of works to the point that it has become an entrenched trademark of relational lore. Unlike Greenberg (1991), who was concerned with reconciling classical drive theory with contemporary relational perspectives, Mitchell not only was not interested in attempting to account for drive theory, let alone reappropriate it within relational psycho-analysis, but wanted to debunk it entirely. Here he introduces a major flaw to his theory, for he jettisons the primacy of embodi-ment. What becomes of our corporeality in a relational field the-ory if drives are no longer acknowledged as basic constituents of psychic activity? Mitchell's intent is to overturn their importance within psychic life, but he does so through an extreme position of negation—not merely displacement. Mitchell's denunciation of the drives is tantamount to a fundamental denial of our embod-ied facticity.

Mitchell was so unfavorably disposed to the notion of our pre-determined embodiment that it led him to make extreme, inde-fensible assertions such as this: "*Desire* is experienced always *in the context of relatedness*" (1988, p. 3), thus leading Masling (2003) to charge that he was willing to ignore empirically verifiable facts, such as biologically based desires for water, food, sleep, and sex, in order to magnify the differences between his viewpoint and classi-cal thought. Whereas Greenberg throws metaphysics out with the bathwater, Mitchell disregards the biological sciences. Mitchell's (1988) antibiologism is captured in his belief that "even basic bodily events, like hunger, defecation, and orgasm are regarded as experienced through, interpreted in the context of, the sym-bolic textures of the relational matrix" (p. 61). I don't know about others, but for me going to the toilet has always been a solitary activity. It is one thing to experience and interpret bodily events in the semiotic context of meaning signification that can be said to be originally derived from relational-linguistic structures that saturate our cultural thrownness, but it is quite another to suggest that these biologically based processes or urges are not preexistent or instinctually innate.

Pizer (2006) challenges my interpretation of Mitchell's meaning of desire, which Pizer wants to chalk up to a linguistic construct. But what Pizer omits from Mitchell's (1988) text is quite crucial, namely, that Mitchell aligns with the supposition that "we are portrayed *not* as a conglomeration of physically based urges, but as being shaped by and inevitably embedded within a matrix of relationships with other people" (p. 3, emphasis added). Although I agree with Mitchell's last statement, as does Freud, why does Mitchell need to negate biology? Unlike Mitchell, Freud both endorses biologism and the value of social relatedness by offering a holistic, coherent, and internally consistent theoretical corpus, which does not lend itself to the type of false dichotomies Mitchell commits by making such overstatements under the guise of theoretical originality. In fact, Mitchell has been fervently criticized for distorting previous psychoanalytic traditions, magnifying theoretical differences among schools when little or none exist, and using a variety of concepts out of context and selectively to suit his own theoretical needs (see Masling, 2003; Meissner, 1998; Richards, 1999a; Silverman, 2000).

It seems to me that Mitchell was hell-bent on forging his "new" paradigm through negation rather than by seeing how the old could positively inform the new. Perhaps his insight that relationality could have a rapprochement with classical theory came later when Mitchell (2000) became enamored with Loewald, but it does not efface his earlier theoretical commitments that he put to pen. To be fair to Mitchell, if it were not for his untimely death, he may have indeed reformed his theoretical extremism through appropriating Loewald (1970), who found more harmony in the "relational character" (p. 292) of drive theory.

Pizer (2006) pushes the issue further by prioritizing relational experience while subordinating embodiment. He states, "An alternative point of view (closer to Mitchell's) would argue for relational experience to be regarded as the basis of experience and for embodied experience to be contextualized in relational experience" (p. 195). Notice Pizer says that relational experience is the "*basis* of experience" (emphasis added). Here he is essentially saying the same thing as Mitchell without considering the philosophical predicaments he generates. For example, following the same tenor of other relational theorists, he offers no philosophical defense of the mind–body problem that adequately accounts for mind–body dependence. According to most reasonable people I know, it is generally uncontested that "if you ain't got a body, you ain't experiencing nothin'." Pizer, Mitchell, Hoffman, and others may rightfully think they are "constructing" how they *conceive* of embodiment, which I do not object to nor necessarily see as problematic, but they are certainly not constructing their material facticity *ex nihilo*. Embodiment logically and developmentally precedes "constructive," linguistic thought. I think the relational community has more thinking to do on this subject.

FREUD'S RELATIONAL THEORY OF MIND

Freudian drive theory is an ontological treatise on unconscious organization, human motivation, and psychic development. Unlike Mitchell, Freud was deeply engaged in the problem of nature, hence the empirical *and* speculative investigation of our embodiment. Freud had to account for our embodied, sentient life within human motivation and behavior in order for psychoanalysis to be legitimately viewed as a human science, so his solution was to develop a philosophy of organic process that could potentially account for all forms of psychic and cultural phenomena, namely, the doctrine of drives. What sets Freud's drive theory apart from any other theory in the history of psychoanalysis is that he systematically attempts to philosophically address the ontological foundation or *a priori* ground of all psychic activity anchored in unconscious process. Contra Greenberg, it is not enough (let alone sufficient) to claim that everything is relational or intersubjective without attempting to explain how relationality is constituted to begin with, that is, how it comes into being; for this reason alone the relational school can hardly claim to have a sophisticated metaphysical position on the matter. In fact, it was Freud who first explained how relationality was made possible through the transmogrification of the drives.

It is beyond the scope of this critique to offer a justification for Freud's theory of mind, a topic many notable analysts and scholars have addressed elsewhere in considerable length; however, a few points of clarification are in order. Freud (1915a) used the term *Trieb*—not *Instinkt*—to characterize the ontological basis of inner experience, not as a fixed, static, immutable tropism belonging to animal instinct but rather as a malleable, purposeful, transforming, and transformative telic process of directed mental impetus, impulse, or endogenous urge.* *Instinkt* was a word Freud rarely used in the context of the human subject, which he reserved for animal species, and loathed it for its simple equation to material reduction: This is precisely why he deliberately chose the word *Trieb*—more appropriately translated as drive, pulsion,† or impulse—to characterize human motivation. Not only does Freud's thesis on the nature, activities, and transmutations of the *Triebe* answer to the theoretical conundrum of human motivation that still besets psychoanalysis today, but I will attempt to further show that Freud's concept of drive does not at all contradict competing contemporary models favoring beliefs, needs, wishes, and intentionality. On the contrary, he explains how those processes are made possible to begin with.

Freud's technical use of *Trieb* is distinguished from the ordinary usage describing an urge, such as a whim or caprice. Rather, *Trieb* is the *driving force* behind the mind compelled and fueled by unconscious desire. For Freud (1915a), *Trieb* was pure psychic *activity*: Although drives have their source (*Quelle*), hence not simply

---

* All references to Freud's texts refer to the original German monographs compiled in his *Gesammelte Werke, Chronologisch Geordnet. Triebe und Triebschicksale* appears in Book X, *Werke aus den Jahren* (1913–1917, pp. 210–232). All translations are mine. Because many English-speaking analytic audiences may not have access to such texts, I have cited the page numbers to the *Standard Edition.*

† This is the term preferred by Antoine Vergote to emphasize the pulsations of urges emanating from the lived body.

their motivation,* rooted in biologically based somatic processes, the "essence" (*Wesen*) of a drive is its pressure or force (*Drang*), namely, its press, demand, or motion toward action (p. 122). Freud has to account for the question of origin, what I refer to as the "genesis problem" (Mills, 2002a), and this is why he could not omit the importance of our organic (hence constitutional) nature when describing the organization of mental life, what Merleau-Ponty refers to as the question of flesh. The mistake many relational the- orists make is to equate drive with material reduction, a position Freud abandoned after he could not adequately reconcile his psy- chophysical mind ≠ body thesis envisioned in the *Project*.†

Because *Trieb* becomes an expansive bedrock of psychic activ- ity, Freud (1926) stipulated that the dual instantiation of drives properly introduced in 1923 are derived from a developmen- tal monistic ontology (see p. 97; also see Freud, 1932–1933, pp. 76–77): that is, drives are the initial impetus underlying the evo- lution and sublimation of the human soul (*Seele*) and civilization (*Kultur*). What is most interesting about Freud's notion of drive is that he ostensibly introduces the presence of otherness within the very fabric of libidinal and aggressive motivation. A drive has a *telos*, hence an aim (*Zeil*)—It (*Es*) seeks, yearns, pines for satisfac- tion, for fulfillment—which may be sated only through an object (*Objekt*), what Freud mainly considered to be other people, but it

---

* An endemic misinterpretation to many relational critiques on Freudian drive theory is that they often equate the somatic source of a drive with its motivation, the former being biologically conditioned, the latter being pluralistically overdetermined in Freud's sys- tem (cf. Frank, 2003).

† It is important to realize that Freud never intended to publish the *Project for a Scientific Psychology*, written in 1895 and posthumously published, a manuscript he almost burned if it was not for the intervention of his daughter Anna, who wanted to preserve it for his biographers. Freud's early psychophysical project of mental life, a manuscript writ- ten before he established psychoanalysis as a social-behavioral science, was abandoned because he could not reduce the complexifications of mental phenomena, what in the philosophy of mind is referred to as *qualia*, to "quantitatively determinate states of speci- fiable material particles" (p. 295). By the time Freud (1900) published the dream book, he "carefully avoid[ed] the temptation to determine psychical locality in any anatomical fashion" (p. 536), a sentiment he reinforced in his public lectures of 1916–1917 and in 1932–1933.

could be any object or part-object coveted for satisfaction. In fact, Freud says that an object is the "most variable" aspect to drive activity, but he ultimately privileges human connection. In other words, the force or impetus of a drive is to seek human contact and relatedness in order to fulfill its aims. To speak of the destiny of a drive without other people becoming the object of its aims is a vacuous and ludicrous proposition, for a drive without an object is blind and empty. And of course what Freud meant by a human object was in fact a subject, namely, another individual who was separate from the self. Yet Mitchell (1988) avers that "Freud ... eschew[ed] any role for primary relatedness in his theory and reli[ed] instead solely on drive economies" (p. 54). This tenet is fallacious. Let us examine why.

Drive economics never operate in isolation of other mental events and relational aims. This is why Freud insisted that drives undergo transmogrification throughout psychic development and are carried out on unconscious parallel levels of distribution processing, what is customarily referred to as their vicissitudes. Likewise, *Schicksale*, rendered as "vicissitudes," is equally misleading because it implies a passionless, staid mechanism of change rather than the dynamic notion of mutability that belongs to the fate or destiny of life experience. This is what Freud had in mind when he envisioned the psyche as a temporal flux of dynamic events that arise from the most archaic fabric of our corporeal nature, which transforms over time through internal mediations we customarily refer to as "defense mechanisms," itself another unfortunate and misleading aphorism. "Drives and their Fate" comes much closer to capturing the implied meaning behind the transmogrification of inner forces, a process that extends to the most unrefined and immediate expression or derivative of a drive to the most sublimated aspects of human deed and desire. Here there is no simple economy to mental functioning as Mitchell suggests.

Recall that the impetus, force, or pressure (*Drang*) of a drive is internal experiential activity under the press of certain events, events that make themselves felt or known as an urge, wish, desire, or need. It is important to qualify that the source is *not* the motive, only that it is internally derived; motives, on the other hand, are complex phenomena subject to many intervening and emergent interactive effects both internally mediated and externally influenced. Freud (1915a) verifies this when he stipulates, "Although drives are wholly determined by their origin in a somatic source, in the life of the soul [*Seelenleben*] we know them only by their aims" (p. 123). Note that Freud says drives are determined by their "origin" (*Herkunft*), not that all motives are biologically based. The reason why Freud logically situates the source of a drive within our biologically determined facticity is simply because we are embodied beings. We are thrown into a body *a priori*, and hence all internal activity must *originally* arise from within our corporeality mediated by internal dynamics. Here Freud is merely asserting an empirical fact grounded in a natural science framework. Those relational analysts like Mitchell who wish to abnegate the archaic primacy of the body are simply misguided. As a consequence, many advocates of the American middle group devalue the importance of embodiment in favor of relational motives, but they do so based on selective omissions and false dichotomies that fail to acknowledge the indubitable certainty that relationality is predicated on our embodment.* What is minimized if not simply ignored within certain circles is that Freud was in fact the first one to pave a theory of object relations and ego psychology that was interpersonally based on the relational motives of the drives.

Recall that the aim of drive activity is to seek satisfaction. This is the *telos* of a drive, hence its purpose. But unlike the mechanical operations of fixed, predetermined tropisms that are genetically

---

* To be fair to my relational colleagues, there have been some attempts by authors to amend earlier views that the body is of less importance; see Aron and Anderson's *Relational Perspectives on the Body* (1998). But regardless of some relational authors' views on embodiment, the pivotal books that launched the relational movement, namely, Greenberg and Mitchell's *Object Relations in Psychoanalytic Theory* (1983), Mitchell's *Relational Concepts in Psychoanalysis* (1988), and Greenberg's *Oedipus and Beyond* (1991), all position a relational theory by abnegating drive, and thus my critique of their work, I argue, is still legitimate.

hardwired behavioral patterns belonging to some animals and lower organisms, human drives are determinative. That is, they are endowed with a degree of freedom manipulated by the agency of the ego, an ego that operates on manifold levels of conscious and unconscious activity. Freud (1915a) specifically tells us that the aim of a drive may take "different paths" with multiple instantiations; it can be inhibited or deflected, which may be in the service of an ultimate aim; or it can achieve "intermediate" endeavors, can work in tandem with competing goals, and may be combined, coalesce, or merge into a confluence all at once, thus operative on different levels of pressure and meaning (p. 122).

Of course an aim *needs* an object in order to achieve satisfaction, and this is why Freud says an object (*Objekt*) is the "most variable" aspect to a drive, the avenue through which a drive is able to procure fulfillment. Furthermore, an object is "assigned," hence it is not "originally connected" to a drive. In fact an object can be anything, whether in actuality or in fantasy, and can be both extraneous or internal, such as the "subject's own body" (*des eigenen Körpers*) (p. 122). Notice how Freud uses the language of subjectivity when describing a drive and specifically the ego's mediating activity of satisfying its aim. And the overarching preponderance of objects is mostly people and the functions they serve. Drives desire others, hence relatedness.* Here Freud unequivocally accounts for how interpersonal phenomena arise based on the most primordial activities of unconscious desire. Thus not only did Freud account for a relational theory embedded within the process of drive activity itself, he shows the logical necessity and developmental progression from intrapsychic to intersubjective life.

---

* We must acknowledge the multiple motivations and overdetermined processes operative within the drives, including economic and regulatory teleonomic functions, as well as adaptation and defense under the influence of evolutionary currents. Objects are coveted not only for pleasure but also for the function and purpose they serve, and derived modes of relatedness such as emotional connection and love are based on early bonds and identifications with attachments figures.

Therefore, Freud's early thesis on the nature of a drive is a pivotal step in his move toward his mature theory where he concludes that mind is an architectonic, epigenetic achievement that evolves from the most rudimentary expression of the dialectic of life and death—hence from the libidinal activity of Eros to the destructive will of *der Todestrieb*—organized within an unconscious *It* as alien and alienated desire, executed by the agency of the ego, and sublimated through reason, aesthetics, and moral judgment inherent in self-reflective social life. From this vantage point, drives can never be ontologically distinct from relational motives and organizations within the mind, whether this be the binding of semiotic, affective, and wishful connections that attach mental action to an object or person (in fantasy and reality), to the aim of achieving and sustaining the primacy of relatedness with others that the relational school emphasizes.

THE SOCIAL DIMENSION TO CLASSICAL THEORY

Not only is Freud's object relations theory predicated on his seminal 1915 paper, "Drives and Their Fate" (*Triebe und Triebschicksale*), thus making a conceptual clearing for "primary relatedness," he specifically elevates the process of identification, hence an interpersonal dynamic, to the status of a relational phenomenon. Freud (1921) specifically tells us that identification is "the earliest expression of an *emotional tie* with *another person*" (p. 105, emphasis added). An emotional connection is an important ingredient of identification because we simply don't identify with just anyone, as attachment research affirms. There is a selective aspect to identification, and we can see it operating quite unpretentiously during childhood when a child takes his or her parents as an ideal and wants to possess them and/or be like them, often displayed through bonds of affection and play. Later Freud (1932–1933) reiterates this point more clearly: "Identification (*Identifizierung*) … [is] the assimilation of one ego [*Ich*] to another one, as a result of which the first ego behaves like the second in certain respects, imitates it and in a sense takes it up into itself" (p. 63).

Freud goes on to say that it is "a very important form of *attachment* to someone else, probably the very first, and not the same thing as the choice of an object" (p. 63, emphasis added). Here he is deliberately wanting to differentiate the psychic importance and affective value of internalizing a parent or dependency figure rather than merely coveting any arbitrary object for libidinal gratification or having affectionate feelings for someone or something else, such as the family pet. And Freud (1931) specifically concedes that for each gender the mother becomes the original and most important object of identification (see p. 225) "established unalterably for a whole lifetime as the first and strongest love-object and as the prototype of all later love-relations—for both sexes" (1940, p. 188). Here Freud (1940) clearly says that "love has its origin in attachment" beginning with the appropriation of the mother's body (p. 188). If the emotional processes of *identification*, *attachment*, and *love* are not forms of "primary relatedness," then I don't know what would be. From these passages, Freud is clearly describing an intrapsychic process of incorporating the attributes and qualities of another subject (in German, *Person*) encountered through ongoing intersubjective, relational exchange.

Identification, introjection, and the internalization process are all part of attachment processes that are relational in nature (Mills, 2005c), as well as the specific acquisition of values and moral agency that accompany the development of the superego, once again based upon the internalized interpersonal patterns of relatedness that come from familial and cultural life. Freud (1940) is quite clear when he attributes superego development to relational factors:

> Throughout later life it represents the influence of a person's childhood, of the care and education given him by his parents and of his dependence on them—a childhood which is prolonged so greatly in human beings by a family life in common. And in all this it is not only the personal qualities of these parents that

is making itself felt, but also everything that had a determining effect on them themselves, the tastes and standards of the social class in which they lived and the innate dispositions and traditions of the race from which they sprang. (p. 206)

In this pithy yet condensed paragraph, Freud perspicaciously captures the essence of character as an internalized identification with the parents' personal qualities, aesthetics, preferences and prejudices, group loyalties, and revered values. Here Freud is emphasizing the nature of relationships within family life and how the peculiar aspects of certain personality traits and characteristics from one's parents are internalized within the subject, which were in turn historically instilled in one's parents from their own familial and cultural upbringing—what today we may refer to as the transgenerational transmission of family heritage. Elsewhere, Freud (1923) argues how identification is a significant microprocess that influences the choices "determining the form taken by the ego," which makes an "essential contribution" in the formation of "character" (p. 28). Even "the creations of art heighten [one's] identification ... by providing an occasion for sharing highly valued emotional experiences" (1927, p. 14). From this standpoint, psychic life cannot be bifurcated from familial life that resides within a community of others, and communal life cannot be understood unless it takes into account patterns of relatedness based on the types and qualities of relationships that historically constitute society. All of these ontic—hence relational—preconditions are necessary for psychic maturation in general.

It is understandable why Freud would invite misinterpretation and controversy. He transcended his early neurophysiological footholds yet retained his commitment to natural science, wrote in ambiguous fashions augmented by metaphoric prose, and often changed his views over the course of his burgeoning discoveries. Feminists generally abhor Freud for his biologicalization of gender, and humanist reactionaries are sensitive to any form of material explanation. I can see why relational theorists would become confused when reading his early work on drives amongst the backdrop of his evolving theoretical variances. Yet by the time Freud introduced the notions of identification and attachment, such ambiguities are sufficiently remedied. This only points toward a lack of familiarity with Freud's mature texts by relational audiences.[*]

Freud (1921) fully appreciated the *social phenomena* involved in psychic development, and he specifically tells us so:

> Rarely and under certain exceptional conditions is individual psychology in a position to disregard the *relations* of this individual to others. In the individual's mental life someone else is invariably involved, as a model, as an object, as a helper, as an opponent; and so from the very first individual psychology … is at the same time social psychology as well. (p. 69, emphasis added)

Within this same context, Freud emphasizes "the *relations* of an individual to his parents," as well as siblings, friends, love interests, and even his doctor—namely, the psychoanalyst: "In fact all the *relations* which have hitherto been the chief subject of psychoanalytic research—may claim to be considered as social phenomena" (p. 69, emphasis added).

Freud's theses on personality formation and psychopathology further point toward the relational pole of his thinking (see also Frank, 1998a). As early as Freud's (1895) unpublished monograph, *Project for a Scientific Psychology*, he states, "It is in relation to a fellow human-being that a human-being learns to cognize" (p. 331). Here Freud anchors the process of cognition and thought to the contingent relations with others that serve as a mental model of mimesis and identification necessary for learning acquisition. During his early writings, Freud also emphasized the role of trauma and seduction on the developing psyche, hence becoming a determining factor in the ontogenesis of neurosis. With regard

---

[*] According to the Program Coordinator of the Institute of Contemporary Psychoanalysis in Los Angeles, where Stolorow is a founding member, there is only 30 hours of seminar time devoted to Freud in both the regular weekday program and the weekend extension program for the whole didactic portion of training. Amazingly, the same amount of hours is devoted to "The Work of Stephen Mitchell."

to the question and nature of personality or character development, Freud (1932–1933) follows the Platonic tradition that the psyche or soul (*Seele*) is composed of the triangular dynamic relation between desire (*eros*), reason (*nous*), and moral agency (*ethos*) under the influence of unconscious mediation. Of course the content and, to a large extent, the qualia or emotional and wishful elements of mental life are broadly based on the internalization of others, the quality and nature of our attachments with our parents, drive and affect regulation, and the burgeoning role of superego maturation. Within the same context, psychopathology is one possible variation of how personality formation transpires, and Freud (1926) specifically situates the source of anxiety within the psychic parameters that inevitably involve others, such as fear of castration, disfigurement, death, moral retribution and punishment, "separation from the mother," "helplessness" and abandonment, loss of the object and the object's love, and so forth (see p. 138). For better or worse, this ultimately means that one would not be "normal," neurotic, or mentally ill unless it did not necessarily involve another person—paradigmatically the mother. Therefore, Freud's theories of psychopathology fundamentally rest upon a relational fulcrum.

Freud was not particularly impressed with having to think the same thing all the time: His ideas went through massive evolutionary changes with regard to both theory and technique, and by the time Eros was elevated to a supraordinate drive to account for narcissism, libidinal object love, self-preservation, and that of the species (1940, p. 148), the role of relationality was an indissoluble aspect of his mature theory of human nature.

But it may be argued that relational concepts were implicit in Freud's early work all along: Oedipalization is based on coveting one's parents, to possess them, to extract their desired attributes, to *be* them. The nature of defense always involves an interlocutor, a subject through which drive derivatives are directed, withdrawn, or renounced. Projection and projective identification, for example, are attempts to expel the other and the other's desire that have become incorporated within the self through interpersonal encounters. Transference is the recapitulation and enactment of encoded, patterned forms of early relatedness that were internalized and subsequently played out in the whole fabric of the subject's relations with other people, which are clinically evident in the analytic situation. In fact, civilization throughout the ages has held a transference unto God (Freud, 1927), a primary relation as an exalted communal attachment to an idealized object, abstraction, and/or belief system that may be said to occupy most of the world population. Furthermore, Freud's (1930) treatise on civilization is none other than a testament to the conflictual nature of human relationships. In the end, with objective certainty, the social character to Freud's theories of human nature cannot in good conscience ignore the relational dimension to personal existence.

THE INTERPERSONAL NATURE OF CLASSICAL TECHNIQUE

In the consulting room as well as in his collegial interactions with others, Freud acted like a man who exuded attentiveness, charm, quick wit, tact, perspicaciousness, and at times interpersonal warmth. He was purported to be sensitive and caring toward his patients, for example, feeding a patient when hungry, issuing loans to those in need, and acting genuinely compassionate during moments of a patient's vulnerability. He offered advice when asked and at times went out of his way to advocate for support and defend both patients and colleagues. Of course, his benevolent demeanor and attitudes coexisted with other competing and sometimes contradictory elements of his personality, as they do with most people, but they nonetheless do not erase the historical documentation that he related well with others. Freud was a very good listener, often penetrating deeply into the crux of the matter with a gentle bedside manner. Moreover, his methodological papers on psychoanalytic technique show irrefutable evidence that he was concerned with fostering an empathic interpersonal ambiance by being sensitive to the relational parameters of treatment.

Despite the fact that Freud did not use terms such as *interpersonal* or *intersubjective*, Lothane (2003) rightfully points out that therapy was always characterized in terms of dyadic, interpersonal manifestations in all aspects of the treatment, including managing resistance, transference, working-through, and the free associative method. Freud (1912b) defines one facet of technique as the analyst's ability to "turn his own unconscious like a receptive organ towards the transmitting unconscious of the patient" (p. 115), hence arguably a dynamic that is accomplished by the analyst's simultaneous attunement with his own subjectivity and the subjectivity of the patient. Yet Mitchell (1988, p. 297) and others (cf. Hoffman, 1998, pp. 97–102) still misrepresent Freud's depiction of the analytic encounter by referring to the analyst as a "blank screen," when Freud (1912b) actually said that the analyst should be "opaque" (*undurchsichtig*) to his patients, hence invoking the metaphor of a "mirror" (*Spiegelplatte*) (p. 118). There is nothing blank about opacity, and a reflective surface is hardly a screen. Take another example: Transference is the reiteration of the internalized presence of another person, hence a relational enterprise, which Freud (1916–1917) flatly tells us depends upon "the *personal relation* between the two people involved" (p. 441, emphasis added), namely, the analyst and analysand. We *relate* to our internal objects, that is, the internalized subjectivity of another. It should be quite clear that from Freud's own writings he establishes relatedness as a primary role in personality development and the clinical encounter.*

Classical psychoanalysis has many humanistic commitments that are either overlooked or displaced in the general psychological literature, and this displacement is reinforced by the extreme polarity relational psychoanalysis attempts to construct between

---

* George Frank (1998a) nicely enumerates many of Freud's technical papers where Freud invokes the "personal" dimension to treatment. For the sake of brevity, I have listed only a few examples here.

the two schools. This is an unfortunate and misguided myth per-
petuated by a radical misunderstanding of the nature of Freudian
inquiry and technique. For example, empathy has always been
an important dimension to analytic practice, and it is crucial for
making advances in the working alliance. Empathy is described
by Freud (1921) as "the process ... which plays the largest part in
our understanding of what is inherently foreign to our ego in other
people" (p. 108). Earlier, Freud (1913) referred to this as "sympathetic understanding," which is the ability to form an effective
transference through "proper *rapport*." He says, "It remains the
first aim of the treatment to *attach* him to it [the transference] and
to the person of the doctor. To ensure this, nothing need be done
but to give him time" (p. 139, emphasis added). Freud continues
to tell us that this process leads to an attachment to the therapist
through linkages to certain imagoes in the patient's past that are
associated with affection and understanding, and this technical
approach "carefully clears away the resistances that crop up at the
beginning and avoids making certain mistakes" (p. 139).

Freud argues that it is only through empathic attunement
and understanding that more positive transferences and feelings
of affection will develop and help mitigate the resistances that
threaten the therapeutic alliance. He emphatically warns against
taking a judgmental or moralizing stance or acting as an advocate
for another party the patient experiences conflict with, such as a
parent or spouse, for it will only serve to form a violent resistance
to forming a bond with the clinician.

Within many clinical accounts of empathy, the emphasis falls
on being attuned with the affective processes of the patient.
Following Freud's (1921) claim that a "path leads from identification by way of imitation to empathy" (p. 110), Helene Deutsch
(1926) believes that empathy is initiated by a temporary identification with the other. Regardless of the debate surrounding the
question, definition, and problematic consensus of what exactly
constitutes empathy, on some level identification (whether tran-
sient or partial) is a key ingredient in the capacity to relate to and

understand the inner processes and experiences of the patient (see Fliess, 1942; Furer, 1967). As a relational strategy, empathy is a necessary and indispensable aspect to any psychoanalytic treatment. Following Freud, we must strive to maintain the empathic attitude ("sympathetic understanding") toward the patient (thus implicitly siding with the patient) in the service of maintaining rapport and the positive alliance. Even in the context of providing interpretations, Freud believes that the "personal influence is our most powerful dynamic weapon" (1926b, p. 224) in bringing about mutative therapeutic changes in the patient based on one's "relation to the doctor" (1916–1917, p. 445).

A brief perusal through Freud's technique papers shows a remarkable wealth of attunement to the dynamics of transference, recommendations for conducting psychoanalytic practice, rules governing dream interpretation, beginning the treatment, dealing with unresolved trauma and working through painful affect and pathognomic conflict, and preventing erotic countertransference enactments. It goes without saying that all these technical reflections presuppose the interaction between two human beings and that Freud's technical strategies are relational in focus. Although having its genesis in a real source (viz., a relational encounter), transference is the imaginary relation to an internalized object and its representations, hence fantasized motivational and behavioral scenarios involving relationships with other significant people. Freud (1912a) refers to them as "stereotyped plates" in which we imbue the world and all human relations with certain anticipatory expectations, inherent properties, and behavioral fantasies. He is particularly keen on warning the doctor against acting out on his amorous affections based on erotic desires stimulated by the patient in order to keep "the counter-transference in check" (1915, p. 164). Here Freud is astutely aware of the human factor involved in conducting therapy. If it were not for our own needs for affection, companionship, sex, and love for other people, we would not need such caveats. But this is human nature, and we are obliged to notice and respect the fact that we are relational animals.

Freud's (1912b) highly referenced paper "Recommendations to Physicians Practising Psycho-Analysis" is packed full of guidelines, directives, and suggestions that are sensitive to the relational parameters of treatment. His first technical rule is how to listen. By adopting an "evenly suspended attention," one becomes interested in all aspects of the patient's associative productions that slowly reveal subterranean factors peculiar to each person's psychology mediated by the analyst's unconscious reception of the patient's unconscious disclosedness. The next is the "fundamental rule," which is a "demand made on the patient" to be honest and disclose whatever comes to one's mind without censorship, "criticism or selection" (p. 112). Here an ethical imperative is bestowed on the patient, which becomes integral to a working alliance. Just as rapport and sympathetic understanding facilitate the establishment of trust, safety, and attachment, the analytic dyad cannot function effectively without the cooperation of the patient's pledge to honesty (also see Thompson, 2004).

In several places in his writings, Freud discusses the "cooperative relationship" (1940, p. 173) or the "real relationship" (1912a, p. 100) that exists between doctor and patient. In another technique paper, "On Beginning the Treatment," Freud (1913) outlines many nuances of how to first communicate to the patient about entering into psychoanalysis, including the pragmatics of establishing a professional business relationship. And of course these technical rules for practice do not occur in a vacuum: They necessarily require the relational negotiation of two agencies participating in mutual collaboration. A good example of this is on setting the fee. I suppose if Freudian theory was truly a "one-person psychology," then the question of fees would never come up.

THE MYTHS OF A "ONE-PERSON PSYCHOLOGY" AND THE "ISOLATED MIND"

When Freud's theoretical corpus is taken as a whole, the relational tradition's criticism that Freud's theory and method is a "one-person" rather than a "two-person psychology" (see Aron, 1996; Greenberg & Mitchell, 1983; Mitchell & Aron, 1999) becomes an untenable claim. Furthermore, accusations that Freud's view of the mind is "monadic" (Mitchell, 1988, p. 3) and "isolated" (Stolorow & Atwood, 1992, p. 12), thereby collapsing into "solipsism" (Mitchell, 2000, p. xii), may be interpreted as sophistry. The myth of the isolated mind attributed to Freud is in fact a mythology orchestrated by contemporary theorists. The biggest disagreement I have with Stolorow and his colleagues is their constant inaccurate references to Freud's model of the mind as an "isolated Cartesian container." Here I do not think that they fully understand Descartes's overall project. Stolorow et al., as well as Mitchell, constantly refer to terms that accuse Freud of adhering to a solipsistic, isolated, and monadic theory of mind, when Freud neither believed nor stated any such thing in his writings. These are unwarranted accusations and fallacious conclusions. Stolorow, Atwood, and Orange's rendering of Descartes is something one might find in an introductory philosophy textbook replete with inaccuracies and pithy summations. In their collaboration *Worlds of Experience* (2002), they barely engage what Descartes *actually said* in his texts, relying instead on secondary sources and commentaries, and as a result they misinterpret his project. Any Descartes scholar would find their interpretation of Descartes to be elementary at best.

Stolorow et al. (2002) maintain that the Cartesian mind is "estranged" (p. 2) from the external world, essentially alienated, sealed off, and solipsistic, a philosophical proposition they extend to Freud. Stolorow (2010) continues to maintain that "the Freudian mind remained a Cartesian worldless subject, a container of mental contents, radically separated from the surround" (p. 6). This is not the case. In fact, Stolorow's whole claim to originality is based on a fallacy of logic, specifically, a non sequitur, hence an inference or conclusion that does not follow from the premises; in this case, a false premise attributed to Freud—one he never espoused, and neither did Descartes for that matter.

If Stolorow and his colleagues studied the *Meditations on First Philosophy* with precision, they would likely concede that they have made unwarranted generalizations. In my opinion, they fundamentally misunderstand what Descartes said and what he intended to convey. In the Synopsis to the *Meditations*, and in his letters of reply to his critics, Descartes clearly defends himself against the accusation that he is a solipsist. Rather, he is making a *categorical distinction* between the human soul or mind and the body—he is not saying that they are estranged or alienated from one another. Here the reader should know that for Descartes, the body is extended in space and is part of the natural world, albeit by Stolorow et al.'s interpretation they are completely separated.

Descartes begins his meditations by using a skeptical, epistemological methodology of doubting everything as a tool to overturn unquestioned presuppositions of his time, only to conclude that he is certain of his own inner subjective processes and eventually the external world, but this does not mean that the inner and outer, subject–object, self and world are estranged from one another. On the contrary, he goes on to argue that mind and nature, psyche and substance, consciousness and reality are interconnected. Descartes (1641) specifically says in his Synopsis, summarizing the Sixth Meditation, that "the mind is proved to be really [categorically] distinct from the body, but is shown, notwithstanding, to be so closely joined to it that the mind and the body make up a kind of unit" (p. 11). In the Sixth Meditation, he further states that mental activity, such as "sensory perception and imagination, cannot be understood apart from some substance for them to inhere in, and hence cannot exist without it" (pp. 54–55). Here Descartes specifically says that mental operations are embodied. He continues to say that there is a "union" and "intermingling of the mind with the body" (p. 56). In fact, he refers to the "whole self" as "a combination of body and mind" (p. 56), which are "united" (p. 59). In other words, mind and body are interdependent: You cannot have one without the other. Therefore, it is illegitimate to say, as Stolorow et al. do, that the mind is "estranged" from body, hence apart from the "natural world."

There are in fact many connections to the mind, body, and nature in Descartes's overall philosophy—not just the subject matter of the *Meditations*—that challenge Stolorow et al.'s claims, the details of which are not important to make my point in this context. Having said that, in summary, it is incontestable that although Descartes does argue that it's possible that the mind (soul) could exist independent of the body (so that in a technical sense they are really distinct substances), he understands the human being to be an intimate *unity* of mind, body, and world and respects (even highlights) the role of embodiment in experiential life, especially moral life. The two main texts in rich support of this understanding are *Passions of the Soul* (written a couple of years before his death) and the correspondence he had with Princess Elizabeth of Bohemia (written around the same time, circa late 1640s).

Stolorow's (2011) most recent collection of essays attempts to delineate a post-Cartesian psychoanalysis by continuing to misrepresent Freud. In essence, he builds a straw man, manufactures unwarranted false dichotomies, and throws red herrings that purportedly repudiate "the dehumanizing causal-mechanistic assumptions of Freudian metapsychology" (p. 2) for a more humane existential psychoanalysis. This inflammatory language serves as a beacon to create the impression that Freud's theoretical corpus was itself dehumanizing, when it may be persuasively argued that Freud himself was a post-Cartesian. Not only does Stolorow continue to make unsupported assumptions based on a lack of textual evidence, he repeatedly casts aspersion on classical theory by importing value judgments that distort metapsychology. Stolorow simply throws Freud into a Cartesian container when he fails to appreciate that Freud was a dialectician—not a dualist—and that the Freudian mind and world participate within a developmental monistic ontology (see Mills, 2002a, 2010). Psychoanalytic audiences unfamiliar with the history of Western philosophy will simply assume Stolorow is correct because his position is offered *ex cathedra* and designed to appeal to emotion (viz., we are existentially created and not mechanistically determined!) rather than presented as a balanced and conscientious view of the evolution of Freudian thought.

What is absolutely inconceivable is that by Freud's own words, which I just previously expatiated, he cannot possibly be a solipsist who favors a view of the psyche as existing in isolation from other people. Yet this is, in my opinion, the intersubjective and relational propaganda that has been uncritically circulating in psychoanalytic publications for the past three decades. It is only because psychoanalysts are not philosophers, and hence would not have formally studied the classic texts of Western philosophy, that these fallacies made it past a blind review process; for if philosophers were evaluating these manuscripts for publication, they would have surely caught such atrocious errors in misrepresenting Descartes.

When people closely examine even the secularity of the relational platform, many take a nihilistic critique of classical psychoanalysis based on misinterpretations (and sometimes blatant distortions) of Freud, omitting what he actually said in his mature texts—let alone reading them in German and thus erecting a foundation of theoretical novelty based on straw man arguments. Not only is this not accurate scholarship, but it conditions the next generation of students, mental health professionals, and analysts to erroneously conclude that Freud's views were fundamentally flawed, antiquated, and reductionistic, without having to bother to read Freud's texts directly to decide for themselves— simply because credible authorities dissuade them from doing so. I believe this also sends the wrong information to the public, who are generally naive about the historical terrain defining theory and practice, let alone psychoanalytic politics.

What is unnecessarily unfortunate is that these invented schisms between classical and relational viewpoints, which serve only to differentiate contemporary approaches from previous schools under the guise of betterment and novelty, create more polarization and tension rather than unity and collective identification despite having many shared affinities based upon a common calling. George Frank (1998a) rightfully concludes, "This polarization only contributes to the fragmentation in psychoanalytic theory today" (p. 141). What is of further irony, perhaps in part unconsciously informed, is that although relational analysts advocate for the value of relatedness—not opposition or difference—many relational writers use the language of objection and exaggerated difference to advance their cause.

In addition to these adumbrated criticisms, I have often speculated that the current preoccupation with Freud bashing by some mainstream American psychoanalytic psychologists identified with the relational movement is due, in part, to an unconscious renunciation and disidentification with what classical theory represents to a collective group narcissism identified with particular contemporary ideals. What I particularly have in mind is a *transference to theory* demonstrated by the virulent need to reject Freud, who is retroactively seen as a cold, depriving, critical father figure for the projective fantasy of the unconditional acceptance, warmth, nurturance, empathy, and reciprocal recognition from an idealized loving mother (*qua* ideal object) who forms the symbolic role model for a way of being in the consulting room. From my perspective, this *transference ideal* personifies the relational turn. In some ways we may not inappropriately wonder if this is due, in some cases, to an unresolved Oedipus complex from within this collective group informed by pre-oedipal dissatisfactions that continually strive to recover the lost presence of an idealized, albeit fallible mother, what Ferenczi intimates in his correspondence to Groddeck as possessing "too little love and too much severity" (Ferenczi & Groddeck, 1982, p. 36). In other words, the symbolic internalized function of an idealized internal (maternal) object is more appealing than the symbolic austerity of the paternal factor. Although there are many historically documented reasons to conclude that Freud had at times an intractable personality, this is not good enough or a sufficient reason to discredit—let alone jettison—his ideas without giving them their proper due. It is with equal understanding and personal longing why the maternal function is such a prized commodity within symbolic preferences informing our unconscious identifications with particular revisionist theoretical and technical priorities. And if attachment theory is correct, we may appreciate even more deeply why we are compelled to value this symbolic ideal.

4

Therapeutic Excess

THE VALUE OF RELATIONALITY IN CLINICAL PRACTICE

George Frank (1998a) argues that the relational tradition has overstated its claim to providing an original contribution to the field, instead giving the "appearance" of a unique position when it is merely the reappropriation of old paradigms with a makeover, what Giovacchini (1999) calls "old wine in murky bottles." I would say that this is not entirely the case. From the standpoint of redefining therapeutic intervention, analytic posturing, and technical priority, relational analysis is a breath of fresh air. Having questioned, disassembled, and revamped the classical take on neutrality, anonymity, and abstinence, analysts now behave in ways that are more personable, authentic, humane, and reciprocal rather than reserved, clinically detached, socially artificial, and stoically withholding. Although it is indeed difficult to make generalizations about all relational clinicians, which is neither desirable nor possible, one gets the impression that within the consulting room there is generally more dialogue rather than monologue, less interpretation and more active attunement to the process within the dyad, more emphasis on affective experience over conceptual insight, and more interpersonal warmth conveyed by the analyst, thus creating a more emotionally satisfying climate for both involved. No longer do we get an image of the sober, cerebral, emotionally sealed-off analyst who greets the analysand with a curt social acknowledgment, then walks back to his chair saying nothing, standing in thick uncomfortable silence with an expressionless face waiting for the patient to lie on the couch or sit down. Rather we imagine the analytic encounter aspiring toward an interpersonal ideal of relational fulfillment and mutual recognition that serves a nurturing and validating function for both the patient and the therapist, similar to the consummate holding environment envisioned by Winnicott or a milieu of optimal empathic attunement identified by Kohut, with the supplementary exception that the analyst is also recognized, or at least acknowledged, as being a human subject with a distinct personality and needs.

In a recent article delineating the differences between Freudian and relational psychoanalysis, Henry Friedman (2010) defines the classical school as adhering to an overarching theory and method of practice that

> follows technical guidelines that are aimed at elucidating drive derivatives originating in the infantile period of drive stages, including all the aspects of both libido and aggression that are expressed as wishes and defenses against awareness of those wishes. The desired analytic stance … requires that they minimize the participation of their affects and personal beliefs in the analytic dyad. They strive for a stance that includes careful attention to remaining "neutral" or non-reactive to the patient's emotional needs and demands, in the service of going deeper into the transference manifestations that otherwise would remain concealed or absent from the process. The analyst's emotional responses are seen as countertransference problems that can and will lead to enactments, which are seen as detrimental to the process. (p. 143)

This summation of the Freudian position emphasizes clinical theory sensitive to deciphering drive derivatives as the expression of wishes, conflicts, and defenses against them, as well as the technical instruction to remain "nonreactive" to the patient's psychological needs. Any emotional reaction or responsiveness on the analyst's part is seen as countertransference enactments that are deemed "detrimental" to the treatment. The goal of analysts' involvement, it seems, is to "minimize" their participation as a *real person* in favor of a technical stance of "going deeper." At face value, this approach appears to be the exact opposite from contemporary perspectives that displace drive theory for the primacy of relatedness and believe that emotional responsiveness and personal disclosure by the analyst is what is most mutative and curative. Friedman (2010) continues,

> Ultimately, analytic competence is defined as the ability of the analyst to remain in possession of his or her analyzing instrument, which is neutral, non-gratifying, and always aware of the presumed deeper origins of the patient's responses to him or her. A reactive and responsive analyst, in this view of analysis, is destined to destroy the possibility of analyzing the emerging transference, which is seen as the core of any treatment that can rightfully be called psychoanalysis. (p. 143)

This passage unambiguously asserts that the analyst should remain nonreactive, nongratifying, and nonresponsive, or otherwise it will "destroy" the treatment. He implies that anything short of this analytic comportment would not be rightfully called "psychoanalysis." Relational analysts would surely charge Friedman with espousing an uncritical traditionalism that dogmatically presumes that the only way to conduct so-called proper analysis is the "old-fashioned way." This furthermore ignores normal developmental needs to feel connected to another person, recognized, and validated as a human being, whereby each individual relates to another authentically and nonartificially. If we were to follow the classical prescription to the letter, we could easily imagine psychoanalysts acting completely unnatural, where they belie their real lives and personalities for an automation of technique that is manufactured, contrived, or feigned, which would likely appear entirely insincere to a patient. Furthermore, this portrayal of the classical analyst by a classical analyst further perpetuates the mythology of the omniscient one who knows, like a sage or religious chieftain possessing Gnostic access to Truth ordained by orthodoxy.

In my opinion, relational and intersubjective viewpoints have convincingly overturned the dogmatic inculcation of Americanized classical training and encourage free thinking, experimentation, novelty, spontaneity, creativity, authentic self-expression, humor, and play. And here is what I believe is the relational position's greatest contribution—the way they practice. There is malleability in the treatment frame, selectivity in interventions that are tailored to the unique needs and qualities of each patient, and a proper burial of the prototypic solemn analyst who is fundamentally removed from relating as one human being to another in the service of a withholding, frustrating, and ungratifying methodology designed to provoke transference enactments, deprivation, and unnecessary feelings of rejection, shame, guilt, and rage.

Today's relational analyst is more adept at customizing technique to fit each unique dyad (Beebe & Lachmann, 2003; Greenberg, 2001), what Bacal (1998) refers to as a specificity of intervention choice, and rallies against a blanket standardization or manualization of practice. Because of these important modifications to methodology, one may not inappropriately say that a relational approach can be a superior form of treatment for many patients because it enriches the scope of human experience in relation to another's and validates their wish for understanding, meaning, recognition, and love, what may very well be the most coveted and exalted ideals that make psychoanalysis effectively transformative and healing. In short, unlike the caricature of the classical analyst, the relational practitioner treats the patient as a real person who has needs, conflicts, and wishes that the analyst is obliged to address and, if possible, meet or fulfill simply because it is the humane thing to do.

Traditionalists and contemporary Freudians may have a legitimate criticism that the new view analysts gloss over the goal of uncovering unconscious conflicts, but in their defense, they would likely say that uncovering unconscious material for the sake of pure discovery is not as therapeutically important as other pursuits. To be fair to the classicists, however, in enumerating various criticisms, contemporary practitioners by and large could be accused of (a) not focusing on the deeper stratification of unconscious structure and their dynamics processes; (b) largely failing to focus on the genetic past and their symbolic manifestations in the transference; (c) being inattentive to unconscious fantasy; (d) being too permissive in maintaining a permeable treatment frame, one that largely lacks contained or well-defined boundaries, including consensual rules for participation; and (e) focusing too much on the here and now, where the emphasis is placed on co-constructing a relationship rather than exploring the patient's dynamic past. But in practice, this is much more likely to be a matter of emphasis.

In response, the contemporary practitioner would likely question the value of unconscious interpretation as a primary therapeutic goal over the lived reality of the present moment that is far more pressing and important to the client. Here, interpretation for the sake of interpretation out of the analyst's need to pursue truth or to be right, to interject self-importance in the session, or to trump the patient's take on his or her own inner experience is not deemed to be the main mission of analysis. In fact, the principle of the primacy of interpretation that traditionally characterizes the technical method of psychoanalysis could be the very bane of treatment for many patients simply because it is not helpful. Not only can premature or imposed (let alone intrusive), adduced interpretations drive patients away from treatment because of their misattunements or stinging exposures based on a lack of tact, they can arguably be clinically counterindicated. The last thing patients want is their analyst to analyze with a hammer.

The *interpretive imposition*—the calling card of shame—is often an authoritarian epistemology foisted upon the analysand as an illusory objective observation toted under the banner of truth, when it is simply superimposed power on a dubious subject. The personal (sometimes narcissistic) need for the clinician to spew forth gems of wisdom, or point out unconscious motives based on the analyst's internal muses (*qua* constructive fantasies) and passing them off as so-called quasi-scientific facts, perpetuates a hubris that betrays the spirit of psychoanalysis as a catalyst for self-knowledge. A methodology that privileges interpretation over self-discovery, disclosedness, and unconcealment, what the ancients refer to as *aletheia* (ἀλήθεια), undermines the value of self-exploration as a confrontation with the dialectic of truth and uncertainty.

What patients remember the most about you is not necessarily what you say but how you relate to them, how you model a way of being; this is what gets internalized and transmuted within psychic structure. No one wants to be related to as a thing. Traditional approaches, whether intended or not, implicitly foster (if not encourage) a detached scientific, experience-far observer paradigm, whereas the relational approach sees the inherent value of being real and genuine and fostering an experience-near, coparticipant observer stance, whereby the patient is related to as a nonobjectified person.

It becomes difficult to define the overall purpose or meaning of therapy because the clinical encounter is always mediated by context and contingency. For rhetorical purposes, if I had to pinpoint the essence of treatment, I would say that therapy is a *process of becoming*, a process of creative self-discovery, a process that requires the presence and influence of the other. Therefore, therapy is about forming and being in a relationship, one that is healthier and more genuine than what patients know only too well in their private lives. Having the opportunity to say what they truly think, and feel how they truly feel, is one of the most beautiful experiences and more curative dimensions of analysis, and having this recognized, understood, and validated by another person serves to encourage and instill a new set of values and ideals for what it truly means to have a fulfilling relationship. When this occurs naturally and developmentally over time, the patient comes to identify with and pursue a new way of being that is modeled on authentic relationality.

ON THE QUESTION OF THERAPEUTIC EXCESS

Despite these noted strengths, relational analysis has generated a great deal of controversy with regard to the question and procedural role of analyst self-disclosure. On one hand, relational approaches break down barriers of difference by emphasizing dyadic reciprocal involvement, which naturally includes the analyst having more liberty to talk about his or her own internal experiences within the session. However, the question arises: Where do we draw the line? Of course this is a question that may only be answered from within a well-defined frame of analytic sensibility, is contextually determined, and open to clinical judgment. But this question has led many critics of the relational turn to wonder about the level of what Jay Greenberg (2001) refers to as "psychoanalytic excess" or what Freud (1912b) called "therapeutic ambition." Equally, we may be legitimately concerned about the undisciplined use of self-disclosure, countertransference enactments, uninhibited risk taking, and flagrant boundary crossings that have the potential to materialize within this evolving framework of analytic practice. Although I believe that most relational analysts are very sound clinicians, it is incumbent upon us to flag potentially questionable or experimental practices in order to bring them into a frank and open discussion on exactly what constitutes a legitimate execution of analytic method (if there is such a thing). Recall that the earliest relational analysts within Freud's inner circle were borne out of extreme and excessive forms of experimentation: Jung, Rank, Ferenczi, and Groddeck displayed palpable sexual transgressions under the illusion of analytic treatment, and they were also advocates of mutual analysis (Rudnytsky, 2002), which is not unlike the current trend (with qualifications) to return to an emphasis on mutuality, reciprocity, and equality.

On one hand, relational analysts are commendably brave to report case studies where their own internal processes and intimate experiences are discussed openly in professional space, which I find of great service to the community because it breaks down oppressive taboos surrounding restrictive attitudes on analytic disclosure, self-censorship, and dishonesty among colleagues and creates a clearing for acknowledging the value of the analyst's phenomenology in analytic work. On the other hand, we are introduced to material that evokes questions of potential misuse. There is always a danger with the overexpression of personal communications, countertransference disclosures, and the insistence on providing reciprocal revelations that may reveal more about the needs of the analyst rather than of the patient. Although relational analysts operate with degrees of variance and specificity with regard to the employment of self-disclosure, this description from Lewis Aron (1999) may serve as an example:

> I encourage patients to tell me anything that they have observed and insist that there must have been some basis in my behavior for their conclusions. I often ask patients to speculate or fantasize about what is going on inside of me, and *in particular I focus on what patients have noticed about my internal conflicts* ... I assume that the patient may very well have noticed my anger, jealousy, excitement, or whatever before I recognize it in myself. (pp. 252–253, emphasis added)

This statement leaves the reader wondering who is the one being analyzed, thus raising the question of whether a relational approach could subtly be in the service of the analyst's narcissism. Having said that, for anyone who knows Lew Aron, he is far from being a narcissist. In fact, he is a very warm, genuine, intelligent, and caring human being. But my point is that his words could easily be misinterpreted and taken as a permissible stance to encourage our patients to focus on us rather than on their own internal processes. I admit that self and other—inner and outer—are never cleanly separated; however, this technical recommendation places an emphasis on the assumption of mutual internal conflict and a direct encouragement on the part of the analyst for the patient to explore such conflict in the analyst.

Presumably, Aron (1996) is conducting his practice under the guidance of mutuality, what he specifically says is "asymmetrical" or what I prefer to call proportional. The acceptance of mutuality within relational discourse is often unquestioned because of the systemic emphasis on dyadic reciprocal relations, dialogic exchange, and the value of the analyst's presence and participation in the therapeutic process. This is given and uncontested. But we may ask, What do we mean by mutual? Is everything mutual, or are there independent forces, pressures, and operations at play that are defined in opposition to difference? When relational analysts employ the notion of mutuality, do they really mean equality, such as having the *same* relationship, or are they merely inferring that something is shared between them? Modell (1991) refers to mutuality as a form of "egalitarianism," specifically canceling the notion of difference in favor of equality. In fact, relational analysts often equate mutuality with equality, when I believe we need to make fine distinctions between mutuality and equality.

Equality implies that there is no difference between each subject in the dyad, that they are identical, and that they have the same value. This position seems to ignore the substantial individual differences that exist between the analyst and the analysand, not to mention the power differentials, role asymmetry, and purported purpose of forming a working relationship to begin with. Here mutuality merely means existing in relation to another subject who, despite harboring individual differences, still shares collective values and qualities that define us all as human beings, but they are far from being equal (*aequalis*). Individualities exist while concurrently participating in a collective shared universal. We all have competing needs, agendas, defenses, caprices, ideals, and wishes, and these clash with those of others. So mutuality is merely a formal category of coexistence, not the qualitative implications it signifies. This is why I prefer to refer to analytic mutuality as defined through proportional exchange, whereby a patient, namely, one who suffers (*patiens*), seeks out my professional assistance as an identified authority and pays me a large fee to help. There is nothing equal about it: I'm not the one being analyzed or paying for treatment.

One cannot help but wonder how the overtly self-disclosing analyst reconciles the tensions that inevitably occur when the patient's personality via the therapeutic process radically resists wanting to know anything personal about the analyst at all, let alone the analyst's "internal conflicts." Here I have in mind patients with histories of developmental trauma, attachment disruptions, abuse, and/or personality disorders who are generally mistrustful of any kind of relationship. And narcissistic analysands will be the first to let you know that they are not paying you to talk about yourself, let alone demand mutual recognition. Of course we as analysts want to be recognized and appreciated by our patients, not only because the desire for recognition is a basic human need but because our work is laborious and we wish some gratitude. Despite how intrinsically rewarding our work can be, we often serve as a filter and container for a plethora of pain, hate, and rage with some emotional cost to ourselves; therefore external validation is affirmative and rewarding. But we must be mindful that we need to be sensitive to the patient's unique needs and not foist or superimpose our own for the sake of our desires for gratification despite identifying with a certain therapeutic ideal. In saying this, I realize that our ideals sometimes tend to betray the reality or pragmatics of how we conduct ourselves in the consulting room, because we are human, and every intervention is governed by contextual dynamics. Of course we want to be recognized by our patients, as we strive to recognize and validate them. When this happens naturally and unfolds organically from within the intimate parameters of the treatment process, it becomes an aesthetic supplement to our work and, moreover, to our way of being, which speaks of the depth of attachment therapeutic relatedness affords.

COUNTERTRANSFERENCE AND SELF-DISCLOSURE

Abend (2003) has questioned the purported advantages of analyst self-disclosure, particularly alerting us to concerns over radical self-revelation. Ehrenberg (1993), for example, radicalizes the emphasis on countertransference disclosures and argues that direct articulation of the analyst's own experience is the fulcrum for analytic work. Perhaps unintended by her, we do not require much effort to imagine how this dictum could potentially lead to disastrous consequences, including unethical behavior and gross boundary violations. At a conference where I was present, Barbara Pizer (2003) delivered a shocking confession to a bewildered audience that she had broken the confidentiality of a former analysand to her current patient (who was in previous treatment with Pizer's analysand) by implicitly revealing that her former analysand was sexually abused.

After I first mentioned this incident (Mills, 2005a), Stuart Pizer (2006) accused me of professional misconduct and committing an illegal act, where I allegedly made "spurious and baseless allegations of ethical impropriety" (p. 195) against his wife, which he further claims are "untrue" and "libelous" (p. 196). Not only did I witness such events as an audience member, but the whole conference presentation was taped. Because Pizer's charges against me are so contemptuous, I am forced to provide irrefutable evidence to clear me of such allegations. Here is what Barbara Pizer (2002) says in the transcript from her taped verbal presentation at the conference in question:

> Actually, the vignette I am about to relate comes from a brief treatment between Kate and myself that begins with a broken frame. I had gotten to know her in another context. I supervised her for two years beginning in 1988. At that time she came recommended to me by her colleagues; also by Ariel, her therapist, whom I had once known well and to whom I felt deeply attached, even though, given life's circumstances, I had not spent time with her for over a decade. In the course of working with Kate, a gifted clinician herself, working with deeply disturbed patients, I came to learn of her own traumatic past, which included severe neglect, sexual abuse, repeated abandonment, and ultimately a hospitalization ... Kate felt finally rescued by Ariel.

Pizer goes on to explain that 14 years after their supervisory relationship had ended, Kate called her in a frantic state concerning Ariel, still Kate's therapist, who had unanticipatedly suffered a stroke. Kate was immediately plummeted into crisis and sought out Pizer for help. The therapeutic work, which lasted for a few months, delved into Kate's multiple traumas and psychic fragmentation associated with, among other things, Ariel's illness and felt-abandonment of her, as well as the uncertainty surrounding Ariel's prognosis and recovery. Pizer focuses on a particular intervention she delivered while Kate was dissociating in session. Here is what Pizer tells the audience:

> Heart in mouth, I do something I have never done nor ever wish to do again. I say that in spite of current circumstances, there is in fact an underlying continuity containing us here, and now is the time to speak out loud about it. I tell Kate that way back in the '70s when Ariel was still a psychology student in training, we were engaged in a process similar to the process that she has been engaged in with Ariel. Ariel was my analysand.

Although I concede that Barbara Pizer did not explicitly say that her former patient was "sexually abused," she nevertheless did communicate, in her own words, that she had told her current patient that the patient's previous analyst was at one time Pizer's analysand. Moreover, she told the patient that her previous analyst went through a similar process in her therapy with Pizer. The current patient had a trauma history including "sexual abuse" and was a previous supervisee of Pizer's. In my opinion, it is very reasonable to conclude that if my analyst had told me that my previous analyst was her patient in the past and that my previous analyst went through a similar process that I went through in the moment of reliving painful traumatic material in session, I would immediately conclude that my previous analyst was also a victim of sexual abuse. Although Pizer informs us that Kate returned to continue her therapy with Ariel when she had recovered from her rehabilitation and that they both expressed gratitude and reassurance that Pizer did not do them any harm, it still does not annul the fact that Barbara Pizer broke the rule of confidentiality that governs the practice of our profession.

Having said this, despite Pizer's betrayal of her previous patient's trust, to me her intentions portray a genuine care and anguish for her current patient's suffering. She was emotionally compelled to say these words in a moment of therapeutic crisis where two people were palpably distressed. She appeared to respond authentically following her own clinical intuition. Was this countertransference? I will let the reader decide.

Now before the reader passes judgment, it is very important to keep in mind how the context that supports such an intervention influences the analyst's disclosures. But regardless of the circumstances surrounding the intervention, it becomes too easy to see how therapeutic excess can have potential detrimental effects.

Other relationalists have forayed into what certainly looks like excess, at least out of context, including disclosing erotic feelings (Davies, 1994), lying to patients (Gerson, 1996), and even screaming while invading personal body space (Frederickson, 1990). Wilber (2003) confessed to a patient that he had had a sexual dream about her, and she reportedly became furious. In a highly controversial paper, Jody Messler Davies (1994) confessed her own sexual longing for a 27-year-old male graduate student, which in her words was "pushed along by this young man's adamant need to deny the reality that he could be the object of a woman's sexual desire" (p. 166). Torn between her own countertransference reactions and the need to be "honest,"

> I said to the patient one day, "But you know I have had sexual fantasies about you many times, sometimes when we're together and sometimes when I'm alone." The patient began to look anxious and physically agitated. I added, "We certainly will not act on those feelings, but you seem so intent on denying that a woman could feel that way, that your own mother might have felt that way, I couldn't think of a more direct way of letting you know that this simply isn't true." The patient became enraged beyond a point that I had ever seen him. I was perverse, not only an unethical therapist, but probably a sick and perverted mother as well. He thought he needed to press charges, professional charges, maybe even child abuse charges; how could I help him when my own sexuality was so entirely out of control. He was literally beside himself. Unaware of what he was saying, he could only mutter, "You make me sick, I'm going to be sick. God, I'm going to throw up." (p. 166)

Despite appearing incredibly exhibitionistic, to her credit, I admire her grit and honest revelation in reporting this vignette. If we cannot have honest disclosures in psychoanalytic writings and professional communications about what we actually say in sessions to our patients, then we cannot have honest professional discourse either.

But what happened to the patient? The patient ends up weeping while punching "his fist into his palm repeatedly." Davies's subsequent commentary on her intervention minimizes any "serious unresolved countertransference pressures" and instead argues that her intervention "represented one of the most therapeutic alternatives" (p. 167). Her argument is that therapy is a real relationship between two people and not merely some one-way internal relation that belongs solely to the intrapsychic life of the patient's mind but rather a "mutually constructed, intersubjective playground ... and perpetual interaction between two actively engaged participants" (p. 168). Although this is arguably the case, does it necessarily follow that her intervention was "one of the most therapeutic alternatives"? From her description of how the patient acted following her self-disclosure, it can be argued that it represented one of the *least effective* things to say. Davies continues to defend her position under the rubric of honesty. She concludes, "Within such a scenario, the analyst oftentimes *must* speak the dangerously charged words for the first time" (p. 168, emphasis added).

Must we? In the province where I live and work, if I, as a male therapist, disclosed that I have "sexual fantasies" for my female patient, not only could this be construed as sexual abuse, I could potentially be arrested.* With regard to the consequences of

---

* In Section 4 of the Regulated Health Professions Act, 1991, under Subsection 3, "Sexual Abuse of a Patient," it states, "In this Code, 'sexual abuse' of a patient by a member means, (a) sexual intercourse or other forms of physical sexual relations between the member and the patient, (b) touching, of a sexual nature, of the patient by the member, or (c) behaviour or remarks of a sexual nature by the member towards the patient. 1993, c. 37, s. 4." Last amendment: 2009. Notice that Davies's remarks would clearly fall under paragraph (c) of this clause under Ontario legislation.

Davies's intervention, I am once again left wondering, Whatever happened to the patient? She does not tell us whether he stayed or eventually bolted from treatment (which is what I would predict). Could you possibly repair such a rupture after telling a patient about your lust? Is honesty for the sake of honesty a sufficient justification supporting this type of intervention? Furthermore, is it always necessary to be honest when making self-disclosures? In other words, do we want to be this truthful? And if so, what therapeutic benefit would this have?

Apparently Davies has a penchant for confessing erotic desires to her patients. In another article (Davies, 1998), she admits that she was flirting with her male analysand after he called her on it in session. Regardless of context, the most salient question becomes, Why is she flirting in the first place?

Suffice it to say that these are some examples of therapeutic excess that alert our attention to the possibility of attribution of error in contemporary technique. Of course there is a theoretical distinction between truth and honesty and our *choice* to verbally disclose certain internal processes to an analysand. I admit that I am rather conservative about these matters, preferring to foster a safe climate for self-reflection, emotional release, and pathological containment, whereby the patient is not burdened by my "inner conflicts." But this does not mean that risqué or "dangerously charged words" *ipso facto* are not legitimate to say in certain circumstances. They may very well be—and necessarily so. The problem becomes defining a uniform or universal touchstone on which to make such choices. In fact, it is precisely the *criteria* of what is appropriate or inappropriate to say that is lacking consensus, which is indissolubly laced to the *context* that influences the appropriateness of that decision in the first place. Indeed, intervention choice is contingent on such criteria, as criteria are contingent on context. And because we lack a clear guidepost on what criteria to follow under contingent circumstances, we may be eternally begging the question if we tarry on this path much longer. Here I think the more important issue for debate becomes not the particular verbalizations of what therapists say in session but rather the question of *permissibility* itself.

Admittedly, I have been using Davies (as well as other relational authors) here in a self-serving fashion as examples to accentuate my concerns about therapeutic excess in relational discourse. I have no doubt that she is a very good clinician based upon the authentic spontaneity described in her sessions when emotionally charged variants are introduced without warning. If we were to focus only on the content of these aforementioned interventions without taking into account the context and the overall process of treatment, then these enactments could be deemed as unethical, if not outrageous. I myself would be guilty of this on many occasions, which many of my colleagues could claim are countertransference dramas at best. For example, I am not ashamed to admit that I had dropped my afternoon responsibilities to pick up a bipolar patient who was suicidal from his apartment, loaded up his dogs in my minivan, and drove him to the hospital after taking his dogs to a kennel and helping him shop for personal toiletries. Nor do I think it was unprofessional of me to visit a patient late in the evening in the ER after he attempted suicide and then visit his wife and child that same night to debrief them and help contain their trauma. The patient particularly enjoyed my unannounced visit the next day when I brought him his favorite food of freshly cooked Polish kielbasa after he had been checked into the psychiatric ward. Despite my ancillary criticism of my colleagues, my main point here is to draw increasing attention to how relational analysts are bringing their own personalities into the consulting room, presumably under appropriate discretion guided by clinical intuition and experienced judgment, as well as having the courage to discuss their countertransference enactments in professional space.

It has been argued time and again that it is far too easy for someone outside the lived analytic encounter to become an armchair quarterback and call all the plays after the game. Although certainly no intervention is beyond scrutiny or reproach, what strikes me about some of these therapeutic transactions is their humanness and authentic spontaneity despite seeming excessive. The hallmark of a relational approach to treatment is that it approximates the way real relationships are naturally formed in patients' external lives, including the rawness, tension, and negotiability of the lived encounter, with the exception that the process falls under analytic sensibility. This is why the relationalists demand we be malleable in the treatment frame rather than apply a rigid, orthodox, or authoritarian procedure, because malleability is necessary in order to cater to the unique contingencies of each dyad; this necessitates abolishing any illusory fixed notions of practice that can be formulaically applied to all situations.

I believe most analysts can buy into this premise, but regardless of its pragmatic value, it still begs the question of method. If every intervention is contextually based, then it is relative and subjectively determined, hence not open to universal applications. The question of uniform technique becomes an illegitimate question because context determines everything. The best we can aim for is to have an eclectic skill set (under the direction of clinical judgment, experience, self-reflectivity, and maybe even wisdom) to apply to whatever possible clinical realities we may encounter. But perhaps I am being too naive or idealistic in assuming that every analyst is capable of achieving this level of professional comportment. Here I am wondering how this revisionist relational methodology affects training, supervision, pedagogy, and practice. Hoffman (1994) tells us to "throw away the book" once we have mastered it. Fair enough. But what if a neophyte were reading the relational literature and took such a statement literally? What about reliability and treatment efficacy if there is no proper method to which we can claim allegiance? Could this not lead to an "anything goes" approach conducted by a bunch of loose cannons justifying interventions under the edict of relationality—a modern-day "wild analysis"? Yet the same potential for abuse exists when applying any approach rigidly, whether it is a formal procedure, orienting principle, or general technical considerations; thus the question of method will always remain an indeterminate question, with some approaches being more justifiable than others.

PRINCIPIA ETHICA AND THE QUESTION OF METHOD

The question of method and its ethical ramifications is certainly not an issue confined to the relational movement. It is as old as the discipline itself. For example, Freud used to analyze his colleagues while going for a walk, had his patients stay at the same spa when he and his family took their annual vacation, kept his pet chow in the office during sessions while he smoked like a stove, and once accepted payment of a sack of potatoes in lieu of money. Imagine the stir this would create today.

Take, for example, the conventional practice of conducting or remaining in long analyses. I have often felt that long analyses are the product of transference neuroses and are ultimately unhealthy for patients because they promote dependency, passivity, conformity, and complacency, and hence they reinforce neuroticism. This type of indoctrination can lead to a pathological reliance that eclipses critical thinking, discourages autonomy or creative living, and stifles feelings of transcendence and personal freedom. The direct or implicit encouragement of a protracted treatment is also self-serving for analysts because they reap financial gain that augments their annual income and material quality of life. Granted that we all have to make a living, but are protracted analyses an example of what Irwin Hirsch (2008) calls "coasting in the countertransference"?

Let me continue to play devil's advocate. Have the patient and analyst become "just too cozy"? Could this mutual comfortableness be construed as an unconscious conspiracy? In fact, it could be argued that it is psychologically detrimental for an analyst to imply—let alone encourage—a patient to remain in extended therapy that has already lasted for several years (not to mention decades). When it is not explicitly encouraged or suggested, implicit forms of approval may be conveyed through unassuming attitudes, such as not asking patients about their thoughts concerning treatment duration or offering the placid excuse that the clinician was waiting for the analysand to broach the topic—only then to have the analyst analyze the patient's need or motive to bring up the issue in the first place. This of course shuts down the inquiry or, even worse, pathologizes the need to question the duration of analysis, which then throws it back on the patients as their neurotic issue. Or broaching the topic of termination could readily be seen as premature or conceived as resistance or the desire to flee based on an unconscious enactment.

Keep in mind that Freud conducted short analyses in the early days of establishing psychoanalysis as a behavioral science and that today analytic institute training requirements are largely responsible for establishing lengthy treatments based on the A. A. Brill medicalization model of psychoanalytic training. It is also conceivable that the contemporary training requirements to become psychoanalysts in North America are what is largely driving the continuation of extended treatments. Most clients cannot justify the gain or benefits of a long analysis based upon the personal cost involved, in terms of both lifestyle sacrifices and financial expense. Analytic candidates, on the other hand, are willing to pay and stay in treatment because they want the credential. Is it the analytic candidates who are largely sustaining this market condition, perhaps even comprising, aside from the wealthy, the preponderance of extended analyses themselves? As long as there is an institutional expectation that analytic candidates must complete a mandatorily extended personal analysis coextensive with their seminars and supervision hours, then this requisite itself molds propositional attitudes favoring lengthy treatments.

And how about treatments that last beyond the mandatory institute requirements? It is not uncommon to observe how power differentials within institute governance may contribute to expectations around frequency and duration of treatment, especially if one's personal analyst is also a training and supervising analyst at the candidate's institute and has direct evaluation over the candidate's performance. If protracted analyses are encouraged by the executives and faculty of training institutes, does this not reinforce the notion that patients should stay in therapy for as long as possible and that the candidate is not conducting so-called true analysis unless these conditions are emulated? And does this not instill an expectation—let alone an attitude—of dependency rather than autonomy? Shouldn't psychoanalysis be a catalyst for individuation and the actualization of personal freedom—for living one's life authentically and to its fullest potential? In short, one must grow up and fly from the nest.

Rebecca Curtis (2007) openly wrote about her personal analysis with the late Stephen Mitchell with surprising honesty. Although she in many ways focused on Mitchell's classical technique—itself a surprise—she also acknowledged that she took his class at the institute while simultaneously being in analysis with him. Mitchell also requested her to write an article for *Psychoanalytic Dialogues* during her treatment, presumably while he was editor. But to his credit, as Curtis tells us, he "thought it was not appropriate for me to keep seeing him, given I clearly was not finding him helpful" (p. 299). Perhaps this is a good example of how a relational attitude is sensitive to the actual needs and preferences of the analysand rather than hammers away with resistance or transference interpretations. Here the pragmatics of patient–therapist fit must be the central locus when working together successfully as an analytic dyad.

In contrast to the relational analyst, let us examine an intervention from a more traditional approach. Wilfred Bion (cited in Klein, Heimann, & Money-Kyrle, 1957, p. 229) offers an example of his work with a schizophrenic whom he had been seeing for 5 years in a 5-day-a-week analysis:

Patient: I picked a tiny piece of my skin from my face and feel quite empty.
Bion: The tiny piece of skin is your penis, which you have torn out, and all your insides have come with it.

Patient: I do not understand … penis … only syllables and now it
    has no meaning.
Bion: You have split my word "penis" into syllables and now it has
    no meaning.
Patient: I don't know what it means, but I want to say, "If I can't
    spell I can't think."
Bion: The syllables have been split into letters; you cannot spell—
    that is to say you cannot put the letters together again to
    make words, so now you cannot think.

It goes without saying that, like the examples listed from the relational literature, we don't know the nature or quality of Bion's relationship with his patient or the historical or developmental contingencies, what the past content of sessions revealed, or even the affective, unspoken, or behavioral cues of the current context that may be influencing Bion's choice of intervention. We may even concede that, in principle, we have no way of knowing what is beneficial or detrimental in this therapeutic exchange or if the patient would necessarily be in a position to know himself. But what is clear is the authoritative tone, hubris, and brazen certainty in which Bion delivers his interpretations, what Thompson (2004) calls "messages from the gods" (p. 118). Perhaps this is merely an artifact of his classical training, his personality, or both. After all, he was a tank commander in World War I. But he was also analyzed by Melanie Klein, herself analyzed by Ferenczi and Abraham, thus modeling the way analysis "should" be done. Let us examine a vignette from her work.

In Klein's (1961) *Narrative of a Child Analysis*, she analyzes a 10-year-old boy named Richard whose treatment took place during World War II. Based upon her careful case notes recorded after each appointment, this is what transpired during the *very beginning* of the fifth session:

> Richard began by saying that he felt very happy. The sun was shining. He had made friends with a little boy about seven years old and they played in the sand together, building canals. He said how

much he liked the playroom and how nice it was. There were so many pictures of dogs on the walls. He was looking forward to going home for the weekend. The garden there was very nice but, when they first moved in, "one could have died" when one saw the weeds. He commented on Lord Beaverbrook's change of job and wondered if his successor would be as good.

Mrs. K. interpreted that the playroom was "nice" because of his feelings about her, the room also standing for her. The new friend represented a younger brother. This was bound up with his wish for a strong father who would give Mummy many babies (the many dogs). She also interpreted his concern that, if he pushed Daddy out ... he would take Daddy's place but would be unable to make babies and hold the family together. He was also happy because he was going home and, in order to keep the family life friendly, he wished to inhibit his desire to take Daddy's place. The weeds stood for himself when he upset the family peace by his jealousy and competition with his father. He has used the expression "one could have died" when referring to the weeds, because they represented something dangerous.

Richard sneezed and became very worried. (p. 34)

Klein goes on to interpret Richard's purported fantasies of primal scenes, penises, dangerous internal objects, and *his wish to have intercourse* with her and his mother. It comes as no surprise that the boy became horrified and immediately wanted to flee from the anxiety she engendered with her interpretations. From this description alone, it is palpably clear that she has superimposed Freudian oedipal theory on the treatment scenario. If the relational camp is to be overly criticized for therapeutic excess, then what should we make of this intervention—therapeutic ambition, overzealousness, excess, or wild analysis? Whether Klein was correct, semicorrect, or incorrect in her interpretations is not the point; we must seriously question whether deep interpretations *in this context* are the most effective form of treatment, especially with a child. Most relational analysts who place currency on the forms of relatedness that are cultivated in the session would surely conclude that this analytic method is abusive and potentially traumatizing to patients. In fact, by today's standards, it would constitute child abuse.

Equally alarming is Lacan's (1973) technical innovations, which many analysts find unacceptably experimental and careless, if not patently egregious, invalidating, and damaging to patients (Mills, 2003a). Take for example his variable-length sessions (*seances scandées*), sometimes lasting as little as 5 minutes, in which he would spontaneously and capriciously terminate a session abruptly, hence telling patients to leave his office because he was bored with their associations.* Of course this technical strategy was said to be justified under the theoretical assumption that it is productive to "surprise the unconscious." In today's society, this is a good way to invite an ethics complaint and lose business at the same time. No wonder he was blamed for the suicide of some of his analysands (Haddad, 1981) and eventually excommunicated from the psychoanalytic community (see Lacan, 1964) for his perverted technique.

Of course there are many other important historical figures in psychoanalysis on whom we may focus in critical and even condemning ways, which makes the phenomenon of therapeutic excess in relational technique look rather benign. Recall that Ferenczi had some of his patients sit on his lap like a baby and kissed others on the lips, while Jung slept with some of his patients, which later turned into a love affair with his eventual wife, Emma Jung, and Toni Wolff, his paramour, who inconspicuously lived with the Jung family for decades until her death.

Many commentators have suggested that the early analysts who engaged in the sexual exploitation of their patients or committed boundary violations were acting out their own conflicts in response to unresolved trauma. Peter Rudnytsky (2002) offers a relational critique of the attachment and loss, developmental disruptions, and object relations pathology inherent in the writings of Ferenczi, Rank, and Groddeck that arguably find counterparts in the real-life

---

* It is speculated that Lacan's experimentation with technique had something to do with a rather humiliating experience he had in 1936 at the Congress of the International Psycho-Analytical Association in Marienbad, where Ernest Jones had cut him off in midsentence just shortly into his presentation, a painful experience Lacan reportedly remembered for the rest of his life.

histories of these men who were themselves victims of early abuse. Even Jung confided to Freud in a letter on October 28, 1907, that he was sexually assaulted as a boy, which contributed to his " 'religious' crush" on Freud (see McGuire, 1974, p. 95). The transference unto Freud arguably would have fueled some of these tendencies to act out with patients by his early adherents as well. For example, Rudnytsky criticizes Freud's androcentrism, personal narcissistic traits, prejudicial views on women and gender, phallocentrism, countertransference, and overidentification with his Jewish facticity, thus highlighting his proclivity to project his own psychic agenda into the intrapsychic lives of his analysands and place demands for loyalty on his followers who desired his acceptance.

Rudnytsky traces the rise of Rank from his unwavering orthodoxy to Freud in the initial years to his renunciation of the primacy of the unconscious and the force of genetic explanation in human motivation for his own predilection for the will predicated on a philosophy of consciousness. What is rather tragic about Rank is how his early work was so innovative and noteworthy whereas his later work set out to devalue and repudiate his earlier psychoanalytic allegiances based, in part, on his embittered reaction to the narcissistic injuries he suffered from Freud and his fellow "brothers," which eventually ended in Rank being expunged from Freud's inner circle. The experience must have been sorely humiliating. Before he was excommunicated, whereby experiencing prolonged conflict with Jones, Abraham, Freud, and Ferenczi, he even sent letters of apology to the members of the committee. In one such letter of December 20, 1924, he showed deference and groveled for their forgiveness with a shameful confession, only to be mistrusted and shunned even more. We get the impression that Rank ascends as the most promising young scholar of the humanities to devolve into a rather rueful and contemptuous, acting-out adolescent who needed to rebel and defile Daddy because he himself was kicked out of the house.

Since the English publication of Ferenczi's *Clinical Diary*, Ferenczi's insights have become more recognized and influential among contemporary psychoanalytic circles, only with his atrocious boundary violations left out (one hopes). Ferenczi is given more generosity in Rudnytsky's sympathetic critique than in those of the other analysts, perhaps, in part, for his emphasis on pre-oedipal development and his relational turn away from Freud's metapsychology, thus showing how Ferenczi anticipated many key elements that preoccupy psychoanalysis today, including the role of trauma, love, attachment, and loss; countertransference; mutual analytic co-construction; the primacy of intersubjectivity; empathic attunement; and a general warmth and respect for patients, that are often omitted from the caricatures that accompany the staid, classical analyst. Rudnytsky's analysis of Ferenczi's *Clinical Diary* is a humanistic one, showing a vulnerable, emotionally maimed man pining for recognition from Herr Professor, secretly revealing his script of confessions, as well as the revolutionary ideas that Ferenczi developed with regard to theory and technique. It is no accident that Ferenczi placed so much emphasis on trauma and forgiveness, because he was himself a victim of childhood sexual abuse, as were Rank and Jung, as well as highlighted the nature of internalization and the role of internal objects on psychic development (see Rudnytsky, 2002, p. 129, fn 4). Equally, Rudnytsky shows how Ferenczi suffered from his own developmental traumas only to theoretically champion the primacy of love as the proper avenue for analytic healing, a poignant wish that is embedded in his own self-analysis.

Now enters Groddeck. Groddeck is an odd sort of bird in psychoanalysis: He was the director of a small sanitarium in Baden-Baden, Germany, but ironically had a psychotic break near the end of his life and was hospitalized in Medard Boss's institution. Groddeck befriended Ferenczi and in fact treated him at his clinic where Ferenczi took extended annual visitations, thus influencing Ferenczi's own shifting theoretical and technical innovations. We may not inappropriately say that Ferenczi found in Groddeck the maternal tenderness he did not receive from Freud. Once proclaiming to be a "wild analyst," he is probably most famous for his theory of unconscious forces emanating from "The It" (*Das Es*), the term Freud appropriated for his mature tripartite theory of mind. *The Book of the It* is Groddeck's treatise on unconscious processes, but what is most interesting about this work is that it is written as a novel. Writing the book in epistolary form, Groddeck casts his autobiographical persona in the character of Patrik Troll, who writes 33 letters to an unnamed lady friend (mainly a composite of his second wife, a former patient he married, but also Freud as well), discussing everything from masturbation to God. In fact, Groddeck candidly propounds the centrality of masturbation in human life and the meaning of sexual symbolism in myth, social institutions, and Judeo-Christianity; reinforces the thesis of somatic conversion as compromise formation; offers a feminist critique of Freud's phallocentrism; and privileges the role of the maternal object in psychic life over the oedipal father. These themes echo the writings of many contemporary relational authors, one of whom is Michael Eigen (2006), who self-discloses, "To masturbate is to see God. All through childhood I masturbated, day and night, many, many times a day, constantly" (p. 17).

I suspect that if we wanted to dig further into the personal life histories and professional actions of the early analysts, we would find all sorts of objectionable material that would bear on the question of method and ethical comportment. But what is unmistakable is that these early analysts who deviated from Freudian stricture postulated key theoretical refinements and participated in an analytic praxis that are forerunners of the relational movement today.

Since its inception, psychoanalysis has always received criticism for not measuring up to the propounded status of a legitimate "science." But clinical case material is what we mainly rely on as legitimate sources of qualitative, empirical data.* As Safran

---

* I am not in agreement with Masling's (2003) claim that clinical data are "not empirical" (p. 597) because they rely on the qualitative enactments and analysis of experience, not merely culled from the analyst's clinical phenomenology but also empirically investigated by psychoanalytic psychotherapy researchers including Gill, Hoffman, Luborsky, Strupp, and Safran, just to name a few.

(2003) points out in his survey of psychotherapy research, there are many empirically derived conclusions that address the question of treatment efficacy. Once taking into account the patient's developmental and life history, we may be alerted to the following conditions that remain the major criteria with which to evaluate the merit and/or limitations of a treatment and the specific interventions employed: (a) the qualitative degree of the working alliance, including (but not limited to) the level of trust and capacity to form an attachment with the analyst; (b) mutual agreement with regard to the process and goals of treatment; and (c) the patient's assent to professional authority as indicative of his or her level of satisfaction (with or without symptom improvement).

As I have stated elsewhere (Mills, 2005c), in my opinion psychoanalysis is ultimately about process over anything else—perhaps even above technical principles, theory, and interventions—for it relies on the indeterminate unfolding of inner experience within intersubjective space. In our training we learn to cultivate an analytic attitude of clinical composure, optimal listening, data gathering, hypothesis testing, critical reflection, clarification, and reevaluation—all of which conceptually and behaviorally guide the analytic process. Process is everything, and attunement to process will determine if you can take the patient where he or she needs to go. The analyst has the challenging task of attending to the patient's associations within particular contexts of content and form, perpetuity versus discontinuity, sequence and coherence, thus noting repetitions of themes and patterns, and the convergence of such themes within a teleological dynamic trajectory of conceptual meaning. The clinician has to be vigilant for competing, overlapping, and/or parallel processes that are potentially operative at once, thus requiring shifts in focal attention and process. There are always realities encroaching on other realities, and affect plays a crucial part. Observation becomes a way of being that requires listening on multiple levels of experiential complexity—from analyzing manifest to latent content; detecting unconscious communications; recognizing resistance, defense, drive derivatives (i.e., unconscious desire), transference manifestations, and differential elements of each compromise; tracking the dialectical tensions between competing wishes, fantasies, and conflicts with close attention to their affective reverberations; listening at different levels of abstraction; and ferreting out one's countertransference from ordinary subjective peculiarities to tracing the multifarious interpersonal components of therapeutic exchange. Given such complexity and the overdetermination of multiple competing processes, I hardly think psychoanalytic technique is capable of being manualized by following a step-by-step method.

For the record, I am not making any ethical charge, nor am I showing any malice or ill will toward anyone in the relational field for simply taking their words seriously. I have critiqued people who I find have something of value to say, even if my disagreements have generated bad feelings. If I did not think these issues were important, then I would not have bothered wasting my time commenting on them. My intent is to stimulate noteworthy attention and serious debate about these ideas and practices so our profession can continue to prosper and advance.

I have been criticized by several relational analysts (Jacobs, 2006; S. Pizer, 2006; Stolorow, Atwood, & Orange, 2006) for reporting clinical events out of context. One point I want to convey in my adumbrated and excerpted examples of "excess" is the overdetermined motivations and multiple implications embedded within an intervention. Here the reader will observe the dialectical tension between my praise for the technical liberation the relational tradition has introduced and the potential for ethical concern and admonishment. The main issue here becomes a serious inquiry into the ground, breadth, and impediments to psychoanalytic method. This is an important area in the relational field that needs continued discussion and debate (also see Aron, 1996; Brice, 2000; S. H. Cooper, 1998; Ehrenberg, 1995).

Marilyn Jacobs (2006) in particular believes that I am accusing the relational field of an "inherent risk" of therapeutic excess that leads to unethical behavior based upon a theoretical orientation that guides such conduct. She is essentially charging me with a theory–method confound, namely, that I accuse relational theory—indeed the whole relational tradition—of "determining" the analyst's behavior in the consulting room, concluding that I am saying that relational "theory" "prescribes" "unethical" behavior (pp. 189–190). This is not the case.* By definition, theory and method are differentiated classifications, and although they may certainly be interdependent, theory in itself does not necessarily "determine" a method or clinical course of action. Nevertheless, the issue she raises sparks important questions for future inquiry among many different psychoanalytic schools, which is not simply relegated to the relationalists.

As I have argued, the relational tradition does not present or possess a systematized view of psychoanalytic theory or practice. When a subdiscipline such as the relational school does not hold a unified theory or methodology, it is particularly open to different interpretations in both theory and practice. There are, consequently, larger degrees of discrepancy in freely translating theory into therapeutic action, let alone uniform technique, because nonsystematization introduces more ambiguity than systematic thought and procedure. This is an undercurrent to the potential degrees of freedom that inform analysts' behavior. Therapists who are identified with any theory must decipher, interpret, and absorb certain conceptual schemas and convert them into directive principles that inform clinical action, regardless of whether the theory justifies the method or vice versa. Theory informs method, but it does not determine method. In fact, it is important to retain a categorical distinction between the two, because a method, in principle, should be able to be potentially applied to

---

* Jacobs (2006) in fact uses the word *suggests* in several places in her reply to my previous discussion on the topic, but she does not cite my actual words. Therefore, her entire refutation is based on a non sequitur that misattributes premises and propositional attitudes to my actual position that I do not hold or state anywhere in my article (Mills, 2005a) she is responding to. As a result, her whole argument against me is based on something that I do not say, hence it is groundless.

diverse and variegated theoretical frameworks that in turn may lend increasing conceptual complexity to explaining therapeutic action. Despite this qualification, adherents of any theoretical model advocate for certain interventions over others that may duplicate, simulate, overlap, oppose, or complement one another, thereby resulting in emphasizing some aspects while deemphasizing others, or they may depart entirely from other technical practices based upon theoretical proclivities. Therefore, it becomes untenable to think that there exists a complete polarization of theory and method, when each dialectically informs the other.

There is a potential for misuse and abuse that exists with any teachings and in any training milieu regardless of one's so-called theoretical orientation. This is certainly no different in contemporary analytic training environs whereby the way one comes to subjectively interpret theory, which in turn affects one's clinical practice, is influenced by faculty, training analysts, and supervisors who advocate for their own perspectives. Such positions may not be devoid of thoughtfulness, clinical judgment, expertise, and experience, but they are biased, necessarily so, by their preferences, whims, and prejudices that oppose other credible points of view. To push this discussion further, I *do* believe, as Jacobs is likewise concerned about, that there is an "inherent risk" of therapeutic ambition in *any* psychoanalytic tradition, not just the relational movement. Throughout the scope of my critique on therapeutic excess, I have accentuated this issue here involving some of the behaviors reported or observed by analysts identified with contemporary relational thought, but this could equally apply to other psychoanalytic traditions as well. Just because I draw attention to and question certain technical practices or theoretical tenets does not mean relational theory is decisively wrong, let alone do I claim it ethically condones or "prescribes" "unprofessional behavior." The issue at hand, in this context, is how one interprets theory, not the theory itself.

5

Contemporary Politics

THE HISTORICAL NASTINESS OF PSYCHOANALYTIC POLITICS

The nature of psychoanalytic politics has always been nasty, cutthroat, and full of dissent. This is to be expected given that the bid for power, control, and narcissistic monopoly that often typifies human nature is what led Aristotle to conclude that man is a political animal. Recall that Freud started psychoanalysis by enlisting a small circle of adherents drawn to his theories, meeting every Wednesday evening at his home to read papers and discuss ideas and cases, many of whom became loyal colleagues, some even friends.* But many did not. It is no secret that Freud could be intolerant of others who offered ideas that were contradictory to his own, leading to several tensions, fissures, and breaks from

---

* He in fact sent a few postcards in 1902 to a select group of people who were enthralled by his lectures at the psychiatric clinic of the General Hospital in Vienna to invite them to form a coterie (what we would now call a study group) at his office (adjacent to his condominium) to discuss theoretical ideas and case studies. This "Wednesday circle," which started out as 4 members—Adler and Stekel among them—grew in number to over 20 people by 1908, with usually no more than 10 members coming at any given week. After dinner, when the circle would gather, Freud's wife would serve coffee and cigars as the group smoked like chimneys while engaging in intellectual discussion, sometimes lasting hours (see Brome, 1967, pp. 15, 18). This Wednesday circle grew in number to such a degree that they formed the Vienna Psycho-Analytical Society and rented a large room once a week at the College of Physicians. When the membership continued to blossom, this naturally led to the formation of the International Psycho-Analytical Association.

key members of his early circle, including Adler, Stekel, Jung, and later Rank and Ferenczi.

There were legitimate intellectual disagreements as well as petty jealousies and rivalries that created factions within the group (Gay, 1988; Jones, 1955), to the point that loyalists developed a secret fraternity designed to safeguard the master's creation, which of course was nurtured by Freud himself (Grosskurth, 1991). In his biography of Freud's early circle, Vincent Brome (1967) tells us that there was "a great deal of gossip, backbiting and malicious talk" (p. 62) that characterized intermember relations, a generalization we could rightfully extend to any political group. At times, the milieu could be quite unpleasant, critical, aggressive, even verbally volatile. For example, Fritz Wittels (1924), once a member of the Wednesday circle, described a particularly hostile meeting where Freud and his supporters

> made a mass attack on Adler, an attack almost unexampled for its ferocity. … Stekel told me that the onslaught produced on his mind the impression of being a concerted one. Freud had a sheaf of notes before him and with gloomy mien seemed prepared to annihilate his adversary. (p. 151)

Jung's defection was worse. Freud was so personally perturbed and threatened by Jung's theoretical independence and international ascendance that at one point he wanted to sever all ties with the Zürich group and dismantle the International Psycho-Analytical Association. After instigating a series of polemical attacks on one of Jung's books, essentially forcing Jung to resign as editor of the *Jahrbuch* and then as president of the IPA, Freud, writing to Abraham, ruthlessly maligned him: "So we are at last rid of them, the brutal, sanctimonious Jung and his disciples."* Freud made it a personal mission to smear his name whenever he could, even calling him "crazy." In his memoirs, Jung (1961) tells us that he was the subject of malicious slander, where Freudians

---

* Freud's letter to Abraham, July 25, 1914; *Letters of Sigmund Freud and Karl Abraham.*

had adeptly circulated sustained rumors that he was schizophrenic, which ultimately damaged his reputation and practice. This unscrupulous rumor had cost him patients, and he also lost students. Jung writes, "After the break with Freud all my friends and acquaintances dropped away. My book was declared to be rubbish; I was a mystic and that settled the matter" (p. 162). But what was even worse is that Jung was branded an anti-Semite, what he attributed to Freud himself, a label he vociferously denied and rebuked; however, it was a stigma that dogged him for the rest of his life.

It is no different now as it was back then; in this way contemporary psychoanalysis is merely an extension of the old, fraught with controversy and dissidence. Only the context happens to be different, where instead of a few visionaries battling over ideas and political leverage, now we have various identified "schools" or "traditions" that are at odds with competing psychoanalytic theories and methodological practices. Whether this be the contemporary Freudians or modern conflict theorists, the neo-Kleinians, the Independents or object relations theorists, the post-Lacanians, the self psychologists, and, most recently in the history of psychoanalysis, the intersubjectivists and relationalists, each self-identified group also has its own subculture of political hierarchy, prestige, and power. To be sure, each camp has its own organizations, forums, training institutes and practices, evaluation and disciplinary procedures, colloquy, publication venues, and, without equivocation, private agendas.

It is often the case that each psychoanalytic subculture has its own modern-day equivalent of "The Committee," namely, a close circle of political friends (and often close personal friends) who share and advance a common cause. And of course political motives and preferences find their way into the governance of any organization, from electing executives and boards of psychoanalytic organizations; to assigning faculty, granting training, and supervising status to analysts at local institutes; to controlling what ideas get disseminated in publication houses, including books, periodicals, and so-called peer review journals (of course depending upon what camp one's peer comes from). Politicians are chosen because they advance "the cause."

Psychoanalysis has been often compared to a religion for its insular operations, secrecy, and unquestioning adherence to orthodoxy based on a guild mentality where a certain designated hierarchy bestows knowledge and so-called wisdom to the uninitiated, much like the oedipal father who indoctrinates his children in the process of his ideological worldview under the guise of *Bildung*. The ancients called this *paideia*. Subjected to such rigid education austerely dictated by dogma, where free speech and opinion are dissuaded, often under the implicit threat of receiving negative judgments or evaluations from superiors, many analysts become conditioned to fear being authentically open about their true beliefs and predilections. Why is this so? Because they fear the tangible political consequences that could follow.

Here lingers a climate of unspoken silence, much like a gnostic or mystic tradition that dare not speak of secret knowledge (*mysterion*, from *myein*, to close [lips and eyes]). Such passivity in the face of political force is often governed by pragmatic concerns that preoccupy the concrete reality of the analyst's life priorities, such as the economics of not receiving referrals from colleagues, the potential blockade of career advancement, the achievement of membership or status in certain organizations, and/or the fulfillment of personal ambitions that include peer recognition and professional acknowledgment. It is very nerve-racking to question let alone challenge politically astute people because of the inherent risk involved in confronting ethically dubious behaviors or questionable practices, having then to deal with the aftermath that is bound to ensue. As a result, many analysts do not speak openly let alone publically about political power differentials and instead become complacent, disengaged, apathetic, or obsequious. Those who do are seen as mavericks, rogues, reactionaries, or dissidents.

DISSIDENCE, COMPLICITY, AND THE WILL TO COURAGE

The beginning days of establishing psychoanalysis as a human science was fraught with controversy, denunciation, outward hostility, prejudice, and even intense animus, to the point that Professor Emil Raimann, a neurologist and assistant at the Psychiatric Clinic in Vienna, harassed Freud relentlessly for 12 years from 1904 to 1916 until Freud complained to the chief to put a stop to the invectives (Jones, 1955, p. 109). Those sympathetic to Freud's theories were censored from publishing papers in journals and lost clinical and academic appointments, and some had careers ruined. Jones even spent a night in jail for asking child patients about sexual matters (Brome, 1967, pp. 33–34). Professionals, academics, and practitioners of all kinds went out of their way to openly persecute Freud, malign his character, have his ideas discredited, and punish those who were affiliated with him or positively inclined toward psychoanalytic thought.

These were virulent times, and the opposition was fierce. With his theories and case evidence largely renounced by his medical contemporaries, Freud was heralded a pervert and was systematically ostracized by Viennese medical circles who were largely anti-Semitic, thereby suppressing publication of his work in leading periodicals and obstructing his appointment to professorship (Gay, 1988). He was ferociously scorned and verbally abused at conferences, and at one neurological and psychiatric congress, a professor from the audience pounded his fist on a table and shouted, "This is not a topic for discussion at a scientific meeting; it is a matter for the police." And this type of outrage happened on more than one occasion.

> During the Neurological Congress in Berlin towards the end of 1910, a famous neurologist, Professor Oppenheim, rose and proposed, in a voice charged with emotion, that they should boycott any institution where Freud's views were accepted. The meeting almost cheered this statement and the hall re-echoed to that kind of enthusiasm which belonged to politics rather than science. (Brome, 1967, p. 32)

Politics indeed. Freud was the subject of constant vituperation, *ad hominem* attacks, and personal vendettas and was accosted by physicians, academe, and the public alike. So much for the early days of psychoanalysis.

Within the pecking order of political affiliation there are always leaders and followers. Freud's inner circle and the larger psychoanalytic membership sheltered him from the mass opinion that he was a charlatan, and he grew very protective of his "new science." Freud was not always comfortable in stewardship positions, instead wanting others to drive the chariot, but he also kept a tight hold of the reigns. It is only natural that his inner circle would gradually grow disgruntled in their own way. Although they embraced the cause, they also had differences of opinion that led to the same forms of political bullying Freud had to endure. Freud's passionate temperament and initial resistance to new ideas did not help matters when others had differing viewpoints.

So it comes as no surprise that some of the early pioneers of psychoanalysis were also major dissidents who splintered away from Freudian theory and practice, such as Adler, Jung, Rank, Ferenczi, Horney, as well as Lacan, just to name a few, to develop their own novel ideas about the psychoanalytic mind and clinical technique. Whether or not dissidents formed their own groups or followings, they had the tendency to become vocal in expressing their disagreements and differences of opinion, which sometimes led to infective, acerbic, and venomous statements designed to politically destroy unwanted rivals. A well-known example of this in the history of psychoanalysis is Anna Freud's antipathy directed toward Melanie Klein. Klein was so controversial that during her lifetime she was both unsettling and monumental—to the point of revolution. Many tried to discredit her unjustly, culminating in the contentious "Controversial Discussions" of the British Psycho-Analytical Society where she went head-to-head with Anna Freud and her followers from 1941 to 1945, what antagonist Edward Glover (1933) later referred to as the "Klein imbroglio," despite the fact that he had previously referred to her work as "a landmark in analytical literature" (p. 119).

Klein is a good example of psychoanalytic bullying. She has been "sniffled at" (Meisel & Kendrick, 1985, p. 182), labeled a "heretic" (Hughes, 1989, p. 44), "branded, vilified, and mocked" (Grosskurth, 1986, p. 3), and even called an "inspired gut butcher" (Kristeva, 2001, p. 229).* In a letter to Jones, Freud writes that despite his "opinion" that the British Society had followed Klein down "a wrong path," he nevertheless conceded that since her observations of children were "foreign" to him, he had "no right to any fixed conviction" (Jones, 1957, p. 197).† Let the ladies battle it out for themselves! And so after the debates solidified, the society arrived at a "gentlemen's agreement": The two factions diplomatically resigned themselves to a mutual, amicable cohabitation within the society, and as an offshoot, an independent, "middle group" was formed.

Here, for the first time in its history, psychoanalysis introduced a permissible space for accepting difference and diversity in the way psychoanalysis could be taught at societies and institutes, and hence a plurality to theory and practice was condoned by the political establishment itself. In retrospect, we can observe how this historic moment set the stage for other opponents, dissenters, visionaries, special interest groups, complementarities, and redirecting shifts in emphasis that eventually led to the spawn of many schools within psychoanalysis, including the object

---

* This quote is attributed to Lacan from Julia Kristeva, who had attended his seminars.
† See letter dated May 26, 1935. But Freud held a grudge that Jones did not back his daughter. Jones himself waffled in his support of Klein while attempting to ingratiate himself to the master. After inviting her to England and paving the way for her reception in the British Society—where Klein was inducted as the first female member—he proved to be an indecisive sycophant. In a letter to Anna Freud, although acknowledging Klein's contributions, Jones writes that she "has neither a scientific nor an orderly mind and her presentations are lamentable" (January 21, 1942, letter to Anna Freud; cited in King & Steiner, 1991, p. 235). But in another letter, Jones is equally unflattering of Anna Freud, who he said had "no pioneering originality" (King & Steiner, 1991, p. 229). For Jones, Melanie was trailblazing yet rueful, whereas Anna was simply banal. It is interesting to note that at one time Jones had romantic inclinations for Anna Freud when she was young and that later in life Jones had his children analyzed by Klein herself (see Grosskurth, 1991).

relations movement, ego psychology, self psychology, and the American middle group who favor relational, intersubjective, and postmodern approaches. But despite the current climate that favors plurality, heterogeneity, and tolerance for difference within psychoanalytic work, there is also a cryptic favoritism that each analyst has with his or her professed, self-identified school(s) of thought that stand in opposition to other schools whose theoretical orientations differ from one's own. And there are many legitimate reasons for such preferences and identifications. But these attitudes can quickly inform prejudices that are acted out in arenas governed by psychoanalytic politics.

Martin Bergmann (2004) tells us that "dissidence is a phenomenon of hubris due to the success of self-analysis" (p. 90). This comment reinforces the notion that the dissident has excessive confidence, self-pride, and personal conviction and that he is not sufficiently burdened by his own neuroses or insecurities to the point that he has the courage to express his mind. Bergmann also points out an unsavory dimension to such hubris:

> All dissidents were convinced that they were right. ... There is much to be said in favor of having convictions. ... But there is another side to conviction where the mind is closed to new ideas, where aggression is directed toward those who hold beliefs, and where a hindrance to further learning and development has taken place. (pp. 92–93)

When this occurs, hubris turns into a breeding ground for political aggression and intellectual myopia. I do not think it is a stretch to conclude that analysts who hold different theoretical models and methodological practices than our own are viewed, either conspicuously or privately, with smug contempt, self-righteous indignation, and intellectual inferiority, sometimes even becoming the object of petty gossip or vindictive rumors, because they are seen as direct threats and rivals to our preferred ways of viewing the world. Perhaps Freud would refer to this as the narcissism of minor differences; here I would argue, as I have done elsewhere (Mills & Polanowski, 1997), that every human being is prejudiced.

We approach competing points of view with prejudice due to emotively preferred identifications that inform our apprehension of any subject matter. This is only natural. And when we anticipate or fear that others will not align with our cause or promote our side, we may become suspicious, guarded, and protective—even hostile. Just as we have a transference to theory (Rangell, 1982), we also have a countertransference to other people's theories, to the point that psychoanalytic camps, groups, schools, or traditions are often openly antagonistic toward others that do not share their perspective. The need to defend our heroes (viz., our esteemed theories) and safeguard them against criticism or exploitation reflects the need to remain attached to our idealizations, to the point that any indication that potentially threatens them, whether in reality or fantasy, is seen as an unforgivable act of dissension. But no amount of blind loyalty, narcissistic arrogance, or felt resistance should impede the pursuit of truth, meaning, and justice, even if we are wrong.

Leo Rangell is one of the few world famous psychoanalysts who has spoken openly about the type of nastiness that characterizes psychoanalytic politics. Having twice been president of the International and the American Psychoanalytic Associations, he has been quite candid about the personal and professional struggles he encountered while in political office, including being the subject of contempt, animosity, mean-spiritedness, rage, personal attacks, and backstabbing, as well as detailing some of the sordid interpersonal tactics that go on behind the scenes, including having to directly mediate verbal diatribes, endure shunning, and confront festering situations that became tumultuous. Even mutual friends could turn on a dime. For example, in describing the personal tension between himself and once close friend, Joseph Sandler, he reports, "For three decades and through many congresses and shared events, our relationship remained strained, hardly more than a nodding" (Rangell, 2004, p. 269). From this brief remark, we can easily imagine how uncomfortable it would be to have to continuously visually absorb the animus from another. But when this goes on and is observed (even discretely or intuitively) in front of professional colleagues and peers who share positions of respect and authority, this can have an affective contagion on the perceptions that mold political sentiment. In his words, Rangell opines "that such small discordances, if they occur in high places, have disproportionate effects on larger bodies. ... I believe that such personal, affective stances play a part in shaping opinions and convictions" (p. 269). And what this translates into is how a political body will be influenced and persuaded by the personalities that affect the governance of that political structure.

Rangell shows an unparalleled act of disclosure in airing dirty laundry and exposing transgressions of psychoanalysts who abused their political power. We should be grateful that he is being honest and forthright in expressing his concerns about the unpleasant and spiteful business that often composes psychoanalytic politics, if not for reinforcing the value judgment that these types of behavior should not be condoned, moreover because he is tacitly encouraging the field to abandon its subterfuge of pretending to be the "analyzed or enlightened one" who is above the depravity of the masses. This is hypocritical self-denial at its finest. When it comes to the dynamics of politics, the psychoanalyst is no different than the common man.

The list of individuals that Rangell (2004) identifies in unfavorable ways includes luminaries such as Anna Freud, Ralph Greenson, and Kohut, among others. The actions of Greenson deserve special attention. Rangell describes him as a man who

> could turn against people unpredictably, humiliating his targets pitilessly. I saw him do this at a party to a physician who had become close to the analytic group, reducing him to a state of helpless embarrassment and physical weakness. Sometimes he apologized the next day—and sometimes the apology only set up the victim for a repeat round. (p. 139)

Rangell reproduces a letter sent to him by one of Greenson's "victims," Lawrence Kubie, who was "mercilessly and needlessly attacked" (p. 139) during a paper presentation at the Los Angeles Society. Kubie writes,

March 1, 1967

My dear Greenson,

I reached home early on Friday morning the 24th. Your apology of the 21st reached me the following morning. A round dozen of our colleagues from both societies had anticipated you by phoning me, and by writing to me to apologize for your behavior, i.e., for its inaccuracy, for its exhibitionism, and for its confusing incoherence. Some said you were drunk. Some said that you had done this before, but never quite as rantingly. (cited in Rangell, 2004, pp. 139–140)

Kubie concludes by telling Greenson, in not so veiled words, that he is a disgrace to the profession and that he needs to seek professional help. This kind of behavior by a prominent analyst is not new. We can easily imagine it going on in Freud's early circle as we observe it today. Here I am further reminded of David James Fisher's (2008) depiction of Bruno Bettelheim, whom he knew personally:

He was a highly serious man with a spirit of gravity about him. He did not suffer fools easily. Impatient, tough-minded, authoritarian, easy to anger, Bettelheim had a need to unmask sentimentality, to cut through phoniness, and demolish soft thinking. He was a proponent of the reality principle and was unwilling to tolerate idealistic or romantic conceptions of the personality, of cultural artifacts, or of history. He displayed an ironic sense of humor and he could be self-deprecating. He intensely disliked pretense and he could be brutally honest, often picking up on an individual's vulnerabilities and inner conflicts, offering searing interpretations. He had an uncanny ability to make one feel understood and, on the other hand, to make one feel exposed, precipitating feelings of shame and guilt. (p. 60)

Setting aside for the moment the developmental backgrounds, personal idiosyncrasies, and familial and cultural experiences that shape personality structure, and the interpersonal styles that convey our affect, motives, and demeanor, I believe it is simply human nature to want to ingress our desire and force our points of view onto others. But some take this to the point of dominance, aggression, and an uncompromising need to control. Rangell (1980) advanced the notion that the political mind is seduced by ambition, power, and opportunism, to the degree that it can lead to a compromise of integrity. When this happens, the subjective (often narcissistic and grandiose) pursuit of personal aims and penchants are chased at all costs, regardless of the effects on others, which leads to unchecked power differentials that cause human suffering. And I would argue that this entails (at the very least) a modicum of psychopathy.

Rangell (2004) further notes, almost in passing,

> While it has been considered ungentlemanly to bring people or personalities into theoretical discussion, ad hominem (and ad feminam) factors, which are always present, are omitted at the expense of completeness. It is ironic that these elements, which are the subject matter of psychoanalysis, should so often be considered off-limits in studies of psychoanalytic history itself. (p. 105)

This irony speaks of a deep taboo but a fundamental insight all the more important to explore. Why is it that some analysts can get away with vitriolic nastiness and political abuse of power and never get called on their atrocious behavior? Why do others stand idly by in complicity like dumbfounded bystanders and watch as detached spectators without having the courage to speak up or get involved? Are they indifferent, disinvested, amused but unperturbed, anxiously cautious, afraid of the repercussions, or intimidated to take a stand, or do they simply lack the guts?

Relational psychoanalytic politics is no different than other special interest groups that have attempted to gain prominence, authority, influence, and delegation or commandeer control over preestablished power structures within the field. In fact, the relational movement is a testament to political savvy and success by the mere fact that it has proliferated in interest and acceptability throughout the psychoanalytic community, has drawn many adherents worldwide, and, as previously discussed, continues to champion antiquated methods of analytic conceptualization and practice that sympathizers simply can't buy. Although relational psychoanalysis is an American phenomenon, mainly represented in the contemporary training institutes, societies, and specialty organizations in the United States, many of which are psychologist based, there is also a burgeoning membership worldwide.

The International Association for Relational Psychoanalysis and Psychotherapy (IARPP), the brainchild of the late Steven Mitchell, boasts a healthy membership of over 1,000 people from nearly 30 countries. Within the United States alone, there are two major journals that favor and/or are friendly to relational thought, including *Psychoanalytic Dialogues: A Journal of Relational Perspectives*, where most of the people whom I critique here either are on the editorial board or have served on the executive, once again including Steven Mitchell, who was the founding editor, and *Contemporary Psychoanalysis*, the journal of the William Alanson White Institute and Society, where the interpersonal school has largely morphed into relational paradigms, an organization where Mitchell graduated from, and those also affiliated with the editorial board and executive fall under the subject of my critique. Although pluralistic in nature, *Psychoanalytic Psychology*, the official journal of the Division of Psychoanalysis (39) of the American Psychological Association (APA), is also friendly toward relational theorists. The relational platform also has two book series with the defunct Analytic Press, now under management of the Taylor and Francis Group. And almost every prominent relational psychoanalyst has strong ties with the Division of Psychoanalysis (39) of the APA.

These fortified allegiances and political connections have many developmental roots and causal motivations, the details of which do not concern us here. But we must keep in mind how this was sparked to some degree by the dominion of psychoanalytic training by the medical community in the United States. Medical-analysts and psychologist-analysts share a historical rivalry that is still alive today, not simply because A. A. Brill institutionally co-opted and monopolized the training requirements of psychoanalysts in the United States—a political move that ensured enduring force by medical practitioners for decades—but also because the clash of egos between the two professions still exists. We may observe this group narcissism conditioned by the quality and so-called superiority of training, social values, occupational prestige, public confidence and trust, and overall respectability medicine has over psychology. Not only were psychologists fed up with being oppressed, and thereby successfully sued the American Psychoanalytic Association for refusing to admit and train "lay" professionals in their institutes, psychologists wanted the same privileges that medical doctors enjoyed. So they created their own training institutes, societies, centers, forums, and associations and organizations (local, regional, national) that sponsor scientific meetings, presentations and panels, colloquiums, workshops, conferences, and publication outlets.

Division 39 (Psychoanalysis) is today one of the largest memberships of the APA, with approximately 4,000 members. It has an annual spring conference with consistent attendance of over 1,000 and has a monthly e-newsletter and quarterly Division newsletter, *DIVISION/Review: A Quarterly Psychoanalytic Forum* (formerly called *Psychologist-Psychoanalyst*), which is truly a journal of its own, sometimes with over 100 pages of print each issue composed of Division news, current events, controversies and concerns, letters, forums, featured articles, membership interests, and pages among pages of book reviews. It is without question the most informative source for member news and current topics of interest that is in print circulation for Division members.

In Division 39, the relational perspective is everywhere: in the APA journal, the newsletter, and the annual conference. The annual conference, usually sponsored by a local contemporary psychoanalytic institute, is dominated year after year by relational, intersubjective, interpersonal, and postmodern perspectives. Most paper and panel presentations cover the same topics and have the same presenters over and over. The invited presenters and panelists are largely relational in orientation, and the more traditional psychoanalytic camps have been so marginalized that one would be lucky to see the words *Freud* or *unconscious* in any presentation titles. Because the contemporary institutes that host the annual conferences control the conference agenda, Freudian approaches, object relations theories, and ego-psychological positions are barely represented. Even self psychology and the interpersonal school have been annexed by relational perspectives to the point that most visible distinctions have vanished. And because contemporary paradigms within the past three decades have gradually fallen in love with the language of philosophy, it becomes equally confusing to know what—if any—distinctions exist within contemporary perspectives.

I would like to share a personal anecdote of my experience at a Division 39 conference that some may find to be in bad taste because of its indiscretion. Although I do not wish to detract the reader from my main arguments in this chapter, the context is important to understand and directly bears on events that transpired afterward, events that I will discuss shortly. At the 2005 conference of the Division of Psychoanalysis (39) of the APA held in New York City, I was chair and moderator of a panel titled "Relational Psychoanalysis: A Critical Dialogue." There I delivered a paper called "Why Freud Was Right: A Response to the Relational School," which was from a brief subsection of my article "A Critique of Relational Psychoanalysis" that was published shortly after in *Psychoanalytic Psychology*. At the conference, as well as in print, I charged the relational school with illegitimate attacks on classical psychoanalysis by radically misrepresenting and distorting what Freud actually said in his original texts. As I argued in a previous chapter, such inaccuracies show poor scholarship and are overstatements that serve to promote an unwarranted theoretical divide between drive theory and relationality, which I allege is due, in part, to informal fallacies construed to politically advance a "new" relational paradigm at the expense of understanding what Freud truly has to offer us.

At the end of the panel presentations and commentary provided by respondent Neil Altman, I was immediately verbally accosted and vilified by Irwin Hoffman and Jody Davies, both of whom responded by yelling at me angrily, thus provoking panelist Roger Frie to speak up. Both Hoffman and Davies were livid, indignant, and emotionally unrestrained in their outrage toward me, and this was all displayed to an audience ambivalently gripped with a mixture of dismay, apprehensive excitement, and anxiety. Despite the fact that they attempted to offer their own arguments against my positions, the affective aftermath of their outbursts colored my perception of their integrity. This is the only time I have encountered hostility at a professional conference for offering a critique of ideas. Not only did I experience their behavior to be rude and uncivil, they fundamentally demonstrated an inability to rationally debate matters of theoretical disagreement or entertain alternative positions to their own without devolving into vitriolic name-calling and character assassination.

It may be said that group loyalties surrounding a particular identification with any school of thought often mirror, perhaps unconsciously, an element of theory exemplified within that school. Contemporary relationalists are no exception. How ironic it is that relational theory purports to value fostering attachment, affective connection, and mutual recognition while at the same time certain analysts who are said to uphold these values can succumb to such behavior.

Of course, it goes without saying that most of the people I have critiqued in this book are conspicuously part of the Division 39 crowd and have held many political positions, including being board, section, and committee members within the Division itself. They are also a visible part of other groups, federations, forums, and formal administrative structures; a part of executives or hierarchies; and/or editorial, teaching, or supervising members of many psychoanalytic organizations, training centers, and university programs, as well as publication journals and book series. These people have power, and they know it. They can squelch a

rival point of view in a number of fashions, some direct and inci-
sive, some circuitous or sneaky, and some downright nasty.

Let us take, for example, Jay Greenberg, the cofounder of the
relational movement, who is also the past editor of *Contemporary
Psychoanalysis,* on the editorial board of *Psychoanalytic Dialogues,*
past editor of the North American Editorial Board for the
International Journal of Psychoanalysis, and current editor of *The
Psychoanalytic Quarterly.* I would like to share a letter I received
from Dr. Greenberg after in good faith inviting him to publish a
book and be on the editorial board of my book series *New Imago:
Series in Theoretical, Clinical, & Applied Psychoanalysis,* an
imprint with Jason Aronson/Rowman and Littlefield Publishers.

November 26, 2007

Dear Dr. Mills,

I decline your invitation to become a member of your Editorial
Board. I have no time to read manuscripts, and do not support the
kind of honorific you seem to be organizing.

Beyond this, I object strenuously to the inclusion of my name
as a member of your board. I can only assume that the others
whose names you have listed have not yet agreed to participate
any more than I have. Further, I assume that you have used me to
lure other members to participate; I consider this is a gross misap-
propriation of my personal reputation. Please remove my name
immediately, and please inform those who received this letter that
I have not in any manner agreed to participate in your project.

Yours truly,

Jay Greenberg, PhD

Does this look like someone who is interested in building relationships? From this letter alone, one must seriously question
whether Greenberg truly practices what he preaches. Greenberg's
hostility is apparent, but his entitlement and grandiose omnipotence is even more astonishing. He actually states that he thinks I
am using his name to "lure" other analysts to be on the editorial
board, as if he is the psychoanalytic poster boy with whom all

other analysts would want to be associated. The readership should know that many respected and prestigious analysts from every major psychoanalytic discipline are part of this interdisciplinary editorial board, including Leo Rangell, Robert Wallerstein, W. W. Meissner, Arnold Modell, Thomas Ogden, James Grotstein, Peter Fonagy, Adam Phillips, R. D. Hinshelwood, Glen Gabbard, Bruce Fink, Polly Young-Eisendrath, Elisabeth Young-Bruehl, Howard Stein, Wilma Bucci, Paul Verhaeghe, Fred Busch, Edgar Levenson, and many others, including two-time Nobel Peace Prize nominee Vamik Volkan and Julia Kristeva, winner of the Holberg International Memorial Prize awarded by the Norwegian government for her contributions to the humanities, arts, and sciences (the prize was for 4.5 million NOR). I suppose Professor Kristeva joined the board only so she could be listed next to Jay Greenberg.

These last examples are essentially benign acts of rudeness, but they are perpetrated by people who hold power and privilege in the psychoanalytic community and who are in positions of evaluating scholarly manuscripts submitted for publication. Just as Kubie was a victim of Greenson's abuse, how impartial of an assessment would I get under Greenberg's editorial thumb? To his credit, however, during a roundtable discussion on the future of psychoanalytic publishing, I asked the panel (who were all editors of major psychoanalytic journals) how they as editors safeguard against editor bias in the evaluation of manuscript submissions, and Greenberg (2011) specifically responded. I was somewhat reassured.

Richard Chessick (2007) speaks of a "failure of nerve" from psychoanalysts to stand up for what is right. Just as Leo Rangell has set an example for speaking up about the incivility of his colleagues, what I wish to champion here is the courage to confront rancor and unfair practices within psychoanalytic arenas, which reflects a broader identification with battling injustice as a moral principle. Following deontic ethics, I see it as a duty. We need to challenge complicity and lassitude, to speak our minds freely without the threat or fear of retaliation, to respectfully intervene when warranted, to put into place institutional sanctions that will allow for parity, to discipline those who abuse their power, and to decry those who are behaving badly.

Psychoanalysts should not be above or beyond reproach when they act inappropriately and disrespect the field. No matter how indiscrete, nonjudicious, or "ungentlemanly" it may be to point out personal actions, attitudes, biases, or events that are of dubious virtue, we should be held to a higher standard as exemplars of dignity, poise, and civility. In my opinion, the personalities, motives, and enactments informing analysts' public demeanor are fair game to analyze, even if we might consider it to be politically incorrect or *ad hominem*. And just as we analyze psychic conflict, maladaptive defenses, and disruptive behavior in the consulting room, it should not be off limits for analysts to point out, question, interpret, and pass judgment on unacceptable behavior that hurts the overall image, respectability, and reputation of psychoanalysis as a discipline.

ANALYSTS BEHAVING BADLY

My previous critique of the relational school has not been well received by relational theorists, if not the relational community in general. When my original critique article first appeared in the Division 39 journal *Psychoanalytic Psychology* (Mills, 2005a), it generated immediate controversy. There was a series of replies by critics, including Robert Stolorow, George Atwood, and Donna Orange (2006), Marilyn Jacobs (2006), and Stuart Pizer (2006), who offered scathing criticism and personal attacks by charging me with failing to live up to scholarly standards, using rhetorical devices to unjustly discredit certain relational authors, taking clinical material out of context, and committing unethical and libelous acts. Following the protocol of the journal, I was given a chance by the editor to reply to these accusations. In turn, I attempted to show that these criticisms largely lacked solid rationale, distorted or ignored crucial textual evidence, relied on *ad hominem* arguments and emotional polemics, and failed to convince me of their genuine merit. I denied all accusations of professional misconduct and drew into question the political motives and intellectual honesty of some key figures identified with the relational turn. Two of these people were Irwin Hoffman and Jody Davies.

This event symbolizes a much larger problem within psychoanalysis. The history of our discipline is replete with competition and contention; divided group loyalties; tendencies toward splitting, envy, and character slander; narcissistic displays of superiority and grandiosity; rigid collective identifications that oppose competing points of view; and political ostracizing under the emotional direction of retribution, abuse of power, and intolerance of difference for perceived transgressions against what any school believes is unadulterated dogma. No wonder critics have bemoaned psychoanalysis for its mismanagement by its adherents (Bornstein, 2001). These politics have fueled splintering and factions in psychoanalysis since its inception, and I doubt it will ever change. But when key leaders of the relational movement succumb to such emotional polemics based on a simple economy of intolerance for difference, it hurts us all as a discipline whose goal is the pursuit of meaning, knowledge, truth, and, potentially, wisdom.

What I believe is fundamentally precarious is the inability to engage leading relational proponents in genuine dialogue about contemporary ideas, despite the fact that they profess to uphold such ideals. Only our discipline can properly appreciate such a contradiction, for it speaks to a broader voice, namely, the echo of human nature. We all get emotionally attached to our ideas because we identify with their value and invest them with personal meaning. When they are challenged we understandably feel threatened and frequently wish to lash out, alienate, or aggress upon our perceived or projected enemy. And we need to have enemies. What would psychic life be like if we all agreed on the same thing? I for one would find it boring. But ideological intolerance of difference is simply unacceptable in any academic or scientific discipline: It does nothing but lead to stasis and exploitive, corrupt power differentials that erode the advancement of any intellectual pursuit. The minute we are prohibited or dissuaded to engage in critique, let alone reviled for doing so, we betray our intellectual integrity as a human-social-behavioral science and lose all credibility as a discipline.

Despite the fact that I was honored with a Gradiva Award from the National Association for the Advancement of Psychoanalysis for the best article written in 2005, the controversy only got worse. Not only was I vilified in print for advancing intellectual ideas, including being accused of lying and committing ethical misconduct and libel by Pizer (2006), which I proved to be fallacious (Mills, 2006), I was further the victim of being politically silenced, which was orchestrated by the manipulative hands of three prominent psychoanalysts.

In an unprecedented tag-team approach, Neil Altman (2007), Jody Davies (2007), and Irwin Hoffman (2007) abnegated my portrayal of their public vituperation at the professional conference just mentioned where Hoffman and Davies verbally attacked me after I delivered a paper to the audience.* This time they had gone so far as to intimidate and persuade the Publications Committee of the Division of Psychoanalysis to have me successfully censored from responding to their published "Commentaries" in *Psychoanalytic Psychology*. Not only did this undermine the purpose and value of democratic debate, it subverted the protocol of this respected and established scholarly journal. What is equally egregious is that they conspired to attack the professional integrity of the editor, Dr. Joseph Reppen. Reppen communicated to me that he was not supported by the Publications Committee who

---

* It should be noted that both Davies and Hoffman admit in writing that they did indeed become verbally aggressive with me at the conference in question. Davies (2007) specifically states, "It is absolutely true that I was appalled by Mills' presentation. ... My anger at Jon Mills and my criticism of him last April had nothing to do with his challenge, therefore, to relational theory in general or to Stephen Mitchell in particular. I criticized Mills—yes in an angry way—for resorting to nasty and unnecessary ad hominem attacks on Mitchell himself" (p. 398). Furthermore, Hoffman (2007) confesses, "I'm sure some may have been put off by our intensity" (p. 402) and "I'm sure I made these points somewhat angrily" and "expressed indignation about Mills ... [who] provoked my rage" (p. 404).

shanghaied the editorial decision process. Not only do these analysts' actions and the complicity of the Publications Committee supplant the notion of academic freedom, it brings our profession into disrepute.

I will not revisit the minutia that transpired at the annual spring conference of the Division of Psychoanalysis held in New York City on April 17, 2005. The veracity of these events can be substantiated by several witnesses who attended the presentation in question.* Roger Frie, who was a panelist along with Neil Altman, has corroborated my portrayal of the events that occurred at the conference. He specifically says, "I experienced first hand the nature of the commentary. I found it unsettling and not appropriate to an academic setting" (2007, p. 5). What is important to emphasize here is not their conduct at the conference but how their political tactics led to a compromise of liberty executed by a democratic board designed to safeguard against the infringement of liberty.

There are three main arguments I wish to advance in this indictment. The first, and this is a minor point, speculatively involves the deliberate and calculated intent on the part of these three analysts to intimidate, manipulate, and essentially abuse their power in order to pressure others to comply with their wishes to have me silenced. The second, the main point, involves the subversion of a free democratic process, and the third is that their collective actions are damaging to the profession.

---

* I was originally led to believe that the whole exchange was recorded and is available on CD (see Sound Images, Inc., 2005). However, as Davies (2007) rightly states, "The question and answer portion about which Mills speaks has been substantially edited by Sound Images, and the sections under dispute are, in very large measure, absent from the CD. We hear much of Mills' response, but it is unclear to what or to whom he is responding" (p. 397). It was unfortunate that this dialogue was not fully captured in the recording; however, it does not annul the fact that several witnesses can attest to its occurrence. Including those who were present are panelist Roger Frie and audience members Jane Tucker, Max Harris, Deborah Luepnitz, Herbert Weiner, Peter Buirski, and Harold Davis. Davis in particular at one point attempted to mediate the conflict from the floor. Of course there were dozens of other people who were in attendance; however, these are individuals whom I specifically remember and/or who spoke to me after the event expressing their astonishment or dismay.

Let us pose the most obvious question: Why would three distinguished psychoanalysts need to eliminate my voice? I simply want to appeal to the intellectual honesty of any reader. Of course most fair-minded people will read between the lines. Dr. Reppen's (2007) brief editorial note published at the end of their essays clues us in:

> The preceding Commentaries are published as a consequence of a condition demanded by Drs. Altman, Davies, and Hoffman, and agreed upon by the Publications Committee of the Division of Psychoanalysis, that there be no response by Dr. Mills to their Commentaries published in *Psychoanalytic Psychology*. This stricture may not be in keeping with the spirit of openness of this journal under my editorship. Nonetheless, readers are free to draw their own conclusions as to the appropriateness of this condition. (p. 406)

Following Reppen's assertions, in my opinion, Drs. Altman, Davies, and Hoffman have committed turpitude by using coercive tactics to depose the journal's protocol and hence materially contributed to censor debate in professional public space. The Division has an obligation to support pluralism and theoretical diversity within our membership in order to allow for a free exchange of ideas, which may be said to constitute its general mission statement. Then why would the Publications Committee acquiesce to such strong-arm politics? I was informed directly by multiple reliable sources of Davies's, Hoffman's, and Altman's systematic efforts at censorship and manipulation over the process of replying to my 2006 article.* There were many circulated rumors, including insinuating lawsuits against the Division and implicitly threatening a mass exodus of relational supporters from the Division's membership if they did not get their way. Reportedly, there were torrents of objections launched against the Division's political governance, and they did in fact complain to the APA against Reppen. In essence, they conjured up the paranoid position

---

* Out of respect for the individuals whom I spoke to directly about these matters, I will protect their anonymity by not mentioning them by name.

and got the Division's executive nervous. Under these circumstances I can understand why the Publications Committee and publications chair and then incoming president of Division 39, Dr. Nancy McWilliams, would be anxious about such a delicate situation, but I cannot accept in good conscience how executives of the Division would succumb to these extorts. Of course they would want to harmonize peace and offer concession with the appeasement of avoiding future bad feelings. I personally harbor no ill will about the Division's actions and can sympathize with the executives' dilemma because they were simply following the reality principle; if I were in their situation, I could conceivably do the same thing. But I cannot remain silent about fundamental abuses of power that are simply scandalous breaches of how we as professionals should act.

It is obvious to me, as I trust it will appear to others, that Davies and Hoffman felt ambushed by my article describing their misconduct, which personally enraged and publicly embarrassed them, to the point that they needed to exert dominance and plot how the readership should come to understand these events. They did so by persuading those in executive power to extinguish my voice and undermine democratic policy. How could 3 out of approximately 4,000 members of the Division overturn publication policy and persuade the Publications Committee to accept such a stricture? How could a prestigious national organization bow to threats and show complicity in academic censorship? It is only because these decisions were made behind closed doors.

Is this the kind of behavior we should tolerate as a professional organization, one that I proudly belong to? Notice that Dr. Roger Frie, who was also a panelist along with Dr. Altman at the talk in question, did not write a reply. He was not included in the fixed agreement with the Publications Committee, obviously because he would have likely reported another story.

Davies (2007) plainly asserts, "I have devoted my entire career to an open exchange of ideas. I welcome critiques of relational psychoanalysis" (p. 400). If this were truly the case, then why would these very words be "published as a consequence of a condition demanded by Drs. Altman, Davies, and Hoffman, and agreed upon by the Publications Committee of the Division of Psychoanalysis, that there be no response by Dr. Mills to their Commentaries" (Reppen, 2007, p. 406)? If Davies was so "devoted" to an "open exchange" and critique of ideas about relational psychoanalysis, then why did she demand my censorship?

It is not unreasonable to speculate that Davies and Hoffman got caught in an awkward position, needed to cover up the deed, and save face by usurping control over the editorial decisions of the journal. Moreover, when an executive committee of a national organization is gaslighted because of paranoiac knowledge, how can that organization claim to be democratic? How does it serve the utilitarian interests of all its members and constituents if such power differentials can easily lead to suppression of academic interchange?

In my opinion, the Publications Committee fell victim to the manipulative politics of those adept at intimidating others and quelling dissent. I could have easily walked away from this issue out of political self-interest, especially knowing the extent to which it may potentially hurt the reputation of the Division as well as my own, but I feel too strongly that this does such a grave disservice to our profession that I cannot simply turn a blind eye. Drs. Davies, Hoffman, and Altman need to be exposed for their actions, and the Division needs to ensure that it will not be intimidated by those who are upset by rivals who criticize their deeds.

The readership should know that this is not the first time Altman and Davies have been accused of advocating censorship. Upset with Morris Eagle, David Wolitzky, and Jerome Wakefield (2001) for criticizing Steven Mitchell, Altman and Davies (2003) charged Eagle and his colleagues of intentionally distorting Mitchell's positions under political partisanship and alluded to the alleged irresponsibility and bias of Arnold Richards, who was the editor of the *Journal of the American Psychoanalytic Association* (JAPA), for publishing their work. In their defense,

Eagle, Wakefield, and Wolitzky (2003) replied with their own allegations that Altman and Davies committed an "*ad hominem* personal attack" in response to their scholarship and, more seriously, that they espouse censorship. In response to Altman and Davies's (2003) choice of provocative words directed at Arnold Richards's "willingness to publish" Eagle et al.'s article, hence chiding Richards and attributing political motives to why "he has chosen to publish" Eagle and his colleagues, they state,

> Altman and Davies imply that our paper so obviously and egregiously distorts Mitchell's ideas that, as editor, Arnold Richards should have refused to publish it. … Altman and Davies make this chilling suggestion despite the fact that, as they must know, the paper was peer reviewed and recommended for publication. … These statements by Altman and Davies are particularly alarming because they are editors of a psychoanalytic journal and have influence over what is published. (pp. 163–164)

Ironically, Altman and Davies reproach me with vituperative language for critiquing Mitchell in virtually the same manner as they did Eagle, and they make the same charges of irresponsibility toward Reppen as they did toward Richards. Is there some pattern here? Although Altman and Davies (2005) denied that they condone censorship, as Eagle, Wakefield, and Wolitzky (2005) point out, they did not "disavow their charge of egregious distortion and attribution of political motives" (p. 268) directed toward their adversaries. This is understandable given that political "turf wars" are nothing new and have dominated the history of psychoanalysis since its inception. What is foretelling, however, is how this event foreshadows Altman and Davies's predilection for accusing political rivals of malfeasance while hypocritically using their political might to bring about the very thing they wish to deny, namely, suffocating an author's voice through the bane of censorship. Not only does this previous exchange with Eagle and colleagues reveal a duplicitous pattern to Altman and Davies's style of relational politics, it furthermore shows their mendacity for claiming to have higher standards and beliefs than what is truly the case.

The bigger issue at stake here is that their subversive conduct vitiates the higher principle of academic freedom that governs an open and representative exchange of ideas. The mere fact that they commandeered and pressured those in office to arbitrarily change the protocol of the journal and displace the independence of the editor, which is guaranteed by the APA, is simply deplorable. Any editor appointed by a democratic electorate is accorded the privilege to determine how he or she wishes to govern the scope of professional activities and editorial decisions. The APA is very clear in its standard contract between the association and its editors. A relevant clause is particularly unambiguous:

> MANUSCRIPTS. As editor, you will have complete authority to accept or reject manuscripts. Your decisions in this area are not subject to review by any office or employee of the APA nor by any member of its governance structure.

Robert Bjork (2000) nicely points out that the reasons behind

> such a policy fosters the freedom of inquiry and expression so necessary for a healthy science. … The lessons of history are clear: When political or other pressures interfere with the autonomy of science, the societal and scientific consequences are grim. APA should reaffirm the principle that a healthy science of psychology requires an open exchange of ideas and findings. (p. 981)

Bjork further informs us that the Council of Editors and the Publications and Communications Board jointly urged the APA to adopt a Statement of Principle that guaranteed a "freedom of inquiry and freedom of expression" where the editor has the right to publish material that others may find to be "surprising, disappointing, or controversial" (p. 983). This principle was indeed reaffirmed by the APA Board of Directors who authorized a vote on the Statement of Principle by the Council of Representatives, which was approved by the council on August 6, 2000.

To paraphrase Santayana, history is doomed to repeat itself if we do not make a concerted effort to heed its call. If we were to generalize what happened here with the Division 39 journal and apply this scenario to any other context involving an editorial-governed, peer-review periodical, then academe would simply become a bankrupt endeavor. In the end, Reppen is maligned by Davies, Hoffman, and Altman for allowing an author to have a voice, only then to snuff that voice in order to get the last word. By burking the issue they also deceived the readership by obstructing access to the whole truth.

Think of the ramifications this has on the future of psychoanalytic publishing when potentially any author could be censored for having differing opinions or rival political allegiances or for simply writing something controversial. The general readership of the journal was duped because the content was subjected to contrivance and censorship. Academic freedom rests upon the fundamental principle of liberty of speech, particularly even if one does not agree with a competitive viewpoint.

The official stance of the Publications Committee was that Reppen should not have allowed me to publish the details of Hoffman's and Davies's behavior at the conference,* but there is no recorded documentation about how the decision was made, let alone what criterion was employed to determine that Reppen had indeed employed poor judgment. In the minutes of the April 23, 2006, meeting of the Publications Committee, submitted by secretary Dr. William MacGillivray, where the matter was discussed, what is stated under the terse paragraph titled "Complaint to the Publications Committee" is the following: "The consensus was to allow the aggrieved parties [Altman, Davies, Hoffman] to report their complaints and to not allow a response [by Mills] to their letters" (p. 2). Here the "consensus" by the committee members who were present at the meeting made a decision to condone censorship. There was no formal vote.

The "aggrieved" claim was that Reppen was irresponsible for publishing such "grossly misleading" (Hoffman, 2007, p. 403) "blatant distortions" (Davies, 2007, p. 398) of what really transpired.

---

* Correspondence from Nancy McWilliams.

Davies goes on to say that these communications were "one-sided renditions of hallway conversations" (p. 399), when they were not. They were public actions whereby both the content and the venue of the exchange centered around a critique of ideas at a conference. Therefore, these communications are intellectual property and subject to report. The issue here is not whether you agree that Reppen should have or should not have published my commentary but that he has the right as editor to make autonomous decisions immune from verbalized and felt threat or persuasion in the spirit of intellectual liberty. Notice that Reppen is so committed to fair-mindedness and a libertarian process that he allowed three authors to disparage his actions and good name in print under the rubric of nonpartisanship. If we are to follow the tenor of their main collective argument that Reppen should not have published my article on grounds of *ad hominem* polemics, then their commentaries never should have seen the light of day.

A minor point, but one worth raising, is that even if others may perceive intellectual arguments to be *ad hominem*,* would not an authentic and unimpeded exchange of ideas be necessary in order to bring all facets of an argument to the table? In other words, even if there were unanimous consent that a particular written statement was indeed *ad hominem*, would this automatically mean that it *should not* be published? In the spirit of democratic exchange, it follows that *nothing* should be omitted from the public domain unless you subscribe to some form of thought control.

The reader should be reminded not only that many disciplines publish *ad hominem* material but also that this practice is part and parcel of the discipline itself. The field of politics is the most conspicuous example where polemics and negative indictments take center stage in convention and advertising campaigns, which often informs the fulcrum of information that is disseminated to the public. In the humanities, including philosophy, critical

---

* It should be noted that most criteria of determining *ad hominem* complaints are subjectively defined and not procedurally specified in order for there to be any objective judgment or consensus to begin with.

theory, and sociology, not to mention literary and art criticism, where *ad hominem* critiques and emotional polemics are rampant in peer-refereed publications and reviews, it is common practice to observe outright denigration and personal attacks on authors and artists, citing colleagues they disagree with fervently who are also political and academic rivals. No one in these disciplines is crying foul. There is no censorship there, because they embrace democratic exchange under the banner of free speech.

Another point: Why should the personal actions of analysts be exempt from discussion when they take place in professional public space? We analyze these behaviors in our patients, so why should it be off limits in the literature? I do not agree that politics should supplant completeness let alone stifle debate in representing differing points of view.

This incident is ultimately not about me or them, nor is it about the inappropriateness of airing personal grudges or even the publication choices of the editor. It is about the greater philosophic *principle of freedom*, and this intimately becomes a moral question. If we accept the notion that knowledge is expanded based upon an unencumbered exchange of ideas no matter how controversial or unsavory the subject matter may be, then we must be committed to the principle of academic fairness, honesty, and an unobstructed free flow of thought. In *On Liberty* (1859), John Stuart Mill makes an eloquent point:

> We can never be sure that the opinion we are endeavoring to stifle is a false opinion; and if we were sure, stifling it would be an evil still. ... First, the opinion which it is attempted to suppress by authority may possibly be true. Those who desire to suppress it, of course, deny its truth; but they are not infallible. They have no authority to decide the question for all mankind and exclude every other person from the means of judging. To refuse a hearing to an opinion because they are sure that it is false is to assume that *their* certainty is the same thing as *absolute* certainty. All silencing of discussion is an assumption of infallibility. Its condemnation may be allowed to rest on this common argument, not the worse for being common. (pp. 76–77, emphasis in original)

Following Mill, the best way of sanitizing corrupt ideas is by exposing them to the daylight of human critique and opinion. If you hide competing viewpoints, then certain ideas—particularly biased ones—retain their influence and corruption over others because unrecognized truths linger behind the veil of censorship. And it does not take much of an imagination to see the peril of where this could potentially lead if political structures adopt arbitrary policies of garroting certain voices while promulgating others.

Because this issue transcends any one individual, it is the principle of democracy that becomes undermined. The Division is ultimately responsible because it allowed its constituents to preempt and terminate an open discussion rather than allow the dialogue to play itself out naturally in print. Regardless of the intentions of the Division to end a bad feud, which I accept in good faith, they violated academic freedom by superimposing a stricture that subverted the original protocol of the journal established by the editor, which further sets a dangerous precedent for eliminating dissent. These political lapses in judgment not only compromise academic freedom but ultimately demonstrate that the Division is not truly a democratic entity when it can arbitrarily elude upholding equity.

The greater issue at stake here, it bears repeating, is the principle of a free colloquy of ideas without censorship, coercion, or intimidation of the editor and the Publications Committee, who should operate autonomously in their decision-making governance. When this process is superseded, it affects and hurts us all. When you let a select group of people abuse power, conspire to censor free thought, and adulterate a representative commerce of ideas, then we no longer have access to facts, competing truths, and multiple points of view that inform our comprehensive framework of knowledge. Remaining silent about these inequities implicitly condones their actions and perpetuates abuse of power. Furthermore, and perhaps equally important, this constitutes a major threat to our scholarly and scientific discipline and the integrity of psychoanalysis as a political institution. If these analysts are not challenged for their actions, then they will be left to continue to band together and bully and abuse anyone else who poses a threat to their own cherished group loyalties and collective guild.

Such abuse of power has been brought to our attention in several influential and timely psychoanalytic writings (Dorpat, 2006; Raubolt, 2006; Reeder, 2004; Shaw, 2006), which call for an end to this virulence and antisocial, contemptible behavior that continue to be tolerated in psychoanalytic institutes, societies, and professional organizations such as Division 39 of the APA. I for one take these works seriously and see that we have a professional and moral obligation to challenge subversive practices when we encounter them in order not to sustain the unjust mistreatment of others. If left unchecked, this type of behavior will only serve to pollute, fracture, and harm our discipline, which may likely incur further marginalization and public disgrace.

What is apparent to me from Altman's, Davies's, and Hoffman's tactics leading to their written commentaries is that they did not seem to be aware of the inappropriateness of their actions. They demanded the censorship of an author, maligned the editor, advocated for the subversion of a democratic process, and tacitly held the Division hostage under the rumored threat of retaliation. I seriously doubt that the psychoanalytic community will take a public stand on this issue, given that certain individuals will have to go out on a limb—only to endure anxiety and face uncertain consequences—but it should. If further power imbalances are continuously sustained with no repercussions to those who transgress, then it will be to the detriment of us all. We must preserve the integrity of free dialogue without the anathema of censorship, which if left unchecked will erode our profession. If we do not collectively advocate for an unencumbered exchange of ideas under the rubric of academic freedom, we will be no more credible than any fundamentalist religion based on unquestioned dogma and emotional prejudices.

6

Psychoanalysis and Its Critics

What constitutes psychoanalysis? This question continues to be a perennial debate.* In fact, it is rather bewildering that after 100 years since Freud established the discipline, no current consensus exists. Perhaps this becomes an empirical criterion that may help us chip away at the obfuscation and rhetorical quibbles that underlie our ambivalence in self-definition. Analysts have historically emphasized certain facets of theory and praxis that differentiate our discipline from other psychological sciences, including questioning whether or not psychoanalysis is a science at all, as well as whether analysts truly follow a replicable method. The bifurcation typically becomes the following: Does psychoanalysis adopt a set of theoretics or philosophical presuppositions that all analysts can agree upon (at least in principle), and do we follow a

---

* I realize that answering this question is tantamount to a grail quest; however, I attempt to provide an adumbrated definition of psychoanalysis that centers on the question of the discipline's categorization as a human science. Here I shall concern myself with a narrow scope of interest in demarcating a conceptual arena that lends coherent explanation to the theoretic-methodological categorization of psychoanalysis rather than with the special activities, qualities, and attributes that make up a psychoanalyst. By focusing on the central question of what constitutes psychoanalysis, that is, what defines its essence, I wish to avert engaging the ongoing debate surrounding what constitutes a psychoanalyst. These issues are politically saturated with subjective predilections and group loyalties that inform self-definition and do not adequately address whether a consensus can be reached on the essential categorical characteristics that define our profession. Instead, I will attempt to provide a modest argument for why psychoanalysis should be interpreted within a human science model, yet one guided by a consilient attitude. The virtue of psychoanalysis is that it transcends any dichotomy of value that is attached to either a scientific or a humanities paradigm.

certain technical procedure that would classify the process as distinctly psychoanalytic? And is the question of theory to be sectioned off and classified as a science or part of the humanities? Or even converged (some would say conflated) into a synthesis whereby psychoanalysis becomes a human science, despite the fact that it may necessarily deviate from conventional scientific explananda?

At the other extreme, does psychoanalysis devolve into some type of philosophical paradigm, hermeneutic, or perhaps even an esoteric order, exclusive guild, or religion ensconced in mystification and bred by indoctrination? On the technical side of things, does psychoanalysis really follow a method, one that can be repeated, even a loosely defined one based on orienting principles? And do psychoanalytic practitioners really behave in a fashion that follows a certain operational procedure, one that further gives tangible results subject to observation, verification, and replication? Or do we really do what we feel is best in the moment in the private chambers of our consulting rooms? Hardly the criterion of science. But human—all too human, something that science itself cannot deny is part and parcel of its own discipline.

TOWARD AN OPERATIONAL DEFINITION OF PSYCHOANALYSIS

Is it possible to provide a clear and concise operational definition of psychoanalysis that may be met with broad consensus from the psychoanalytic community?* Let us propose three tiers of inquiry

---

* Central to the debate surrounding the equivocal definition of what constitutes psychoanalysis is simultaneously the question, What constitutes a psychoanalyst? That is, what special activities, qualities, attributes, and so forth make up a psychoanalyst? In other words, what gives one the right to call him- or herself a psychoanalyst? I will not be concerned with the ongoing debate surrounding professional identity, form and style of technique or specific clinical praxis, whether one uses the couch or a chair, the number of analytic sessions conducted per week, the training requirements that govern psychoanalytic institutional life, or the criteria employed by credentialing bodies when they confer such a designation. These questions often evoke the narcissism of minor differences and will only distract us from the task at hand. Here I am more interested in demarcating a conceptual arena that lends coherent explanation to the theoretic-methodological categorization of psychoanalysis rather than the formal designation of what we may properly call a psychoanalyst.

that examine the specific definition and explication of psychoanalysis as

1. a theory of mind and culture, and
2. a method of clinical treatment, but also
3. a general method of observation regarding human phenomena further related to
   a. individual psychic dynamics (viz., intrapsychic events, personality formation, wishes, fantasies, conflicts, defenses, etc.),
   b. social behavior (viz., attachment processes, intersubjective dynamics, interpersonal motivations, etc.), and
   c. collective social life (viz., linguistic practices, communal political-economic structures, culture, religion, ethnic heritage, etc.).

The subtiers of inquiry in propounding a general definition of psychoanalysis as a theory and method may be further explored

i. in relation to the specific theoretical postulates that undergird psychoanalytic thought, that is, what distinguishes it from other psychological theories (e.g., the study of unconscious mental processes), and
ii. as a form of clinical treatment that is delineated by its specific methodological procedures and employed technical principles, such as the capacity to confront resistances, analyze the transference, and interpret unconscious motivations and repetitions that influence subjective thoughts, fantasies, and behaviors. For the sake of parsimony, here I will mainly address the broad considerations of how psychoanalysis is situated within the sciences and humanities.

The first division of our inquiry concerns theory. And here the question of theory is broken down into (a) *General Psychological Theory*, or theoretic models applied exclusively to human experience, and (b) *Clinical Theory*, namely, which presumptive principles and processes are operative in the clinical encounter and how those dynamics influence treatment and the analytic relationship. In general, psychoanalytic theory should (ideally) be

1. coherent,
2. explanatory,
3. generalizable, and
4. pragmatic, namely, is it useful?

The second division of inquiry concerns method. And here the question of method centers around clinical activity on the part of the analyst that is (a) *Procedural*, namely, does it follow a clearly definable course of action or set of established modes of professional conduct, and if so, is it (b) *Prescriptive*, that is, does it follow a set series of steps or strategies designed to achieve a desired goal? Or is it malleable? Is there a built-in margin of freedom for each subject executing a methodological process to alter such rigid requirements laid out by a purely prescriptive directive? In the reality of clinical practice, no respectable analyst would claim to follow a rote step-by-step recipe governing professional conduct. Because the human intellect is not a computer or mechanical-technical processing system, variation and execution in method is an uncontested empirical fact. This necessarily means that method and its execution will always fall under the rubric of subjective judgment, because any methodological institution is derived and driven by human experience and personal preferences. Hence method is necessarily predicated on prejudicial inclinations and biases in its execution, despite the fact that it conforms to certain analytic sensibilities or attitudes governing therapeutic orienting principles informed by theory.

To what degree is theory and method arbitrary, contextual, contingent, personalized, exploratory—hence experimental and nonconclusive? Does theory only provide parameters for explanation and meaning, or does it guide method? If so, are theory and method necessarily the same thing? Does a theory of mind and culture stand in relation to universal theoretical postulates that apply to individual and collective motivation and behavior? And if so, how does it stand in relation to individual and cultural differences, social and biological discrepancies, historical and gender variances? How does it stand in relation to clinical process?

These are difficult questions to sustain. Can a psychoanalytic theory actually operate outside of therapeutic parameters? And can a method, in theory, transpire without relying on theory? One could conceivably affirm the former while questioning the latter. A theory (or metatheory) could certainly be applied to human thought, motivation, and action, either individually or socially, whether it transpires in a therapeutic environment or not. The issue becomes, Does it adequately satisfy the criteria of *coherency*, *explanation*, *generalizability*, and *pragmatism*? But can a methodology actually be executed devoid of any theoretic directing the method or procedural actions themselves? Every discipline has a set of theoretical orienting principles guiding inquiry, research, and methodological process, whether presumptive or not. Is this notion of criteria any different for psychoanalysis?

The specific variances and emphases placed on theoretical nuances that compose the different schools within the history of psychoanalysis (from classical theory, to object relations models, ego psychology, the French school, the American interpersonal tradition, modern psychoanalysis, self psychology, contemporary Freudian and modern conflict theorists, to relational, intersubjective, and postmodern approaches) do not concern us here. The reader, I presume, is sufficiently familiar with these distinctions that we do not need a discursive treatment of this subject matter. Regardless of the theoretical parameters, differences, and discrepancies that define psychoanalysis, we must ask, What kind of categorical classification system or set of methods and theories does the discipline as a whole fall under? This question has typically been characterized by the scientific versus philosophic binary or the naturalism versus humanities debate regarding a proper definition of psychoanalysis. It is here that we should revisit the historical criticism against psychoanalysis from the standpoint of objections from philosophers who either support or refute the scientific versus philosophic dichotomy.

PSYCHOANALYSIS AND ITS CRITICS

> Some investigators ... who are unwilling to accept the unconscious, find a way out of the difficulty in the fact that ... in consciousness ... it is possible to distinguish a great variety of gradations in intensity or clarity. ... The reference to gradations of clarity in consciousness is in no way conclusive and has no more evidential value than such analogous statements as: "There are so very many gradations in illumination—from the most glaring and dazzling light to the dimmest glimmer—therefore there is no such thing as darkness at all"; or, "There are varying degrees of vitality, therefore there is no such thing as death." Such statements may in a certain way have a meaning, but for practical purposes they are worthless. This will be seen if one tries to draw particular conclusions from them, such as, "there is therefore no need to strike a light," or, "therefore all organisms are immortal." Further to include "what is unobservable" under the concept of "what is conscious" is simply to play havoc with the one and only piece of direct and certain knowledge that we have about the mind. And after all, a consciousness of which one knows nothing seems to me a good deal more absurd than something mental that is unconscious. (Freud, 1923, p. 16fn)

Freud is heralded as one of the most influential yet disputed thinkers of the 20th century, having radically affected and transformed our shifting conceptions of mind, human nature, science, religion, civilization, and gender. It has been said that no one since Jesus has been so compelling or controversial.[*] Ricoeur (1970) refers to Freud's work as a "monument of our culture" (p. xi), and Wollheim (1971/1990) says he "revolutionized ... the world" (p. x). Just as Kant is attributed with initiating the Copernican turn in philosophy, so is Freud credited with turning our understanding of human psychology on its head.[†] Whether we admire or vilify, adore or detest him, we may reason with or against him, but we cannot reason without him.

Freud's ideas have become commonplace even among popular culture: Nowhere can we turn without being reminded of his

---

[*] This was attributed to Freud by the narrator of A&E's *Biography of Sigmund Freud*.

[†] Lacan (1977) compares the significance of Freud's discoveries to that of Copernicus (see *Écrits: A Selection*, pp. 114, 295).

legacy. Currently psychoanalysis enjoys a central focus of contemporary European, North American, and South American intellectual life. We may especially observe a resurgence of interest in Freud studies among the humanities and social sciences, including philosophy, literature, social-political theory, anthropology, psychobiology, ethology, cultural theory, history, religion, feminist thought, art and film studies, semiotics, neurocognitive science, and the history of ideas. Within the field of psychoanalysis, however, Freud has largely devolved into contemporary perspectives. Because the history of psychoanalysis has produced several post-classical movements,* there is a culture of narcissism that informs divided group loyalties. Plagued by challenges from within its own governing institutional practices, as well as from waning public interest in analytic treatment, psychoanalysis has endured a century-long evolution from Freud's original vision. Adding to these challenges, Freud's theories have become so fundamentally distorted and misinterpreted by generations of English-speaking commentators that he is radically misunderstood even within psychoanalysis today. But whether he is renounced or subsumed, psychoanalysis is merely a footnote to Freud.

Philosophy as a discipline remains largely oblivious to the psychoanalytic movement and is equally slow to embrace the potency and ramification of Freud's ideas. But with increasing attention—both sympathetic and critical—psychoanalysis continues to generate profound philosophical consequences for the way we come to understand and live our lives. With respect to Freud, like Plato, one does not have to espouse everything he said in order to appreciate how certain aspects of his thought resonate within us all. Yet some of his more controversial assertions have provoked derisive attacks, including vulgar polemics, leading to modifications, extensions, critical revisions, and redirecting shifts in emphasis. This is particularly the case for certain universal pronouncements

---

* For an in-depth historical overview of the evolving paradigms within the psychoanalytic domain, see Mills (2000a).

that invite reactive critique and outrage, such as his thesis of innate bisexuality; the claim that we all harbor incestuous, homicidal, and suicidal desires; the notion that dreams—no matter how disturbing, as well as jokes, slips, and symptoms—are the fulfillment of a wish; and perhaps most provocatively that the belief in God is merely the childhood illusion of an exalted father in the sky: It is no wonder why he generates controversy. Freud is particularly hated for his views on women, the cultural disparagement of non-Western societies, and his abhorrence of religion—perhaps in part explaining the unease surrounding the Freud exhibit, *Conflict & Culture*, sponsored by the Library of Congress, which was delayed for years because of political protest.

Freud remains deeply embedded in our time if not for the simple fact that he is threatening. Many people, I would say most—from the average citizen to the intellectual—are afraid of his ideas; that which we fear we must defend against in some way, from pure denial to extreme, sometimes ludicrous attempts to justify why Freud was wrong.* One reason why he generates such emotive contention is that he shatters our cherished ideals—that which we hold most dear to us—and as a result evokes anxiety, hostility, and psychic terror. But Freud ultimately threatens us with knowledge about ourselves—that about which we wish to know nothing whatsoever—knowledge that can potentially disrupt the way we experience and understand our inner worlds.

How can one think the unthought? This is precisely the question Freud attempts to explain by positing the existence of an unconscious ontology. Philosophy has traditionally assumed an ambivalent attitude toward the psychoanalytic unconscious,

---

* See Richard Webster's (1995) *Why Freud Was Wrong: Sin, Science, and Psychoanalysis* for an account of Freud-bashing. In my opinion, this work is an irresponsible, untenable, and misinformed attack on the main tenets of psychoanalysis under the guise of scientific idolatry that denigrates Freud while deifying Darwin. Certainly this is not new criticism but one here presented more for sensationalism rather than based on philosophical merit (also see Cioffi, 1998). Some philosophers have gone so far as to deny the existence of the unconscious altogether (e.g., Webster; also see Miles, 1966; Sartre, 1943/1956), which Freud (1923) would merely reply is "absurd" (p. 16fn).

from questioning its epistemic verity to denouncing its existence altogether. Although Freud has been championed by some philosophers such as Richard Wollheim, John Wisdom, Jonathan Lear, and others, Donald Levy shows how many of Freud's critics have repeatedly focused on very selective and prejudicial arguments that have misunderstood key theoretical concepts and have neglected the broader domain of psychoanalytic inquiry. In *Freud Among the Philosophers*, Levy (1996) undertakes a comprehensive philosophical defense of the psychoanalytic conception of the unconscious against four major critics of Freud, namely, Wittgenstein, James, MacIntyre, and Grünbaum. Because Levy is a philosopher who critiques philosophers who have been identified as critics against psychoanalysis, his work is particularly instructive for psychoanalysts who may not be aware of these issues. Scrutinizing the claims that psychoanalysis is mythology, incoherent, self-contradictory, and scientifically unverifiable, Levy exposes selective philosophical biases and misunderstandings that have dominated Anglo-American philosophy's critique of psychoanalytic doctrine.

Levy initially examines Wittgenstein's thesis that psychoanalysis is essentially a mythology because it imposes a predetermined explanation through interpretations. Interpretations are imposed on mental states that reduce them to something familiar or conventional, whereby the criterion of truth or correctness of the interpretation is determined by a person's accent or agreement. Wittgenstein further concludes that psychoanalysis is a reductive enterprise that fails to account for individuality and personal meaning, which is diffused and lost in generic interpretive technique, an insipid claim that is frequently and unjustly launched against Freud.* Here Wittgenstein fails to account for the myriad

---

* As noted earlier, Freud (1895) is often misunderstood to be a reductive materialist, relying on his unofficial and immature views espoused in the "Project for a Scientific Psychology" (p. 295). Freud realized that he could never offer an adequate theory of mind solely from a neurophysiological account and by 1900 had officially abandoned his earlier materialistic visions for a psychological corpus (cf. p. 536).

kinds of interpretation that withstand generalization as well as the nature of resistance and defense, free association, transference, dreams, and symptom formation as valid criteria for evidence of unconscious mentation. When juxtaposed against these aspects of psychoanalytic theory, Wittgenstein's critique is myopic and shallow. But in all fairness to Wittgenstein, his ideas expressed in his *Blue Book* and in *Lectures and Conversations* were notes and private conversations he had never intended to publish. Therefore, the question of his philosophical rectitude is moot.

William James, on the other hand, systematically attempts to annul the very concept of unconscious ideation in *The Principles of Psychology* and asserts that the very notion of unconscious ideas is unintelligible and may not be appealed to under any circumstance. James's central argument is that the unconscious is a dispensable concept because fleeting conscious ideas may offer the same explanatory force without appealing to unconscious mental activity. For James, unconscious processes are reduced to brain states. Like Wittgenstein, James fails to address pivotal concepts of psychoanalytic lore, such as the nature of dreams and parapraxes, which make his alternative explanations deceptively easy. But we must remember that James published the *Principles* in 1890, five years before Freud established psychoanalysis as a formal discipline. Furthermore, James was a very pluralistic and ambivalent thinker and was not especially impressed by the need to think the same thing all the time. In *The Varieties of Religious Experience*, James (1902) writes as a phenomenologist, which naturally leads him to a deeper appreciation of the role of the unconscious (see p. 207). And by 1909, he endorsed Freud at Clark University after delivering his famous *Five Lectures*.*

Levy further examines Alasdair MacIntyre's arguments against Freud set forth in his book *The Unconscious*. Among

---

* Earnest Jones and Peter Gay report such an account in their biographies of Freud. However, for James, there was always a tension between his sympathy for philosophical theology and psychoanalysis' hostility toward religion (cf. Jones, 1955, p. 57; Gay, 1988, pp. 211–212).

many analytic philosophers who have lambasted psychoanalysis for its dubious scientific status, MacIntyre claims that the unconscious is unobservable and is thus an illegitimate object of science. Because of MacIntyre's narrow emphasis on repression, a concept he misunderstands, Levy demonstrates that like Wittgenstein and James, MacIntyre ignores key psychoanalytic concepts and methodological procedures that lend substantial support to the legitimacy of an unconscious ontology. According to MacIntyre, because the unconscious is beset by a lack of clarity regarding its observability, the problem of unverifiability precludes its epistemological justification and its explanatory force. Following in the tradition of Popper, who claims that psychoanalytic theory is nontestable, hence unfalsifiable, MacIntyre questions its scientific credibility and its predictive value. Yet he selectively ignores the nature of resistance, transference, and free association that when brought into the context of interpretation has substantial predictive value that may be verified or falsified as in other scientific models. Furthermore, any science has a problem with prediction for it presupposes fixed-causal laws, thereby attenuating the notion of freedom, a reductive and dogmatic ontic assertion that psychoanalysis does its best to avoid.

We may interpret MacIntyre's arguments to imply that observable entities (including processes and properties) may be attributed only to consciousness and that the observability of unconscious processes is illusory. MacIntyre makes an ontological commitment when he asserts that the unconscious is inherently unobservable, hence its essence may never appear nor is there any possibility of it becoming observable. Although Levy challenges this thesis, mainly appealing to clinical observation, he further objects to MacIntyre's distinction between observables and unobservables, for to know that a process is absolutely unobservable, one would have to know that no method or technique could ever make the process experienceable. Furthermore, to maintain that an essence can never appear is to disavow its existence all together. Hegel eloquently dissolves this dilemma when he equates appearance with essence, for nothing could exist unless it is made actual. Therefore, unconscious essence does not remain hidden behind the transcendental real; instead it manifests itself *as* conscious reality.*

Levy's final critique examines Adolf Grünbaum's assault on the scientific credibility of psychoanalysis for lacking controlled experimentation and empirical validity, thus creating a chasm between objective and subjective knowledge claims. Levy points to a false dichotomy between Grünbaum's intra- and extra-clinical distinctions and reproaches his rejection of clinical evidence. In refuting the claim that psychoanalysis is foreclosed from the possibility of having scientific status, Levy reinforces the notion that Freud's critics have repeatedly focused on very selective and prejudicial arguments that have repeatedly misunderstood key concepts and have neglected the broader domain of psychoanalytic theory. In my opinion, this could be largely due to the fact that philosophical critics are not clinical practitioners, so they lack the practical education and experience that comes with psychoanalytic training. It is here where I wish to further engage this debate by juxtaposing and defending a dialectical account of psychoanalysis that adequately accounts for both scientific and philosophical parameters.

---

* From *The Encyclopaedia Logic*, Hegel (1817a/1991) makes this clear:

> Essence must *appear*. Its inward shining is the sublating of itself into immediacy, which as inward reflection is *subsistence* (matter) as well as *form*, reflection-into-another, subsistence *sublating itself*. Shining is the determination, in virtue of which essence is not being, but essence, and the developed shining is [shining-forth or] appearance. Essence therefore is not *behind* or *beyond* appearance, but since the essence is what exists, existence is appearance. (§ 131, p. 199)

In the *Phenomenology of Spirit*, Hegel (1807/1977) also shows that the coming into being of higher forms of subjectivity is mediated by their previous appearances. "The inner world, or supersensible beyond, has ... *come into being*: It *comes from* the world of appearance which has mediated it; in other words, appearance is its essence and, in fact, its filling" (§ 147, p. 89).

THE SCIENTIFIC VIABILITY OF PSYCHOANALYSIS

From its inception, psychoanalysis has been criticized for not being a legitimate science. I suppose the validity of this claim fundamentally rests on what we mean by science (Latin *scientia*, from *scire*, to know). Although there are many people who have rejected the scientific viability of psychoanalysis, or have neutered it to the status of "pseudoscience" (Cioffi, 1998), it is Adolf Grünbaum who deserves our special attention. For nearly four decades, the general thrust of his attacks is unwavering in content and focus and reiterates his point that psychoanalysis is not a true science. Following Levy, I wish to offer a modest defense of psychoanalysis as a human science and argue that Grünbaum commits a category mistake in comparing psychoanalysis with the physical sciences, and hence he upholds a standard of scientific inquiry that cannot be applied to our field. As a philosopher, and hence not a clinician, he furthermore lacks a proper epistemology of knowing how to appropriately evaluate the validity of clinical data and focuses on select aspects of Freudian theory he uses as a straw man to unjustly refute the whole discipline of psychoanalysis itself.

Grünbaum may arguably be psychoanalysis' most tenacious—and staunchest—critic. What sets him apart from other critics such as Frederick Crews, however, is that he has more substance, breadth, and sophistication to his critiques. Analysts reading one of his latest contributions (Grünbaum, 2006) may likely become immediately defensive, derisive, and provoked by his wholesale dismissal of our profession. Perhaps this was part of Grünbaum's intent given that he customarily writes as a polemicist with a dramatic flare of negation. The broad structure of this particular essay is to first put in their place everyone who challenges him or has disagreed with his work in the past, only to quote his numerous publications to establish his unquestionable authority. He then proceeds to denounce key aspects of Freudian theory with obsessive scrutiny, only to conclude that there is no scientific credibility to psychoanalysis whatsoever.

After reading his trenchant polemic, when all is said and done, one is left with the overall conclusion that "there is not one damn shred of scientific evidence to psychoanalysis—period." How does an analyst begin to respond other than reactively denounce Grünbaum's propositions as preposterous? There is a cornucopia of empirical evidence in the cognitive neurosciences, the attachment field, infant-observation research, developmental psychology, clinical psychopathology, and the therapeutic process that are corroborations, validations, extensions, revisions, and emendations of Freud's contributions, work Grünbaum chooses not to mention or engage in this context. He also chooses not to mention the modifications and radical shifts in theory and practice since Freud's time. Given that he is thoroughly familiar with the history of psychoanalysis, it is surprising that in an anniversary issue of *Psychoanalytic Psychology* devoted to Freud's legacy, he would further omit any substantial discussion with regard to the broad spectrum of theoretical orientations and traditions that have emerged from Freud's work, which now compose the psychoanalytic domain. Notwithstanding the empirical (hence scientific) research that has emerged in psychoanalysis since Freud's time, Grünbaum remains focused on Freud and stays very close to the text.

We could offer a lengthy bibliography pointing to the scientific merit of Freud's theories and therapy,* but admittedly this would fail to address Grünbaum's arguments, and I imagine he

---

* The American Psychoanalytic Association (2009–2010) has recently launched a public advocacy campaign on their Web site intended to educate the inquirer and consumer on the scientific viability, theoretical coherence, and treatment efficacy of psychoanalysis and psychoanalytic therapy where they list scores of empirical studies of efficacy and effectiveness in psychodynamic treatments, including primary studies, reviews and meta-analyses, and methodological issues, as well as empirical studies of psychoanalytic process and empirical studies of psychoanalytic concepts (see www.apsa.org/Programs/Research/Empirical_Studies_in_Psychoanalysis.aspx). Despite this large contemporary database, it should also be noted that Fisher and Greenberg (1977) provided a metareview of over 1,800 empirical studies in *The Scientific Credibility of Freud's Theories and Therapy*, which yielded overwhelming support for the scientific viability of psychoanalysis over three decades ago.

would draw into question the validity of that database anyway. Regardless, his arguments should be taken very seriously and addressed through scholarly rigor if our profession wishes to continue to advance, but I am not inclined to engage him on this tedious level given the limited scope of this project. Here I will confine myself to a few remarks. What I hope to offer for reflection is how Grünbaum's understanding of psychoanalysis (a) is skewed, (b) lacks a proper epistemology from within the framework of clinical practice, and (c) is based on a misguided application of natural science to the behavioral and social sciences, as well as the humanities, where psychoanalysis is said to have its proper home.

Grünbaum's career-long critique is notably intimidating and erudite and likely to be overwhelming to those not learned in his discipline. There is a logical acumen to his specific criticisms despite his blanket generalizations and categorical abnegation of Freud's theoretical corpus. But there is also an overall straw man to his sweeping dismissal: By ruminating on the minutia of specific aspects of Freud's theories, he generates the false impression that the whole Freudian edifice is precarious, when Grünbaum is actually focusing on a select set of problematics and then making an unwarranted generalization—as if his criticisms debunk the entire body of psychoanalytic knowledge and practice.

Grünbaum has us believe that Freudian theory and technique is essentially bankrupt despite the fact that Freud is arguably the father of modern-day psychotherapy and psychiatry. It may prove useful to recall that Freud was the principal person to establish and articulate the basic technical principles of psychotherapy, including establishing rapport with patients; forming a therapeutic alliance; pointing out defenses and compromises in the service of resistance, self-protection, and repetition; forming an authentic manner of relatedness with patients; examining the transference; interpreting unconscious wishes and conflicts; and reaching the affect as part of the working-through process. Freud formulated a broad edifice of normative human psychology and psychopathology upon which clinical diagnoses still largely rest today and introduced what is generally considered to be the most complex theory of mind and human nature that rivals any competing school of psychology. Psychoanalysis has infiltrated academe throughout the world, particularly in the humanities and behavioral sciences, not to mention the fact that many psychoanalytic concepts are an indelible part of popular culture. No small feat indeed. Then what are we to make of such a totalistic refutation of a discipline that not only has survived over a century of evolution and fine-tuning but in many remarkable ways holds prominence in many parts of the contemporary world?

It is important for the reader to understand the particular philosophical tradition that Grünbaum is coming from, along with his imported biases, and how this shapes the context of his overall critique. Grünbaum represents a very conservative perspective known as philosophy of science that is closely identified with the analytic tradition, here the term *analytic* meaning the Anglo-American philosophical tradition where the gold standard of logic, argument and clarity, and scientific methodology corners the market on truth and objectivity. This tradition is often opposed to the European continental tradition of philosophy where the nature of subjectivity and culture is both celebrated and deconstructed from within competing contexts of individual experience, society, and linguistic order. These camps often, but not always, have an adversarial relationship, and when certain theoretical differences pose fundamental incompatibilities, we may observe an extreme splitting between each side that is acrimonious and caustic. The structure and tenor of Grünbaum's critique clearly points to his cherished identifications with the tradition he wishes to champion, and he equally conveys a supercilious air of superiority that goes along with the analytic tradition's collective group narcissism. Grünbaum disfavors continental perspectives and is quick to dismiss or devalue hermeneutic, phenomenological, and postmodern interpretations. He unabashedly has his own agenda and mission, which does not mean that it is inherently invalid; however, one needs to be aware of the contentiousness and competition that exists between these two broad divisions in philosophy.

Grünbaum (2006) pulls no punches in attempting to discredit the notion of repression, a dynamic unconscious, the nature of transference, and the free associative therapeutic process. The corollary of his implications is that dynamic mental processes such as unconscious conflicts, relational patterns of repetition, and defensive maneuvers do not actually occur. For any practitioner reading his critique, one may question whether he knows anything about clinical practice or what actually transpires in the consulting room when one person is suffering and seeking relief from disabling symptoms through analytic treatment. Grünbaum is no fool: He is aware and knowledgeable of what clinicians and analysts do, but he does not have firsthand epistemic experience or direct phenomenological engagement with patients, thus his impression of clinical work is bound to be incomplete at best and inaccurate at worst—not to mention the presumably relevant assumption that he has never been in analysis. This is understandable given that he is not a practitioner or a patient, but it is important to stress that he misrepresents and at times distorts what goes on in actual clinical practice. Clinical experience, namely, what it actually means to work with patients, annuls his propositional attitudes.

Just as he reproaches psychoanalysis on its epistemological failures, he himself has certain epistemological vulnerabilities by virtue of the fact that he is not a practicing clinician. This does not debunk his criticism *a fortiori* but only alerts us to his framework of operating conceptually and without professional knowledge of clinical phenomenology. Such vulnerabilities compromise his self-imposed authority and his ability to have a full range of experience where the nuances of verbal and nonverbal disclosure, content and context, affect and emotion, symptom formation, cognitive appraisals, and personal history are ostensibly intertwined into a comprehensive framework of dynamic formulation that properly typifies analytic conceptuality. He is confined only to the written text—his subject of analysis—not the real agency of the person on the couch or the intersubjective system that constitutes the analytic dyad. To properly critique a method, here the method of psychoanalysis, one should be thoroughly familiar with its procedural operations. Reading Freud's technique papers and clinical case studies is far removed from actually being formally trained, not to mention how one can easily get a skewed picture of what actually goes on in contemporary practice.

It goes without saying that the internal motives of an individual's mind are of most interest to psychoanalysts. It is natural to wonder why Grünbaum would spend most of his professional career refuting a discipline unless he felt a personal identification with the need to refute something in himself he finds unsavory. It is not illegitimate per se to consider these variables when assessing the merit of Grünbaum's argumentation, only that it would be in poor taste and unnecessarily *ad hominem* to pursue this line of thinking any further. Let us stay on philosophical ground.

Grünbaum is a philosopher of science and is not a scientist. He has certain ideals and assumptions that don't apply to those actual scientists who conduct empirical work. He does not actually engage in experimentation. Like many philosophers of science, he operates under a theoretical ideal of what science should be like rather than how it is actually conducted. Despite having a degree in physics, he presumably has some illusion that pure objectivity can be achieved through rigorous control of experimental methods, when even the most hard-core natural scientists like experimental physicists would denounce this assumption. In his introduction to Richard Feyman's (1995) book on the principles of physics, Paul Davies writes,

> There is a popular misconception that science is an impersonal, dispassionate, and thoroughly objective enterprise. Whereas most other human activities are dominated by fashions, fads, and personalities, science is supposed to be constrained by agreed upon rules of procedure and rigorous tests. It is the results that count, not the people who produce them.

This is, of course, manifest nonsense. Science is a people-driven activity like all human endeavor, and just as subject to fashion and whim. In this case fashion is set not so much by choice of subject matter, but by the way scientists think about the world. (p. ix)

Science is as much a subjective enterprise as is psychoanalysis.

For Grünbaum, science presumably follows a methodology based on experimentation, verification, and falsifiability of any given theory guiding procedural principles. Following Kuhn and others, if these principles do not apply, then any field of study is not a true science. Given that one cannot directly observe and measure unconscious mental processes by virtue of the fact that they do not appear in themselves to the human eye to be directly observed, controlled, manipulated, and quantifiably measured, then by extension, according to Grünbaum, psychoanalysis does not fit the bill. His entire argument revolves around the notion that psychoanalysis fails as a science—as he defines it. But is he not committing a category mistake on what constitutes science, hence failing to take into account variances and differential modes of inquiry, hypothesis generation and testing, data collection, and differential aspects of procedural self-definition? To me he appears to apply a very rigid definition of what he believes constitutes science and the nature of the empirical. For example, he is wed to the notion that true science can be only experimental in nature. In fact, I would say that he presents a rather skewed picture not only of what genuine scientists define as science but also of that which constitutes the varieties of scientific activity. Grünbaum privileges a certain ideal, presumably under the rubric of pure objectivity, a biased proposition to begin with that begs the question of a legitimate discourse on theory and method.

In actual psychoanalytic practice, the clinician is not concerned about a statistical spreadsheet based on a so-called carefully controlled study where sample populations and control groups are employed, each of which is manipulated by factorial designs. For those of us who have actually engaged in empirical research, we all know how easy it is to manipulate control variables and data in order to get statistically significant results so as to promote our own preferred theories. Factorial manipulation allows us to manufacture data—it does not observe every condition that impacts on or determines such data. An empirical study is confined only to the particular—not the "objective" universal. We make theoretical leaps of faith when treading in those waters. In the consulting room, however, what is both the particular and the universal is the individual patient. The notion of objective science often becomes meaningless, superfluous, or irrelevant for the clinician in the moment of engaging the analysand with his or her own psychic reality.

In psychoanalysis, what is scientifically germane is a particular patient's internal experience in relation to his or her life history, current phenomenology, and attitude toward the relationship with the analyst where the only statistically pertinent sample is $N = 1$. As Paul Verhaeghe (2004) alerts us, "There is no precise unity of measurement for anxiety, for neurosis, and other states. This is the classic problem of reliability and validity. … Consequently, the results still require interpretation, and it is at this point that the experimental field proper is left behind" (p. 14). Insisting that psychoanalysis conforms to a superimposed ideal of natural science fails to properly understand that the study of human subjectivity cannot be sufficiently reduced to such a unit of measurement. And even if it were possible to provide a unity of measurement, let us say of neurosis, it would have to be compared to some ideal normative standard or criteria of nonneurosis or normalcy—itself an impossibility. And even if for argument's sake such a pristine standard existed, the scientist would still be subjectively interpreting his or her object(ive)—whether or not verifiable or falsifiable. Although Freud heralded that psychoanalysis was a natural science, in his day the distinctions within the sciences did not exist as they do now. In light of this fact, Bowman (2002) argues that these antiquated and misapplied notions of physical science and biology under the seduction of positivism serve as a fortified defense against accepting psychoanalysis as a scientific endeavor. I would further argue that this rigid identification with the so-called correct version of science has become an ideology taken over by a false consciousness designed to maintain a pretense of superiority over the humanities. Grünbaum's fundamental argument that psychoanalysis fails as a science rests on a category mistake by virtue of the fact that psychoanalysis cannot be legitimately compared to other hard sciences where clear-cut distinctions of objective criteria correspond to a pure or ideal state, norm, mutually exclusive category, or unalterable point of reference where quantification of measurement is related to an unadulterated and nontransformable standard. In the human sciences, no such standard exists.

Grünbaum seems to be preoccupied with debunking psychoanalysis on the matter of causality, especially on the nature and operations of unconscious motivation. In fact, he is invested in seeing Freud only as a causalist to the point that any other interpretation or application of his theories is deemed illegitimate. For example, not only does he reproach psychoanalysis as pseudoscience, he further fails to give credence to psychoanalysis as a hermeneutic discipline (Grünbaum, 1984, 2004). Does theory of interpretation not bear some relevance to our trade? When Freud uses the language of causality, he is attempting to isolate the elementary processes that give rise to unconscious mental events. He is not addressing the philosophical problem of causality per se but instead addressing a clinical audience accustomed to using a vernacular that attempts to delineate and mark the course of antecedent events that are presumably received, processed, and mediated by mind, which then become catalysts for transformative mental action. This is what Freud meant by psychic determinism. Is not Grünbaum aware of the fact that for Freud, and for the whole field of psychoanalysis, psychic life is overdetermined? Freud was indispensably instrumental in irrefutably showing us how mind is governed by many competing causal forces that operate simultaneously and on stratified levels of dynamic activity and complexity. In fact, any attempt at causal explanations are necessarily subject to the same limitations

Grünbaum uses against psychoanalysis for the simple fact that causality is overdetermined and interdependent on a complex host of contextual relations.

Grünbaum is quick to negate Freud for importing causal claims in his arguments, but he also makes causal attributions himself. In vilifying Freud's theory of repression, Grünbaum (2006) states, "I claim that *factors different from their painfulness determine whether they are remembered or forgotten.* For example, personality dispositions or situational variables may in fact be causally relevant" (p. 267, emphasis in original). Notice Grünbaum uses the signifiers "determine" and "causally" to promote his global and vague thesis that character traits or environmental conditions are primary factors of causation. But of course they are, an obvious point to most of us. At least Freud attempts to account for *how* those forces come into being to begin with and are operative within the individual psyche and, in turn, how intrapsychic dynamics are necessarily social and relational. Furthermore, he articulates how they are indeed collectively embedded and realized historically and culturally. Perhaps Professor Grünbaum would be inclined to tell us how "personality dispositions" and "situational variables" are ultimately caused? Then, in applying the same criteria of science he uses to negate Freud, would he be so kind to tell us, How do you know?

7

Approaching Consilience

HERMENEUTICS AND THE PHENOMENOLOGICAL TURN

Although science requires interpretation to arrive at understanding and knowledge, it is primarily wed to an objectivist epistemology that would resist hermeneutic constructions of the subject. But just as we have seen that science is not estranged from subjectivity, or, more precisely, the individual scientists (subjects) studying the external world (objects), the cognitive processes underlying subjectivity *qua* mentation must necessarily impose interpretations on objects of study, and in this way the subject–object divide is suspended. In other words, if we were to examine the individual personalities of each scientist or *any* theorist, we would conclude not only that their peculiar subjectivities inform their scientific theories but also that structures of subjectivity necessarily participate within universal conditions that make objectivity possible, and this becomes a ground or condition for the possibility of science itself.

When universal cognitive processes that comprise the generic structure of subjectivity (including all its unconscious permutations) become the focus of intellectual investigation, the subject becomes an object of science. And when the object is viewed as an independent microcosm that radically betrays universal classifications due to self-articulation and stylized particularity based on creative self-definition belonging to the existential agent, the individual ceases to be merely an object. Yet each determination requires procedures of interpretation, what we may traditionally attribute to the field of hermeneutics.

When the question of psychoanalysis as a science versus a hermeneutic discipline is raised, this very question presupposes an incommensurate dichotomy and hence reinforces a hegemony whereby each side of difference attempts to exert self-importance over the other, when both have failed to observe the dialectic that conjoins such differences within a mediatory process that attempts a sublation (*Aufhebung*) or integrative holism between the two polarities. If psychoanalysis is to achieve some form of consiliatory paradigm, it must be willing to attempt to explain its activities on multiple plains of discourse with sound methodological coherence. Here I am not concerned so much with a dialectical synthesis of the oppositions of science and hermeneutics as I am concerned about preserving the two methodologies and modes of discourse that have legitimacy within their own frames of reference and perspective purposes.

In Plato's dialogue *Cratylus*, Socrates tells us, "Hermes has to do with speech, and signifies that he is the interpreter (ἑρμηνεύς), or messenger, or thief; or liar, or bargainer; all that sort of thing has a great deal to do with language … he is the contriver of tales or speeches" (408a-b), where "speech signifies all things" (408c). Here Plato inaugurates the role of language and speech through the act of interpretation as the usage of words and creation of meaning within the linguistic field. He also alludes to the inherently misleading, deceitful, and manipulative nature of words and the contortion of meaning, in which Hermes is "always turning them round and round" (408c). What is remarkable is that Plato prefigures 20th-century continental philosophy by 2,300 years.

Hermes becomes our postmodern man, the inventor of language, the quintessential interpreter of meaning through the linguistic determination of thought and understanding.

Today, hermeneutics is broadly classified as the analysis or process of interpretation and the possibility of its conditions. The general or systematic fabric of language, and the particular acts of interpretation, therefore generate the semiotic conditions or ground for the possibility of all understanding. This is the post-modern platform for the linguistic turn in philosophy spear-headed by many German and French hermeneutic traditions. Interpretation intervenes on the representation of its object, its relation to the object, and our relation(s) between our interpretations or commentaries and the object itself (Ormiston & Schrift, 1990). Here interpretation/interpretant as interjection is wed to context and takes as its object its own participation as part of the aims, methods, and techniques of analysis. Hermeneutics therefore takes as its task and object the question of interpretation itself in an attempt to understand the discourse of others and the very condition or ground of discourse itself, leading Kristeva (1990) to conclude that hermeneutics is "a discourse on discourse, an interpretation of interpretation" (p. 99). Following Derrida (1974), interpretations are always instituting reinscriptions of interpretations.

The proposition that "there are only interpretations of interpretations" leads to an inescapable circularity whereby each interpretation could be perennially begging its own question of what interpretation is really about, not to mention *what* interpretation is superior to others, contains more value, is more precise, definitive, or claritive, and so on because it lacks a referent or criterion to which to anchor meaning. If we follow this proposition through to its logical end, this ultimately collapses into relativism because meaning is relative to its interpretive scheme, which further relies on other interpretative schemata for which there are no definitive definitions, conclusive consensus, or universal laws governing interpretation.*

In the very act of asserting an interpretive truth, or the condition of truth, we are engaged in the search of absolute ground, even when there is none to be found, and hence *all* conditions could be overturned with hermeneutic discourse—itself a condition of the ground of grounds. Yet this pursuit becomes a metaphysical enterprise, the quest for first principles. Hermeneutics conditions its own conditions and displaces its conditions in the same breath. If there are only interpretations of interpretations, then objective science is bankrupt because any discovery of the extant world would be solely subject to interpretation rather than accepted as uncontested fact. In other words, if observable reality itself is merely an interpretation or construct, then there can be no facts apart from interpretation. Taken to the extreme, if everything is an interpretation, then there is no such thing as facts.†

But let us challenge this assumption for a moment. Is it merely an interpretive hypothesis that ordinary table salt contains oxidized sodium chloride? Although a mountain has various perspectives in shape and perceptual attributes, this does not annul the fact that it has a certain mass and size. Are there not certain analytic statements, as opposed to synthetic statements, that are, by definition, unquestionably true, such as "All bachelors are unmarried men" or "A triangle has three sides"? Perhaps the hermeneutist would reply that it is precisely through language that such definitions are possible and form a consensus of agreement

---

* One may argue that relativism is necessary because interpretation can take place only within a historical context that relativizes it. I prefer to distinguish the notion of perspectivism from relativism, the former allowing for historical contextualism as well as qualitative variances in subjective experience, whereas the latter denotes the philosophical doctrine that there are no universal truths or intrinsic characteristics about the world, only different ways of interpreting it.

† We may very well conclude that there are no facts apart from interpretation because our epistemological justifications rest on our cognitive capacities to form judgments about any object in question. We are conditioned to interpret since childhood according to our cultural context and the internalization of others' interpretive schemata, which have been historically and consensually validated.

that necessarily requires linguistic interpretation in order to make such statements meaningful to begin with. Mathematicians and chemists have their own language, just as do other disciplines, where they provide certain interpretive truths under the influence of grammatical relativism.

But when interpretations devolve into other interpretations or descend the deferral chain of linguistic signifiers into a combinatory of indetermination as indiscriminate meaning, are we not headed toward the abyss of infinite regress? Are we not arguing in a circle—yet one contained? Both a one and a null—its inconclusive openness and its end, hence its closure? For example, if we say *this* means *that*, then one can say, but that *really means* this, *ad infinitum*. If every interpretation is based on another interpretation, then one can never elude the circularity of interpretation.

We cannot ignore the potential problematics of the hermeneutic turn, despite the fact that we all rely on interpretations to function in the world. Unlike explanation, which sets as its task the function of providing descriptions of events, interpretation conveys and confers meaning.* Interpretation mediates between object and meaning, but it can equally obfuscate our understanding, especially our experience of interpretation. When one raises the question of interpretation and its conditions, that is, the possibility of interpretation, the question itself is already circumscribed and refractory, leading Foucault (1990) to observe that interpretation must always "interpret itself" for it "cannot fail to return to itself" (pp. 59, 67), hence undermining its own conditions and claims to truth. Furthermore, because we mediate, translate, and impose interpretations in accord with our dissimilar and competing desires, intentions, and personal agendas, we may observe Gadamer's (1960) insight that all methodologies of discourse are potentially laced with prejudice.

---

* It may be argued that any explanation of events—especially human actions—necessarily requires interpretation, particularly when making claims about facts and their causal connections, which are sensitive to context. In this way any explanation evokes an act of making something intelligible or understandable.

Frank Summers (2008) makes the claim that "the very nature of psychoanalysis is hermeneutic" because it is an activity engaged in "understanding people" (p. 422). This definition by necessity would make any discipline hermeneutic by virtue of the fact that understanding is an intersubjective enterprise whereby the presence of others is internalized and mediated through self-relation and language, which gives rise to interpretation, understanding, and knowledge even if the scientific object in question is not a human being.* But the distinction he wants to emphasize is between psychoanalysis as intrinsically engaged in understanding human subjectivity and the natural world, the former requiring interpretation, the latter observation. Summers (2004) sees hermeneutics as particularly attractive because it leans toward a human science model where the main goal of analysis is to explain human motivation and uncover meaning rather than take an observational stance concerned with discovering relationships among observable facts (see Ricoeur, 1970), which privileges an objectivist criterion. He concludes, "Psychoanalysis is a paradigmatic hermeneutic science because its target is the meaning of experience" (p. 123). Following Dilthey, Husserl, Heidegger, Ricoeur, Gadamer, and others, whom he tends to lump together under one umbrella, psychoanalytic inquiry is first and foremost concerned with the experiential subject whereby human experience should be the primary object of investigation "as *opposed* to nature," which is the subject matter of the natural sciences (p. 123, emphasis added).

I would argue that it is not necessary to create a binary between experience and nature, for clearly human beings are part of nature and inclusive of anything we classify as natural or belonging

---

* Here I am reminded that for Lacan, what is primary is not the individual but the Other, that is, the symbolic and social functions imbedded within the subject. And for Lacan, the subject is always the subject of the unconscious, and the unconscious is always the Other's discourse. There is always another voice speaking in the patient, a metapsychology of internalized culture, the ontology of symbolic meaning and demand instituted through speech and desire. This is what the Lacanian analyst listens for.

to the natural world, namely, that which is *given*. Just as surely as we are embodied organic beings where we come to take our own nature as its object (i.e., the realm of self-consciousness as metarepresentation), we need not negate human experience as a natural phenomenon or contribute to the hegemony that science constructs in its insistence on the superiority of observation, fact, experimentation, and measurement as opposed to meaning analysis. Although Summers wants to champion hermeneutics as a science, "the methods of which involve rules of interpretation, not observations or their manipulations" (2004, p. 123), I believe it is not possible to ontically separate the two human activities because observation and interpretation are coextensive, simultaneous facets of mental activity, whether they apply to systematic–semantic rules of interpretation or observational–empirical procedures. And psychoanalytic method necessarily requires observation in order to offer interpretations that convey meaning and understanding. We observe by listening, hence focusing on the nuances of the speech act, pointing out patterns and inconsistencies with attention to interrelationships and their correspondent inner relations between thought, feeling, and fantasy, all of which are illuminated through mutual dialogue that aims toward meaning construction.

Equally, "meaning" and "motivation" are not merely "uncovered" or "discovered," which contrarily to Summer's thesis invokes a natural science paradigm of acquiring knowledge and understanding through engagement with the external world where facts are to be accumulated and catalogued. Rather, there is a simultaneous process of creating the found world, to reappropriate Winnicott, whereby there is a contiguous procreativity or generative production belonging to and instituted by the agentic ego. This generative creativity is coextensive with the act of discovering psychic data or unraveling truth (*aletheia*) as unconcealment or disclosedness, namely, that which appears as phenomena (φαινόμενον). Here human experience becomes an overdetermined quest for the desire to know and understand the found given, as well as agentically create, construct, and shape meaning via human dialogue.

It was Dilthey (1923/1979) who proposed the distinction between the human sciences, based upon investigating and understanding the motivations and meanings inherent to the experiential subject or human being, and the natural sciences, which is concerned with the impersonal forces and organizations of nature. Whereas the *Geisteswissenschaften* focus on the science of mental processes and social systems within a class of human events, the *Naturwaschten* focus on the domain of the natural world. Therefore, the bifurcation that is often forged between the human sciences and the natural sciences takes as its premise that nature and human experience are mutually exclusive categories. However, the distinction lies in the methodology each discipline employs.

The subject matter within a human science model is that of the experiential subject and collective social life contextualized within a genus of human events, and impersonal aspects of the natural world are not typically part of its scope or locus. Hence, because human sciences are interpretive and target the meaning of experience, by definition they become hermeneutic. Because psychoanalysis is necessarily predicated on human speech and language and involves the pursuit of understanding human motivation and constructing meaning through interpretive intersubjective exchange, it may be considered a hermeneutic science.

For Dilthey and others, interpretation or understanding (*Verstehen*) becomes a method for investigating the human sciences; however, this is not devoid of certain problems, especially when rules or criteria for understanding may become nebulous. Here it can be argued that hermeneutics never fully escapes the charge of slipping into relativism or recalcitrant subjectivism, given that following certain rules of discourse versus what someone "really meant" can easily be two different things. Likewise, exegetical interpretation of a text or deconstructive praxis, and the application of that interpretation, may readily transform or alter it from its original meaning or purpose. In other words, the

very act of translation itself institutes reinterpretations of interpretations that can potentially spin on in circularity or regress to
a point that meaning is foreclosed from its original signification.

How can hermeneutics escape the charge of its circularity, infinite regress, negation of universals, tacit relativism, and failure to
provide a consensus or criteria for interpretation? How is psychoanalysis able to philosophically justify interpretative truth claims
when they potentially inhere to a recalcitrant subjectivism while
claiming to be objectively valuative?

Despite the ubiquity and centrality interpretation plays within
the psychoanalytic edifice, and the unequivocal significance
the hermeneutical turn has had on our field, we are left with
the conundrum of explaining how interpretation follows a logic
that attempts to offer a compelling case for meaning construction based upon a stylized (contexual), particularized (individual)
method that purports to follow an objective (replicable) pattern of
analyzing human experience, while at the same time eludes any
concrete (universal) criteria on which to judge its epistemological
foundation and efficacy.

In response to the historical tensions and pitfalls associated with
the science versus hermeneutic debate in psychoanalysis, Marilyn
Nissim-Sabat (2009) offers an appealing and cogent series of arguments for adopting Husserlian phenomenology as the foundation
of a new psychoanalytic science that displaces the positivism of a
natural science framework and the potential relativism and subjectivism inherent in a purely hermeneutical approach to psychoanalytic inquiry. Given that contemporary psychoanalysis has
largely adopted the postmodern turn and has found many traditions within continental philosophy appealing for rethinking psychoanalytic theory, it is surprising that phenomenology has not
been given more attention. Nissim-Sabat fills that gap and provides the first sustained argument for why the field should adopt
a Husserlian perspective.

Although proponents of phenomenology are diverse in theoretical scope and focus, and are by no means homogenous,

phenomenology may be said to be first and foremost concerned with the process of experience and how phenomena are disclosed and appear to the human subject via an analysis and description of consciousness. Husserl in particular and phenomenologists in general typically admit to a radical difference between the "natural" and the "philosophical" attitudes, the latter challenging scientific epistemology. Although natural science makes metaphysical assumptions about how things really are in themselves, including discovering objective laws and unchanging "truth," phenomenology suspends its ontological commitments in favor of an epistemological stance that takes concrete human subjectivity and experience as the proper objects of science. For Husserl, this is accomplished by a radical repositioning of our methodological practices that does not privilege the natural science attitude but rather displaces such an attitude through a purely formal investigation into the structures and disclosedness of subjectivity. Rather than assume the existence of natural objects independent of consciousness, Husserl, following Kant and the German Idealists, focuses on how meanings and their relations, rather than things, are constituted via transcendental subjectivity. Unlike the natural scientific attitude that avouches an unadulterated realism that can be observed and measured, the phenomenological subject is never dislocated from its object of study and hence can only make interpretations and convey meaning through its own relations as immediately experienced in the lifeworld (*Lebenswelt*). Here there is no distinction or separation of subject from object, for this contrast is united.

Although there is a complicated set of relationships between science and philosophy, Husserl advocates for a foundational role phenomenology plays in the constitution of any science, indeed, in the possibility for there to be any science at all, including psychoanalysis. To achieve its task, philosophy is required to perform a certain reduction or act of withdrawal from the usual assertions we make about what exists or does not exist in the world. The result of this reduction, suspension of judgment, or bracketing is to reveal the world as a correlate of consciousness. In fact, it is just such a reduction or *epoché* (ἐποχή) that makes phenomenology a descriptive science, the science of pure consciousness as such. In what follows, I will briefly discuss the implications of the phenomenological notion of pure consciousness vis-à-vis the psychoanalytic notion of the unconscious.

Nissim-Sabat carefully prepares her arguments by pointing out the precariousness of naturalism, as well as the advantages of phenomenology over hermeneutics. According to Nissim-Sabat, the natural science attitude is full of unwarranted presuppositions about what is real, objective, universal, absolute, unchanging, and causally deterministic, which ultimately devolves into the bane of material reduction. I particularly find instructive her categorization of scientism as adhering to (a) positivism and naturalism, where science is seen as the only source of knowledge; (b) belief in a mechanistic "billiard-ball model" of causation following fixed universal laws; and (c) affirmation that material and efficient ontological explanations are a sufficient condition for understanding process and reality, hence privileging (d) realism and (e) a correspondence theory of truth, which ultimately have their substance and existence in matter, and the belief that (f) one can have objective knowledge about the world independent of subjectivity or consciousness (p. 44). Although one may object to her broad generalizations to science in general, and Freudian psychoanalysis in particular, she very eloquently shows how these attitudes have formed an indelible foothold in the theoretical corpus that underlies scientism and naturalized views of epistemology and that this furthermore prejudices science in its various investigations and methodologies.

Equally interesting is her analysis of hermeneutics, which is frequently associated with a phenomenological perspective and has been welcomed by many contemporary psychoanalytic theorists. Despite the fact that hermeneutics collapses the subject–object divide, sees subjectivity as necessary to all interpretations, and generally holds an antiscientific posture, Nissim-Sabat argues that it is ultimately subject to relativism because of its disavowal of universals and hence the rejection of the possibility of any scientific law governing interpretation. Another reason, I must reiterate, is that hermeneutics lacks a methodological criterion for which interpretation and meaning are construed and conveyed, hence it cannot escape the circularity of potentially collapsing into a radical subjectivism—or even worse, egoism—where interpretation gives way to subjective caprice guided by self-gratification. Here, she argues, a phenomenological science becomes a more palatable alternative that insulates psychoanalysis from positivism and relativism.*

By dismissing the natural science standpoint, or rather, scientism, natural science's own self-misinterpretation, Nissim-Sabat is also able to reconfigure and reincorporate the hermeneutic tradition within a proper phenomenological attitude that governs our sensibilities regarding interpretive theory and practice. Our object of concern should be the lifeworld and all its variations, which is revealed to consciousness through the phenomenological reduction, hence the systematic bracketing or voluntary suspension of all ontological commitments. This disciplined suspension promises to disclose the psychic field of subjectivity "as a self-sufficient sphere, and thus as a proper object of scientific investigation" (p. 63). By reconceiving psychoanalysis as a non-natural science that places the realm of the psychic as the proper core of psychoanalytic investigations, she hopes to open up an attractive space for psychoanalysis to flourish as a philosophical science of subjectivity.

But in the end, does phenomenology pose its own set of incompatibilities when by definition it centers on the question and structure of subjectivity *qua* consciousness? Can it provide a clearer window into the processes and components of interpretation when its proper object of study is human consciousness

---

* Perhaps Nissim-Sabat is taking too much liberty in separating phenomenology from hermeneutics, for they may be viewed as complementary rather than antithetical. If hermeneutics is more interpretive than descriptive, phenomenology is more descriptive than interpretive: It becomes a matter of emphasis rather than of difference.

rather than unconscious phenomenology? And does this not pose a new set of limitations when the phenomenological method is supposed to bracket or suspend all ontological commitments, which ultimately applies to our collective belief in the ontology of the unconscious?

What would the adoption of the phenomenological method entail for psychoanalysis? First of all, we would have to set aside our theoretical biases and intellectual prejudices about our preferred orientations and simply observe mental phenomena as it shines forth or appears. I could envision a technical process where this would be instructive and even complementary to the free associative method; however, it would be very challenging for most of us to set aside our preferred conceptual frameworks, let alone our ontological worldviews that we import into every subjective act of experiencing. But following the spirit of phenomenology, is this not what science should aspire toward when it makes its observations, engages in data collection, and performs statistical analyses? Is it not supposed to be neutral, precise, and unburdened by theoretic bias when observing and classifying phenomena? Are there really any procedural differences between the two methodologies if they are both based on explicating observable phenomena as they appear to consciousness?

But if we adopt the phenomenological stance, what becomes of ontology? When asked to suspend all ontological commitments, is Nissim-Sabat asking us to do something that we are incapable of doing (at least from a practical standpoint) by virtue of the fact that every human action is prefaced and premised on ontological assumptions we import (especially unconsciously) in our subjective engagement with the world and reality? Here she would say "no," because she is merely advocating for the *suspension of judgments* regarding the ultimate ontology of the world, not that there is a denial of Being per se, only that, following Kant, the ultimate nature of the world is in itself unknowable. In fact, she argues, the phenomenological attitude is what is needed in any viable theory and method of scientificity.

If psychoanalysis does adopt Husserl's phenomenological method, will it have to abandon the belief in an unconscious ontology, and unconscious processes in general, like the ubiquity of transference and defense, which are the historical pillars of psychoanalytic knowledge? Does Husserl (1950) himself make certain ontological commitments when he avers the existence of a transcendental ego that prereflectively performs the acts of *epoché* as analysis of subjectivity *qua* subjectivity, something Sartre (1957) outright rejected? Does Husserl's system (like Sartre's) by necessity reject *in toto* the notion of unconscious operations, or can unconscious mentation be explained within the structures of subjectivity? If, by definition, phenomenology is a science of consciousness, this seems to eclipse any possibility of apprehending or knowing unconscious activity because it is not accessible to conscious experience, and even if it were, it would betray the phenomenological attitude by positing ontological processes beneath (or behind) the veil of consciousness.

But is there any possibility of observing subjectivity that could be conceived as the manifestation or instantiation of unconscious structure? Can we save Husserl from his own contradictions? Husserl barely mentions the unconscious in his writings; however, a cryptic feature of his analysis of the ego entails what he refers to as "passive synthesis" or "passive constitution," which explains the formal mediating and unifying operations of the transcendental ego, what I have called an agentic unconscious ego-organization responsible for all productions of consciousness (Mills, 2010). Although he did not adequately emphasize passive synthesis as the domain of the unconscious, here we may not inappropriately extend Husserl's method to a proper study of unconscious phenomenology.

FROM QUANTUM PHYSICS TO METAPHYSICS

As we have seen, there continues to be a spread of theoretical diversity within contemporary psychoanalytic discourse that may be said to generally coalesce around the scientific versus philosophical conception of psychoanalysis, which largely propounds arguments for a naturalized behavioral science that adheres to an objectivist epistemology and empirical method over a humanities model. In contrast to scientism, where observation, measurement, experimentation, and statistical (mathematical) analysis are privileged, the human science approach emphasizes interpretation and phenomenological description, which focuses on individual motivation, existential meaning, and qualitative experience. Both perspectives and methodological discourses can exist in theoretic harmony, that is, without canceling the other out, but I am afraid that the entrenched convictions of each discipline concomitant with market conditions clamoring for ostensible results interfere with this possibility, at least for now.

Just as psychoanalytic proponents of traditional phenomenology have been relatively few in comparison to postmodern linguistic and hermeneutical approaches, we may also observe a paucity of supporters for more classical forms of natural science, namely, physics. That is, until now. Gerald Gargiulo (2004, 2006, 2010) has advocated for an analogous relationship between quantum mechanics and psychoanalytic conceptions of mind and clinical practice. Although Gargiulo's work may have more utility for clinical theory than for metapsychology, he introduces many novel concepts from physics in an attempt, whether intended or not, to bridge the gap between a natural science attitude and a philosophical one.

Gargiulo (2010) is specifically concerned with how quantum theory, broadly conceived, can offer an alternative, complementary model for conceptualizing clinical experience by comparing the processes of quantum mechanics—not content—to analytic sensibility and technique. His work is important and timely and deserves our serious attention. He informs us that the field of physics "not only addresses the question of measurement but, in the process, necessarily explores the nature of reality itself" (p. 95). Here quantum theory leaves the domain of science and enters the realm of metaphysics. Espousing a nonreductive paradigm that embraces a monistic rather than a dualistic conception of nature, mind, and reality, Gargiulo alerts us to many interesting analogies between the micro and macro world of quantum speculation and experimentation, which could be compared to the latent and manifest content of psychic experience, as well as how psychoanalytic interpretation as the creation of meaning converges with quantum measurements that purport to generate the extant world via observations. As he puts it, "There is no deep reality, that is, there is no *as it is* of the world ... what we measure is all we have" (p. 95). Following the physicists, reality is a construct.

Not withstanding Gargiulo's fine contributions to advancing clinical theory, there are a few philosophical problematics I wish to address. Let us unpack this notion that reality is merely a "construct" or "understood as a construct" (p. 97). It is one thing to conceive of reality via hermeneutical interpretation versus making the ontological assertion that reality *is* constructed. Following Edwin Schrodinger, Mara Beller, Niels Bohr, Werner Heisenberg, and others, Gargiulo (2010) states,

> Quantum physicists speak of *the collapse of the wave function* when, for example, either the position, or the speed, of a proton is established. This is a term that indicates that a measurement has been taken, that is, out of the world of probability/possibility a result has occurred. More specifically and for our purposes more pertinent is the conclusion that the measuring observation causes the actuality of the proton that is observed. That is, the proton exists when it is observed, not before, not after. Strange findings! (p. 96, emphasis in original)

Strange findings indeed. Notice that he says that scientific measurement "causes" "actuality." Further on he summarizes physicists' positions that "a particle does not exist before or after an observation. ... In other words *it only exists* as it is and when it is observed" (p. 98, emphasis in original). Let us meditate on this statement for a moment. This proposition is tantamount to a grand yet crass Idealism, such as ones previously advanced by Fichte and Berkeley, where the physical world is *thought, posited, perceived,* or *willed* into existence. The language of causality and actuality not only imports the mentality that "If I don't observe it, it doesn't exist" but also that *existence itself* is an omnipotent creation of the faculty of mind. How can observation and interpretive thought bring physical matter and energy into existence? How can observation create or, more specifically, how can one *create existence* by merely observing? This would mean that the act of genesis transpires in the moment of observation. More specifically, physical objects in the universe exist *if and only if* they are perceived.

Although we can creatively perceive reality, how can we creatively perceive its transition from a state of nonexistence to generative existence—especially because there would be no state of nonexistence given that everything is born in the moment? In other words, how can mind create the world it observes, only to have it disappear when perception no longer perceives? At face value these propositions seem ridiculous. Is this not the work of fantasy and creative imagination, whereby shared illusion becomes an experiential reality scientists wish to inhabit and repackage as so-called fact, manipulated under a mathematical formula? And how could these metaphysical postulates be passed off as *scientia* to begin with, hence the claim *to know*?

If we are to continue with this line of reasoning, that the world comes into existence with every act of observation and disappears once perception is withdrawn, then how does one approach the genesis problem, namely, the *coming into being* of existence, let alone coherently explain the spontaneous emergence and subsistence of embodied forms of activity that populate our cosmos at every moment? And if consciousness is responsible for the omnipotent causation and propagation of all cosmic activity, then consciousness would also, dialectically, be responsible for its nonexistence. The problematic becomes, if the extant world is dependent upon consciousness, then it would vanish entirely if there were no consciousness. Therefore, the perceptive and volitional causation of disappearance and reappearance would be acts of magical creationism, not simply imaginative construction. And if disappearance of an observable scientific object has a spatio-temporal persistence outside of consciousness (viz., observation and interpretation), then by logical extension there would be a sustained ontological order to the cosmos that is operative and independent of consciousness, a point that some contemporary physicists apparently do not hold.

If being or reality is constructed, and hence does not exist as an ontological presence in itself, then meaning does not exist because it is also constructed and does not emanate from anything onto-logically substantial or subsistent, therefore consciousness does not exist until it is interpretively constructed. But how is that possible if consciousness is required in order to construct? Does it spontaneously generate its own being via self-construction out of nothing? If the world is contingent on construction, and a lack of construction equals nonexistence, then how do we explain the existence of nonexistence? Talk about begging the question. Does not consciousness evolve from a prior ground, from a previous ontogenetic organization that is organic, developmental, and epi-genetic? To sustain this line of argument, because consciousness is required for every act of construction, then it must also construct its own existence or *think itself into being*. But just because we have a thought does not necessarily make it real. In other words, we can't think something *physical* into existence. These are not criti-cisms of Gargiulo per se, given that he is interested in advancing clinical theory, only that they pose serious conundrums the field of physics has the onus to prove.

From what we have seen from contemporary quantum theory, not only is there a suspension of metaphysical realism, or even critical realism, that espouses the notion that there must be some-thing substantial (even if conceived as process, in this context— the energetic stratification of material interactions) behind the veil of appearances, but the real becomes something that is generated *ex nihilo* via consciousness (given that perceptual observation and conceptual interpretation are activities of sensation and cognitive judgment). Here the phenomenological attitude of bracketing or *epoché* is radicalized as the negation of realism for an almighty creationism rather than modestly endorsing the suspension of all ontological judgments.

Although Gargiulo does not make this claim, my reading of the conclusions drawn by the physicists he employs is in essence metaphysical theories masquerading under the authority of science, which *ipso facto* elevates metaphysics to the status of science, when these are truly theoretical speculations that inherit the same conceptual and logical delimitations imposed on any coherent philosophical system. One error appears to be the conflation of epistemology with ontology, whereby interpretive observation as truth claims to knowledge becomes equated with existence itself (i.e., the quantum universe as a measurable object). Put another way, what we know and what *is* can be two entirely different things, although they may be conjoined or dislocated from one another depending upon the context we are investigating. Furthermore, epistemology and ontology are separate philosophical categories that are important to preserve for discursive methodological purposes, for what we know about observable phenomena may be barred from inquiry when the philosophic object in question is not subject to direct observation (e.g., the question of God). Lack of observation, or the potential for such, does not rule out *in toto* the legitimacy of the question or subject matter itself. On the contrary, natural science generally concedes to the limitations its self-defined methodologies impose on any observational stance or standards of measurement it is itself confined by.

It goes without saying that any separation between the human being and reality cannot be ontologically justified because natural science is defined through the ongoing nature of our questioning, hence our subjectivity becomes the ground of "scientific" objectivity. As Gargiulo puts it, "One thing that quantum mechanics has confirmed is that there are no neutral observers. Additionally, building on the quantum concept of nonlocality, we can recognize that we are all part of, interact with, and are manifestations of the reality in which we live" (2010, p. 102). Here I most certainly agree. This is a conclusion made by Hegel over 200 years ago and again popularized in 20th-century Western metaphysics by Alfred North Whitehead and other process philosophers.* It is for this reason that I can envision potential fruitful comparisons between contemporary quantum physics and process metaphysics.

Since Freud, and to some degree Jung and Lacan, I am unaware of any psychoanalyst who has attempted to offer a comprehensive systematic metaphysics. My formal academic studies in philosophy came after my training in clinical psychology and psychoanalysis, and therefore I became immediately enchanted with forming an intimate relationship between these broad disciplines. In a series of works culminating in two books (Mills, 2002b, 2010),

---

* For both Hegel and Whitehead, all aspects of the cosmos, including any dimension of the natural world, space and subatomic organizations, micro and macro orderings, ecosystems, human beings, and social environments, are all interconnected and ontologically inseparable. Hegel (1812/1831/1969, 1817a) established a comprehensive science of the dialectic based on the logic of process. Drawing on Heraclitus's ideas on change, the strife and tension of opposition, and the many within the one, Hegel's dialectical logic is a monistic metaphysical system that attempts to account for all aspects of reality, including nature, mind, science, history, ethics, religion, and aesthetics.

Although it was Hegel who first argued systematically that reality is a process of becoming, it is Alfred North Whitehead (1925, 1929/1978) who is most commonly referred to as the founder of process philosophy. Whitehead (1929/1978) argued that the fundamental activity that comprises and underlies the cosmos is the eternal process of experience constituted through a dynamic flux of microcosmic orderly events, much of which are nonconscious organizations as "drops of experience, complex and interdependent" (p. 18). For Whitehead, process reality comprises a motion of energy continuous throughout nature and is the fundamental building blocks of the universe. Whitehead's system emphasizes the creative and novel advance of nature as a continuously transforming and progressive series of events that are purposeful, directional, and unifying. Like Heraclitus and Hegel before him, Whitehead stresses the dialectical exchange of oppositions that advance the process of becoming. What is particularly interesting is that Whitehead (1925) anticipated the modern physicist conception of nonlocality when he postulated the principle of misplaced concreteness, which is when one fallaciously attempts to reduce a phenomenon to its simple location. In other words, scientists often mistake observable, measurable phenomena for their simple location and make inconclusive causal claims. This fallacy is committed when observable physical locality, such as functional magnetic resonance imaging (fMRI) or positron emission tomography (PET) scans, are equated with the mental functions and representational content we ontologically *infer* to be causal, rather than correspondent, and therefore hastily conclude that mind equals brain. Whitehead in particular has found acceptance among contemporary physicists (see Eastman & Keeton, 2004).

I have introduced a systematic psychoanalytic metaphysics called "process psychology" or "dialectical psychoanalysis," which is largely derived from Hegel's dialectical logic. Having amended Hegel's dialectic to complement contemporary psychoanalytic paradigms, I provide a process account of the coming into being of unconscious agency that conditions the subsequent emergence and organization of all other forms of psychic realty. As a result, I offer a novel treatise on the unconscious mind by explicating the origins of psychic experience. Although Anna Aragno (2008) has nicely argued for a biosemiotic model of forms of knowledge as unconscious communication patterns, I attempt to delineate in a systematic way how unconscious semiotics are the preconditions for subjectivity and mental processes in general, including language, intersubjectivity and social relations, and ultimately human culture. Admittedly lofty in scope and design, dialectical psychoanalysis is therefore concerned with expatiating the ontological conditions that make knowledge and experience possible.

Dialectical psychoanalysis is an attempt to systematically explain how the unconscious generates mind and all facets of psychic reality. Reality is constituted by mind as an agentic process that emerges, grows, and matures from its basal primitive form to more robust configurations of conscious life, self-reflection, and social order. Psychic reality begins as unconscious experience constituted through presubjective and prereflective events that collectively organize into an unconscious sense of agency. The coming into being of this agentic function signals the coming into being of subjectivity, which becomes the fountainhead for future forms of psychic life to materialize and thrive. What this means is that before we can speak of the infant, before we can speak of the mother or the attachment system, before we can speak of culture or language, we have to account for the internally derived unconscious activity that makes consciousness, attachment, and social relations possible.

Process psychology shows how internally mediated relations become the ground and prototype for all external relations, as well as how the structures of unconscious subjectivity allow for inter-subjective dynamics to unfold and transpire. The unconscious is real although it is not an entity. It is more appropriately understood as a *series of spacings* or presencing of certain facets of psychic realty, having loci, shape, and force in the indefinite ways in which they manifest as both the interiorization and the external expression of agentic events. Here we are mainly concerned with the reality of the unseen and the ontological invisibility of unconscious process. Process psychology displaces the primacy of language over the primacy and ubiquity of unconscious mentation, instead radicalizing an unconscious agency that modifies and differentiates itself and disperses its essence throughout its dialectical activities. Here, I believe, science and philosophy become intimately conjoined as a metaphysical enterprise.

For there to be psychic determination or causation, there must be a *determiner* or source of activity that executes this formal act of bringing about mental functioning to begin with, what we may equate with unconscious agency. Freud was never able to adequately answer to the question of a unifying agency because he divided the mind up into competing "agencies," "systems" (1900, p. 537), or "entities" (1923, pp. 23–26), culminating in his mature, tripartite structural theory of 1923. Although Freud did offer an adumbrated attempt to explain how the I (*Ich*) epigenetically developed out of the It (*Es*) as a differentiated and modified agency derived from its initial natural embodiment (see 1923, p. 25; 1926, p. 97), he was not able to explain this developmental process with any precision.

In *Origins: On the Genesis of Psychic Reality* (2010), I offer the first systematic psychoanalytic metaphysics in the history of ideas articulating the birth of psychic agency. Here I argue that structures of subjectivity are themselves conditioned *a priori* by an unconscious agency that is responsible for all forms of mental life to materialize and thrive, including consciousness. My reasoning relies upon the principle of sufficient reason, namely, that there must be an original ground for every mental event that stands in relation to every mental object. Psychic activity does not pop up *ex nihilio*; it must surface from an unconscious organizing principle I have metaphorically called the *abyss*. This unconscious abyss is itself a crude form of agency that performs executive functions and initiates determinate choices and actions through intentional maneuvers we are accustomed to refer to as drive derivatives, wishes, fantasies, defenses, compromise formations, self-states, dissociative enactments, or otherwise anything we may label as belonging to unconscious experience. The locus of this abyss rests within an agentic function that may be properly attributed to an unconscious ego that possesses formal capacities to execute intentional choice aimed toward purposeful ends, what I refer to as unconscious teleology.

How am I to convince the reader that we all possess unconscious agency? Let me begin by asking how could memory, representation, and semiotics be possible? Without an internal executor or agency that performs formal functions of perceptual processing, categorization, retention, synthesis, unification, semiotic linkage, and information exchange, how could human experience be encoded, organized, transmuted, and transmitted via speech and behavior? Where would such activity come from? How could it be carried out if it was not initiated from an inner sense of functional form? In other words, consciousness is neither a necessary nor a sufficient condition for explaining these psychic processes that by definition transpire outside of consciousness. Unconscious productions have a certain force and presence enacted by a formal (impersonal) agentic ego that lies at the heart of all teleological activity. How else could we explain mental events that are operative within psychic regions or territories unknown to immediate consciousness when they appear unannounced? Appealing to neuroscience, biology, or brain discourse gets us nowhere. Cognitive science cannot answer the question of agency because it makes consciousness an epiphenomenon, hence properties of the brain that possess no causal powers of their own. And if we are content in boiling down mind to brain states, then what becomes of freedom and agency?

The coming into being of psychic reality may be understood from the standpoint of a developmental monistic ontology whereby there is a progressive unfolding of desire into an organizing and unifying process system we equate with the unconscious ego as an impersonal executive-synthetic agency. This agency is merely formal, hence it is not a personal agent or subject in any proper sense, which is commonly ascribed to human consciousness or selfhood. The abyss is initially immersed in its own corporeal sentient embodiment and awakens as appetitive motivational longing, its initial Being-in-relation-to-lack. The abyss erupts from its self-enclosed original unity as pulsional desire. Such desirous rupture is in response to feeling its need, urge, or craving to experience and satiate the lack, which takes various initial forms that eventually breach into consciousness as ego proper. Originally, desire takes itself as its initial object through a form of prereflective self-consciousness I refer to as *unconscious apperception*, the pure experiential self-sense belonging to precognitive unconscious thought. The development of unconscious subjectivity ultimately follows an organic process based on a series of dialectical mediations beginning as unconscious apperception and culminating in self-conscious reflection, the sublated domain of conscious human experience. Yet this initial rudimentary process of desirous rupture and apperception constitutes the birth of the human psyche, for mind is an epigenetic, architectonic self-organizing achievement expressed as a dynamic, self-articulated complex totality or psychic holism.

Unconscious mind is a series of spacings that first instantiate themselves as a multitude of *schemata*, which are the building blocks of psychic reality. A schema is a desirous-apperceptive-ideational unit of self-experience that is teleologically oriented and dialectically constituted. Schemata may be viewed as micro-agents with semiautonomous powers of telic expression that operate as self-states as they create spacings within the unconscious abyss. Schemata may take various forms, from the archaic to the refined, and instantiate themselves as somatic, sensuous, affective, perceptual, and conceptual (symbolic) orders within the psyche, each having its own intrinsic pressures, valences, intensities, intentional and defensive strategies, and unconscious qualia.

The microdynamics of schematic expression can be highly individualistic in their bid for freedom, creativity, complexity, and agentic intent and are tantamount to the instinctual and defensive processes we are accustomed to attributing to unconscious mentation in general. The difference here is that schemata are inherently both free and determined, that is, they are self-constituted and determinate within the natural parameters in which they find themselves and operate. This means that schematic expression is highly contextual and contingent, yet schemata exist in a multiplicity of process systems that commune, interact, and participate in a community of events that mutually influence the unique constitution of each schematic structure within the sea of the mind. This overdetermination of psychic processes ensures that unconscious agency ultimately underlies the constitution of all mental functioning.

The multitudinous complex microsystems or communities of schemata evolve from an interceptive source we may properly attribute to an unconscious ego or processor as the locus and executor of subjective agency. Although schemata persist and sustain their existence within the abyss of psychic reality, the unconscious ego is the synthetic unifying agency of mind. Furthermore, it is the unconscious ego that assigns agency to schemata, which allow for their autonomous actions. In this way, agency allows for both unconscious freedom and unconscious determinism, for schemata are autonomous self-organizations that teleologically define and execute their own course of actions. Here emanations from the abyss conform to a sort of *free determinism*, where psychic life arises from and is animated by its own generative forms of self-organization and self-expression—at once given, forged, and constructed. In this way, freedom and determinism are modes of self-causation.

The unequivocal centrality of agency in the constitution of mind becomes a pivotal and indispensible concept for understanding psychic complexity and justifying the existence of determinate freedom. Unconscious agency is ultimately responsible for all aspects of psychic functioning, from the most elemental and primitive to the most sophisticated, because, following the principle of sufficient reason, psychic reality must stand in relation to its original form. From unformulated and inarticulate unconscious experience to reflective self-conscious reason inherent in the formation of self-identity, all psychic activity derives from its original ontological foundations.

CONSILIENT PSYCHOANALYSIS

In our current mainstream topography, the debate still ensues over the question and feasibility of psychoanalysis (and psychodynamic psychotherapy) as a legitimate and helpful form of therapeutic intervention, not to mention its scientific status and theoretical utility for explaining human nature. I have no doubt that psychoanalysis will prevail as the most sophisticated psychological theory we have to date in the history of psychology, although the people in charge—the majority of whom are employed through institutions and corporations in political power, such as academic psychologists, government and research-granting agencies, the medical profession, psychopharmacology companies, and the insurance industry doling out dollars for treatment—will continue to find ways of negating and marginalizing our value out of economic and political self-interest. Despite the fact that psychoanalysis is embraced worldwide as a general psychological paragon elucidating human nature—a testament that steadfastly influences the humanities—and as an empirically effective form of treatment, as long as consensus and opinion are determined by economic and political pressures, psychoanalysis will remain controversial and on the fringe. Although many empirical initiatives in psychoanalysis have been established, mainly instigated by the turn in evidence-based practice to establish its worth and credence, the divide between science and theory has become even wider.

In response, psychoanalysis has joined the game, albeit reticently and in small numbers, to attempt to offer empirical proof of its own that it has something to contribute to both academia and the public at large. We may observe recent developments in the empirical literature in a wide variety of settings that combat such criticism, including the domains of infant and developmental research, attachment theory, dissociation and trauma, clinical psychopathology, cognitive science and neuropsychoanalysis, psychotherapeutic process and defense mechanisms research, personality theory, and applications to sociocultural issues, just to name a few. On the theoretical side of things, advances continue to be made by appropriating knowledge, research methods, interdisciplinary discussion, and descriptive heuristic praxis from other fields where science and the humanities coalesce. Whether there will be fruitful cross-fertilizations between these diverse modes of discourse I cannot predict, but this felicitous direction shows how certain contemporary approaches are attempting to find creative points of connection between the scientific and the philosophical dimensions that continue to preoccupy our field.

It goes without saying that many of my contemporary colleagues will view me negatively for offering this critique. I must reiterate that my primary purpose for doing so is under the intention of advance. Because there is so much that is of importance and value in the relational school, a proper philosophical grounding becomes a necessary requisite in order to lend credibility and validity to its diverse theoretical positions. Ideas without critique are as blind as perceptions without thought, and just as linguistic mediation is a necessary condition for conceptuality, so is self-criticism a necessary dimension for growth and the actualization of further potential.

The politics of psychoanalytic infighting is not a new topic. But it seems to me that the relational school has introduced a new tension within the establishment: With the hermeneutic turn, psychoanalysis is drifting away from its scientific foundations toward philosophy. Bornstein (2001), Masling (2003), Silverman (2000), and Josephs (2001) reproach contemporary psychoanalysis for the abnegation of a scientific framework based on empirically derived research methodology, which is subverted by the seduction of postmodern hyperbole. Although this criticism is not entirely without merit, it also presupposes that psychoanalysis must continue to view itself solely as a scientific discipline modeled after natural-empirical science, a presupposition contemporary analysts have repeatedly drawn into question.

The conception of psychoanalysis as a science was as much a criticism of Freud's time as it is today,* and we can see why the empirical proponents of psychoanalysis—mainly academics—have an invested interest in salvaging psychoanalysis from the bog of illegitimacy. Popper (1972) and Grünbaum (1984) argue that psychoanalysis simply fails as a natural science because it is too private, not open to clinical testing or falsification, and not modeled after physics, whereas Sulloway (1979) and Webster (1995) decry that it must forgo the status of a serious science because it does not conform to Darwinian biology. In a defense of psychoanalysis, Marcus Bowman (2002) argues that outdated and misapplied notions of science and positivism erroneously serve as the main resistance against accepting the value of psychoanalysis as a rational inquiry into the essential conditions of internal human conflict. He claims that critics of psychoanalysis hold on to the illusory hope that human science should be modeled on physical science and/or evolutionary biology when these propositions themselves may be interpreted as category mistakes; distort the real practice of scientific observation, which is based on consensus and agreement; and generally reflect an exaggeration of the authority of science as a touchstone to truth.

Even Freud (1915b) himself recognized the limits to the so-called scientific method: "We have often heard it maintained that sciences should be built up on clear and sharply defined

---

* Freud (1925) states, "I have always felt it a gross injustice that people have refused to treat psycho-analysis like any other science" (p. 58).

basic concepts. In actual fact no science, not even the most exact, begins with such definitions" (p. 117). For anyone actually working in empirical research, we all know how easy it is to statistically manipulate data: "Scientific" reports are primarily based on the theoretical beliefs of the researcher who is attempting to advocate a specific line of argument under the guise of "objectivity." Freud (1912b) saw through this game:

> Cases which are devoted from the first to scientific purposes and treated accordingly suffer in their outcome; while the most successful cases are those in which one proceeds, as it were, without any purpose in view, allows oneself to be taken by surprise by any new turn in them, and always meets them with an open mind, free from any presuppositions. (p. 114)

Hence alerting us to the potential interference of the analyst's subjectivity.

I am afraid that the polarity between psychoanalysis as science and psychoanalysis as hermeneutics will always be a felt tension. On the one hand, disciplines that largely identify with being scientifically (hence empirically) grounded will need to justify their theories through collaborative identification with methodologies that claim to be epistemologically objective, whereas the hermeneutic tradition is invested in their renunciation because they simply can't buy the premise of an objective epistemology. As a result, a stalemate is unavoidable: Each side wishes to annul the validity and justifications of the other rather than seek a complementary union or consilience.* Because psychoanalysis has historically always fought prejudice against its scientific achievements, a phenomenon that dominates mainstream academic psychology and psychiatry, perhaps the relational tradition is finding new momentum in the field because of the felt dissatisfactions inherent in an epistemological scientific framework. And with so many generations of analysts having to labor continually to justify

---

* This word is adapted from Edward O. Wilson's (1998) book *Consilience*, where he attempts to unify the hybrid nature of scientific and hermeneutic knowledge.

their trade to an increasingly cynical public that wants only quick symptom relief rather than insight, it comes as no surprise that the rejuvenation of subjectivity needs to vanquish objective science by making it the contemporary whipping boy. The problem comes when radical adherents for each side attempt to ground their positions through negating the other rather than through seeking the fruitful unification that science and philosophy have to offer one another as a complex holism. Can the two identificatory bodies of knowledge coexist in some type of comparative-integrative harmony or dialectical order? This I cannot answer. Yet I believe it remains an important task to pursue this possibility in order for psychoanalysis to prosper and reclaim its cultural value.

Keith Valone (2005) has advocated for a consilient psychoanalysis whereby he predicts that the future progress of our field will either flourish or fall asunder based upon whether or not we adopt criteria that attempt to integrate "facts and fact-based theory from different disciplines in order to develop a common language and comprehensive explanatory framework" (p. 189). In advancing the spirit of Leo Rangell's (2007) "total-composite theory" as an effort to lend unity to psychoanalytic pluralism, and similarly Brent Willock's (2007) "comparative-integrative psychoanalysis," Valone hopes for a common vision where theoretical integration, "coherence for all disciplines," and "knowledge is ultimately unified" (p. 190).

Despite the fact that this concept is adopted from the work of the distinguished Harvard biologist Edward O. Wilson (1998), where he makes a grand plea for the fundamental unity of all knowledge, this is a philosophical preoccupation that may be said to derive its proper inspiration from Aristotle and later advanced by the great systematic metaphysicians of modern European and German Idealist philosophy. Aristotle was as much interested in the natural sciences as he was in the human condition; therefore, his metaphysics was an attempt to lend unity to all facets that preoccupy collective humanity. The reader should realize that in philosophy there was never a cleavage between science and the humanities (including the subjects of biology, reason, logic, ethics, politics, religion, aesthetics, and psychology) until modern times, when independent disciples were forged based upon sociopolitical, cultural, and economic forces that privileged certain interests and discourses over others. The desire for a comprehensive unity of all knowledge originally belongs to the passion of *philosophos*, literally the love of wisdom.

Whether we strive for complexity in theory building among contrasting disciplines or seek a creative synergy within interdisciplinary relations, we must seriously ascribe to the assumption that social science models are far more complex than natural science models. As Valone (2005) rightfully points out,

> In the social sciences ... such great strides toward consilience have yet to be achieved, nor has there been much effort directed toward consilience. Different disciplines have different languages, different theoretical structures, different analytic methods, and different standards of validity, and often they operate with little awareness or interest in what is being done in related disciplines. (p. 190)

How true. But we should not confound the issue by assuming that all theories are equally valid or plausible (cf. Mitchell, 1993), what Valone refers to as the "postmodern metatheoretical crisis" (p. 198), which ultimately commits us to relativism. We should also not insulate ourselves from knowledge from other disciplines, especially our competitors. Rather, we should be abreast of such developments in order to learn and integrate findings from fields that may have direct bearing on our perspectives, as well as demonstrate that we are not apathetic, grandiose, or narcissistically superior to fields that perceive psychoanalysis to be indifferent to alternative points of view. This is a pragmatic sensibility we should not shirk.

Valone (2005) argues that it is "imperative" and "essential" for our discipline to strive for a grand unified theory through consilient analysis following Wilson's (1998) criteria of (a) parsimony, (b) generality, (c) consilience, and (d) predictiveness. But I am not so sure how a consilient psychoanalysis is possible when competing

discourses, agendas, desires, political structures, collective identity, discipline-specific rivalry, narcissistic group investment, and
personal ego inevitably factor in on any notion of the possibility of
consilience, let alone its probability. In fact, from the standpoint
of probability, I would grant it little hope of success. But I admit
that my pessimism should not spoil the message Valone upholds
with optimism. In fact I applaud him.

Can we incorporate accepted knowledge and facts from other
disciplines into an integrative body of psychoanalytic knowledge
when our discipline may not accept such purported knowledge or
when facts are in dispute? Of course, the answer to this, in part,
depends upon what we mean by *fact*. Given that so-called facts
are often opinions, beliefs, interpretations, inferences, constructive hypotheses, and speculative supplements—not uncontested
truth where there is no outlier of doubt—the presupposition of
the potentiality for a grand unifying theory may be rather dubious. And given that science has a perpetual habit of changing its
mind, hence the facts, can we even trust the self-imposed authority of discipline-specific knowledge without immersing ourselves
in that specific field to determine for ourselves what we think
holds water? Unless one has a passion, penchant, and economic
luxury to study, read, research, and investigate matters for themselves, this is not a very practical imperative to prescribe to our
field. Unless one is a full-time "atypical" academic, this injunctive
becomes more idealistic than realistic.

Despite the receptive openness we may potentially take toward
other disciplines of knowledge where we may exchange ideas
and conceptual schemata and redefine existing theory through a
cross-fertilization of facts and synthetic discoveries, what happens
if these dialogical liaisons clash with other theoretics and methodologies that do not lead to a synergistic integration—let alone
achieve, in Hegel's language, a sublation, whereby disparate data
are comprehensively amalgamated and simultaneously elevated in
sophistication and holistic structure? For example, to use Wilson's
categories, what happens to the law of parsimony when Occam's

razor cannot be applied because the level of theory is too complex, abstract, or abstruse and does not readily fit into an integrative conceptual scheme, let alone translate to other disciplines that have nothing to do with the former discipline? And what happens to the principle of generality when specific results, findings, perspectives, and hermeneutic minutia cannot be applied to all groups or categories under investigation? And if the answer is to persuade and instruct theorists or investigators to make their ideas and methods less abstruse so they can be generalized or universalized to all people, disciplines, and situations regardless of context or historical contingency, then does this not presuppose the superiority of parsimony versus complexity and generality versus contextualism and so hence beg the question of a discourse on method? In other words, how can you persuade a discipline to accept parsimony when it is against the simplicity argument to begin with?

Perhaps a potential solution may be found in embracing a dialectical framework that attempts to unify knowledge without itself claiming to be unified. Here Hegel (1807/1977, 1812/1831/1969, 1817a) may be instructive for a consilient psychoanalysis. As noted in an earlier chapter, Hegel's philosophy of mind or spirit (*Geist*) rests on a proper understanding of the ontology of the dialectic. Hegel refers to the unrest of *Aufhebung*—customarily translated as *sublation*—a continual dialectical process entering into opposition within its own determinations and thus raising this opposition to a higher unity, which remains at once annulled, preserved, and transmuted. Therefore, the term *aufheben* has a threefold meaning: (a) to suspend or cancel, (b) to surpass or transcend, and (c) to preserve. Hegel's designation signifies a threefold activity by which mental operations at once cancel or annul opposition, preserve or retain it, and surpass or elevate its previous shape to a higher structure. Put laconically, and in more contemporary parlance, this is the nature of the intellect engaged in the process of critical thinking.

If consilience is premised on a comprehensive integration and internalization of diverse modes of knowledge culminating in a more unified or grand synthesis, then a dialectical approach would satisfy its criterion. This is what I have attempted to offer in my process account of dialectical psychoanalysis. The movements of the dialectic retain the old as it transmogrifies the present, whereby aimed toward a future existence it actively (not predeterminately) forges along the way. This ensures that dialectical reality is always ensnared in the contingencies that inform its experiential immediacy. Despite the universality of the logic of the dialectic, each movement is always contextually realized. Yet each process, each shape of the dialectic, is merely one moment within its holistic teleology, differentiated only by form. The process as a whole constitutes the dialectic, whereby each movement highlights a particular piece of activity that is subject to its own particular idiosyncratic expressions and modal contingencies. As each valence is highlighted in its immediacy or lived-experiential quality, it is merely one appearance among many in the overall architectonic process of its own becoming. Consilience becomes an orienting principle that is universally driven yet contextually realized, whereby competing modes of discourse and sundry facts are potentially synthetically retained and elevated into a higher unity, whereas others are subsumed or eliminated yet historically preserved within a complex holism we call knowledge.

Following the European continental tradition, I believe it is important to reiterate the point that psychoanalysis is a human science and should not be simply pigeonholed as a natural (hard) science, which consequently elevates the role of subjectivity, negotiation, consensus, and relational exchange when making any observation, interpretation, or epistemological assertion. The implication of this thesis is that any form of science by definition simultaneously becomes intimately conjoined with the humanities. Yet at the same time, any true scientist would not make dogmatic metaphysical statements of irrefutable objective certainty because science (in theory) is always open to the possibility that any theoretical system or methodological framework is an evolving avenue or medium for procuring knowledge, not as fixed, irrefutable determined fact but as a process of becoming. Given that contemporary psychoanalysis is enjoying adventures of change by reappropriating philosophy and incorporating the empirical findings of infant observation research, cognitive neuroscience, evolutionary biology, psychotherapy process studies, traumatology, naturalized epistemology, affect theory, semiology, defense mechanisms research, and attachment approaches, this seems to me to be an auspicious sign for our profession.

It is incumbent upon us to abandon the scientific versus humanities binary and view psychoanalysis as both a humanistic enterprise that is devoted to delving into the depths of human experience and being scientifically sustainable. At the same time, it enjoys the wider parameters of philosophy in not being circumscribed in its questions and objects of study because it is open to posing questions that science itself cannot legitimately entertain because of its self-imposed limitations of observation, experimentation, data manipulation, and statistical categorization that dislocates itself from the concrete study of the lived qualia that define a person's subjective quality of life. No statistical number can come close to capturing the subjective quality of human experience. Although scientific methods may observe, organize, calculate, statistically analyze, and generate predicable patterns of future events, they cannot offer the humanistic understanding and compassion the phenomenal moment affords precisely because science privileges the pursuit of the universal over that of the particular. Although each perspective or domain has legitimacy in its own right, the virtue of psychoanalysis is that it transcends any dichotomy of value that is attached to either a scientific or a humanities paradigm.

Paul Stepansky (2009) recently argued that psychoanalysis has become marginalized and fragmented because it did not pursue a traditional scientific path that more successful, progressive disciplines enjoy largely because psychoanalysis has been insular and obsessed with purity and has embraced theoretical pluralism rather than unifying cumulative knowledge in a consilient fashion consistent with the structure of a mature science. Carlo Strenger (2010), on the other hand, contends that theoretical pluralism is the inevitable result—not the cause—of psychoanalysis' inability to conform to a progressive trajectory of traditional science and has naturally emerged based upon its subsequent marginalization from the mainstream scientific community. Following the hermeneutic tradition, itself a reaction against the methodological restrictions and imposition of naturalism and the requirements of testability, psychoanalysis identified with the more developmental nature of psychotherapeutic process, which relies on narrative in retelling our lives (Schafer, 1976; Spence, 1982). This trend in psychoanalysis, as Strenger points out, led Adam Phillips (1996) to conclude that psychoanalysis is more about forms of conversation than about authoritative knowledge or technique, a project we might say is closer to literary criticism than science. Because psychoanalysis was not destined to become a pure science, it had no choice other than to embrace pluralism. In fact, many contemporary authors "see the reclassification of psychoanalysis as a humanistic discipline as a liberation rather than a loss. … But the price of the hermeneutic conception of psychoanalysis is enormous: It means that psychoanalysis renounces the ambition of producing knowledge about human nature" (Strenger, 2010, pp. 380–381).

We should not make such a hasty generalization. A consilient approach should not be confined to the methodological parameters of science, for knowledge is derived from many methodologies and critical practices, not to mention the fact that psychoanalysis has always made pronouncements about the universal dimensions of human nature. What Strenger nicely points out, however, is that pluralism stems from the fact that we cannot have or expect to have a unified body of knowledge, which perhaps is a deposit from Romanticism rather than the Enlightenment. There will always be value judgments placed on the preeminence of human experience, especially when analysts prize emotion over the scientific rationalism and rationalization of nature. But we should not deceive ourselves into thinking that psychoanalysis offers no synthetic strand that potentially explains all human phenomena, for plurality attempts to do just that: It offers multiple voices and perspectives, each having a degree of validity within its own right, whether that be scientific knowledge or insights derived from the arts and humanities. It is quite conceivable that the multiplicity of perspectives may be categorized and gel into a constellation of organized difference, hence falling under a unifying framework we call knowledge, despite the fact that it is not unified—precisely because it does not claim to be conclusive. And this openness also speaks to the true spirit of science. That is why process—not changelessness—inheres in all disciplines. If knowledge were truly unified, then there would be no further knowledge.

The hermeneutic, narrative, and social constructive trend in contemporary psychoanalysis answers to the existential ponderings we all face in an era of uncertainty despite the fact that credible scientists may tell us otherwise. This truly echoes the sentimentality of psychoanalysis as a human discipline concerned with people's real needs and experiential worlds, namely, their hopes and worries, pleasures and anxieties, longings and despair, desires and suffering. Yet this endeavor takes shape within a broader context of understanding mind, culture, and the universal dimensions of human nature, which falls within the scope of science as a legitimate object of study, where discoveries are made, mysteries uncovered, and new information brought to the light of critical reflection. As long as we stay mired in the narcissism that defines group identity, we will continue to miss the point that there are fruitful connections and interrelationships to be forged by cross-fertilizations and interdisciplinary work where convergences between observation, fact, speculation, and critique become intimately united in a common quest for meaning and knowledge, what the ancients called wisdom.

It should be clear by now that psychoanalysis escapes dichotomization for it is both a science, that is, it is subject to many empirical and qualitative research approaches, and a humanities, where the scientific method, loosely defined, is supplemented by or suspended for other research methods, such as those employed by the social sciences, including phenomenological description, historiography, philology, participant observation fieldwork, interviews, surveys, comparative exegesis, logic, and critical analysis. The dialogue between the social-behavioral sciences and the humanities in particular shows the most promise for expanding and integrating knowledge within a consilient framework, and includes such disciplines as philosophy, anthropology, history, literature, religion, cultural studies, sociology, feminism, gender studies, political thought, moral psychology, art, drama, film, biography, economics, biology, and cognitive neuroscience, hence making a consilient approach broadly appealing and applicable to all facets of human experience. Even if psychoanalysis continues to wane as a form of therapeutic treatment amongst the public, there will always be informed approaches to psychotherapy that continue to engender and sustain psychoanalytic thought. And even if formal psychoanalysis dries up altogether,* Freud's legacy will continue to live on in academe, research in the humanities, and the great cultural works that inspire the intelligentsia, especially those educated in the arts, literature, philosophy, and politics. Even if psychoanalysis remains at the margins, I have no doubt that contemporary paradigms will continue to reinstitute its cultural and therapeutic value.

---

* This is not likely to be the case in many parts of Europe, such as France, or in South America, mainly Argentina, where there is a large psy-culture and where practitioners charge very little for psychoanalysis, similar to what psychoanalytic candidates in training charge patients in North America in order to meet the requirements for graduating from a psychoanalytic institute, fees being as little as $20 a session. Because of national economic discrepancies in urban centers throughout the world, some analysts charge as little as the common wage for a laborer.

References

Abend, S. M. (2003). Relational influences on modern conflict theory. *Contemporary Psychoanalysis, 39*(3), 367–377.

Altman, N. (2007). A lapse in constructive dialogue: The journal's responsibility. *Psychoanalytic Psychology, 24*(2), 395–396.

Altman, N., & Davies, J. M. (2003). A plea for constructive dialogue. *Journal of the American Psychoanalytic Association, 51*(Suppl.), 145–161.

Altman, N., & Davies, J. M. (2005). Constructive dialogue and editorial policy. *Journal of the American Psychoanalytic Association, 53,* 267.

Aragno, A. (2008). *Forms of knowledge: A psychoanalytic study of human communication.* Baltimore: Publish America.

Aron, L. (1996). *A meeting of minds: Mutuality in psychoanalysis.* Hillsdale, NJ: Analytic Press.

Aron, L. (1999). The patient's experience of the analyst's subjectivity. In S. Mitchell & L. Aron (Eds.), *Relational psychoanalysis: The emergence of a tradition* (pp. 243–268). Hillsdale, NJ: Analytic Press.

Aron, L., & Anderson, F. S. (Eds.). (1998). *Relational perspectives on the body.* Hillsdale, NJ: Analytic Press.

Bacal, H. (Ed.). (1998). *How therapists heal their patients: Optimal responsiveness.* Northvale, NJ: Jason Aronson.

Beebe, B., & Lachmann, F. (2003). The relational turn in psychoanalysis: A dyadic systems view from infant research. *Contemporary Psychoanalysis, 39*(3), 379–409.

Beebe, B., & Lachmann, F. (1998). Co-constructing inner and relational processes: Self and mutual regulation in infant research and adult treatment. *Psychoanalytic Psychology, 15,* 1–37.

Beebe, B., Jaffe, J., & Lachmann, F. (1992). A dyadic systems view of communication. In N. Skolnick & S. Warchaw (Eds.), *Relational perspectives in psychoanalysis* (pp. 61–82). Hillsdale, NJ: Analytic Press.

Benjamin, J. (1988). *The bonds of love: Psychoanalysis, feminism, and the problem of domination.* New York: Pantheon Books.

Bennett, M. R., & Hacker, P. M. S. (2003). *Philosophical foundations of neuroscience.* Oxford: Blackwell.

Bergmann, M. S. (Ed.). (2004). *Understanding dissidence and controversy in the history of psychoanalysis.* New York: Other Press.

Bjork, R. A. (2000). Independence of scientific publishing: Reaffirming the principle. *American Psychologist, 55*(9), 981–984.

Blum, H. P. (2010). Object relations in contemporary psychoanalysis. *Contemporary Psychoanalysis, 46*(1), 32–47.

Bornstein, R. F. (2001). The impending death of psychoanalysis. *Psychoanalytic Psychology, 18*(1), 3–20.

Bowman, M. (2002). *The last resistance: The concept of science as a defense against psychoanalysis.* Albany: SUNY Press.

Brice, C. W. (2000). Spontaneity versus constraint: Dilemmas in the analyst's decision making. *Journal of the American Psychoanalytic Association, 48,* 549–560.

Bromberg, P. M. (1994). "Speak! That I may see you": Some reflections on dissociation, reality, and psychoanalytic listening. *Psychoanalytic Dialogues, 4,* 517–547.

Bromberg, P. M. (1998). *Standing in the spaces: Essays on clinical process, trauma, and dissociation.* Hillsdale, NJ: Analytic Press.

Bromberg, P. M. (2009). Truth, human relatedness, and the analytic process: An interpersonal/relational perspective. *International Journal of Psychoanalysis, 90,* 347–361.

Brome, V. (1967). *Freud and his early circle.* London: Heinemann.

Cassidy, J., & Shaver, P. R. (Eds.). (1999). *Handbook of attachment: Theory, research, and clinical applications.* New York: Guilford Press.

Chessick, R. D. (2007). *The future of psychoanalysis.* Albany: SUNY Press.

Cioffi, F. (1998). *Freud and the question of pseudoscience.* Chicago: Open Court.

Cooper, A. M. (2008). American psychoanalysis today: A plurality of orthodoxies. *Journal of the American Academy of Psychoanalysis and Dynamic Psychiatry, 36*(2), 235–253.

Cooper, S. H. (1998). Analyst subjectivity, analyst disclosure, and the aims of psychoanalysis. *Psychoanalytic Quarterly, 67*, 379–406.

Curtis, R. C. (2007). On the death of Stephen Mitchell: An analysand's remembrance. In B. Willock, L. C. Bohm, & R. C. Curtis (Eds.), *On death and endings* (pp. 293–302). London: Routledge.

Davies, J. M. (1994). Love in the afternoon: A relational reconsideration of desire and dread. *Psychoanalytic Dialogues, 4*, 153–170.

Davies, J. M. (1998). Between the disclosure and foreclosure of erotic transference-countertransference: Can psychoanalysis find a place for adult sexuality? *Psychoanalytic Dialogues, 8*, 747–766.

Davies, J. M. (2007). Response to Jon Mills: An open letter to the members of Division 39. *Psychoanalytic Psychology, 24*(2), 397–400.

Davies, J. M., & Frawley, M. G. (1999). Dissociative processes and transference–countertransference paradigms in the psychoanalytically oriented treatment of adult survivors of childhood sexual abuse. In S. Mitchell & L. Aron (Eds.), *Relational psychoanalysis: The emergence of a tradition* (pp. 269–299). Hillsdale, NJ: Analytic Press.

Dennett, D. (1991). *Consciousness explained.* Boston: Little, Brown.

Derrida, J. (1974). *Of grammatology* (G. C. Spivak, Trans.). Baltimore: Johns Hopkins University Press.

Descartes, R. (1641/1984). *The philosophical writings of Descartes, Vols. I–III* (J. Cottingham, R. Stoothoff, & D. Murdoch, Trans.). Cambridge: Cambridge University Press.

Deutsch, H. (1926). Occult processes occurring during psychoanalysis. In G. Devereaux (Ed.), *Psychoanalysis and the occult.* New York: International Universities Press, 1970.

Dilthey, W. (1923). *Introduction to the human sciences* (R. J. Betanzos, Trans.). Detroit: Wayne State University Press, 1979.

Dimen, M. (1991). Deconstructing difference: Gender, splitting, and transitional space. *Psychoanalytic Dialogues, 1*(3), 335–352.

Dorpat, T. (2006). Covert methods of interpersonal control. In R. Raubolt (Ed.), *Power games: Influence, persuasion, and indoctrination in psychotherapy training* (pp. 93–118). New York: Other Press.

Eagle, M. N. (2003). The postmodern turn in psychoanalysis: A critique. *Psychoanalytic Psychology, 20*(3), 411–424.

Eagle, M. N., Wakefield, J. C., & Wolitzky, D. L. (2003). Interpreting Mitchell's constructivism: Reply to Altman and Davies. *Journal of the American Psychoanalytic Association, 51*(Suppl.), 163–178.

Eagle, M. N., Wakefield, J. C., & Wolitzky, D. L. (2005). Eagle, Wakefield, & Wolitzky respond. *Journal of the American Psychoanalytic Association, 53*, 268.

Eagle, M. N., Wolitzky, D. L., & Wakefield, J. C. (2001). The analyst's knowledge and authority: A critique of the "new view" in psychoanalysis. *Journal of the American Psychoanalytic Association, 49,* 457–488.

Eastman, T. E., & Keeton, H. (Eds.). (2004). *Physics and Whitehead.* Albany: SUNY Press.

Ehrenberg, D. (1993). *The intimate edge.* New York: Norton.

Ehrenberg, D. (1995). Self disclosure: Therapeutic tool or indulgence? Countertransference disclosure. *Contemporary Psychoanalysis, 31,* 213.

Eigen, M. (2006). *Lust.* Middletown, CT: Wesleyan University Press.

Ellis, B. (2002). *The philosophy of nature: A guide to the new essentialism.* Montreal: McGill-Queen's University Press.

Ferenczi, S., & Groddeck, G. (1982). *Briefwechsel 1921–1933* (Pierre Sabourin et al., Eds.). Frankfurt: Fischer, 1986.

Feyman, R. P. (1995). *Six easy pieces.* Reading, MA: Addison-Wesley.

Fichte, J. G. (1794). *The science of knowledge* (P. Heath & J. Lachs, Eds. & Trans.). Cambridge: Cambridge University Press, 1993.

Fisher, D. J. (2008). *Bettelheim: Living and dying.* Amsterdam/New York: Rodopi.

Fisher, S., & Greenberg, R. P. (1977). *The scientific credibility of Freud's theories and therapy.* New York: Basic Books.

Fliess, R. (1942). The metapsychology of the analyst. *Psychoanalytic Quarterly, 11,* 211–227.

Fonagy, P. (2000). Attachment and borderline personality disorder. *Journal of the American Psychoanalytic Association, 48*(4), 1129–1146.

Fonagy, P. (2001). *Attachment theory and psychoanalysis.* New York: Other Press.

Fonagy, P., Gergely, G., Jurist, E. L., & Target, M. (2002). *Affect regulation, mentalization, and the development of the self.* New York: Other Press.

Fosshage, J. L. (2003). Contextualizing self psychology and relational psychoanalysis: Bi-directional influence and proposed syntheses. *Contemporary Psychoanalysis, 39*(3), 411–448.

Foucault, M. (1990). Nietzsche, Freud, Marx. In G. L. Ormiston & A. D. Schrift (Eds.), *Transforming the hermeneutic context: From Nietzsche to Nancy* (pp. 59–67). Albany: SUNY Press.

Frank, G. (1998a). On the relational school of psychoanalysis: Some additional thoughts. *Psychoanalytic Psychology, 15*(1), 141–153.

Frank, G. (1998b). The intersubjective school of psychoanalysis: Concerns and questions. *Psychoanalytic Psychology, 15*(3), 420–423.

Frank, G. (2003). Triebe and their vicissitudes: Freud's theory of motivation reconsidered. *Psychoanalytic Psychology*, *20*(4), 691–697.

Frederickson, J. (1990). Hate in the countertransference as an empathic position. *Contemporary Psychoanalysis*, *26*, 479–495.

Frederickson, J. (2005). The problem of relationality. In J. Mills (Ed.), *Relational and intersubjective perspectives in psychoanalysis: A critique*. Northvale, NJ: Jason Aronson.

Freud, S. (1894). The neuro-psychoses of defence. In J. Strachey (Ed. & Trans.), *The standard edition of the complete psychological works of Sigmund Freud* (Vol. 3, pp. 43–61). London: Hogarth Press.

Freud, S. (1895). *Project for a scientific psychology*. In J. Strachey (Ed. & Trans.), *The standard edition of the complete psychological works of Sigmund Freud* (Vol. 1). London: Hogarth Press.

Freud, S. (1900). *The interpretation of dreams*. In J. Strachey (Ed. & Trans.), *The standard edition of the complete psychological works of Sigmund Freud* (Vols. 4–5). London: Hogarth Press.

Freud, S. (1912a). The dynamics of transference. In J. Strachey (Ed. & Trans.), *The standard edition of the complete psychological works of Sigmund Freud* (Vol. 12, pp. 97–108). London: Hogarth Press.

Freud, S. (1912b). Recommendations to physicians practising psychoanalysis. In J. Strachey (Ed. & Trans.), *The standard edition of the complete psychological works of Sigmund Freud* (Vol. 12, pp. 109–120). London: Hogarth Press.

Freud, S. (1913). On the beginning of treatment. In J. Strachey (Ed. & Trans.), *The standard edition of the complete psychological works of Sigmund Freud* (Vol. 12, pp. 121–144). London: Hogarth Press.

Freud, S. (1915a). Instincts and their vicissitudes. In J. Strachey (Ed. & Trans.), *The standard edition of the complete psychological works of Sigmund Freud* (Vol. 14, pp. 111–140). London: Hogarth Press.

Freud, S. (1915b). The unconscious. In J. Strachey (Ed. & Trans.), *The standard edition of the complete psychological works of Sigmund Freud* (Vol. 14, pp. 161–215). London: Hogarth Press.

Freud, S. (1916–1917). *Introductory lectures on psycho-analysis*. In J. Strachey (Ed. & Trans.), *The standard edition of the complete psychological works of Sigmund Freud* (Vols. 15–16). London: Hogarth Press.

Freud, S. (1921). *Group psychology and the analysis of the ego*. In J. Strachey (Ed. & Trans.), *The standard edition of the complete psychological works of Sigmund Freud* (Vol. 18, pp. 65–144). London: Hogarth Press.

Freud, S. (1923). *The ego and the id.* In J. Strachey (Ed. & Trans.), *The standard edition of the complete psychological works of Sigmund Freud* (Vol. 19, pp. 1–68). London: Hogarth Press.

Freud, S. (1925). *An autobiographical study.* In J. Strachey (Ed. & Trans.), *The standard edition of the complete psychological works of Sigmund Freud* (Vol. 20, pp. 1–76). London: Hogarth Press.

Freud, S. (1926a). *Inhibitions, symptoms and anxiety.* In J. Strachey (Ed. & Trans.), *The standard edition of the complete psychological works of Sigmund Freud* (Vol. 20, pp. 77–178). London: Hogarth Press.

Freud, S. (1926b). *The question of lay analysis.* In J. Strachey (Ed. & Trans.), *The standard edition of the complete psychological works of Sigmund Freud* (Vol. 20, pp. 179–258). London: Hogarth Press.

Freud, S. (1927). *Future of an illusion.* In J. Strachey (Ed. & Trans.), *The standard edition of the complete psychological works of Sigmund Freud* (Vol. 21, pp. 1–58). London: Hogarth Press.

Freud, S. (1930). *Civilization and its discontents.* In J. Strachey (Ed. & Trans.), *The standard edition of the complete psychological works of Sigmund Freud* (Vol. 21, pp. 59–148). London: Hogarth Press.

Freud, S. (1931). Female sexuality. In J. Strachey (Ed. & Trans.), *The standard edition of the complete psychological works of Sigmund Freud* (Vol. 21, pp. 225–243). London: Hogarth Press.

Freud, S. (1932–1933). *New introductory lectures on psycho-analysis.* In J. Strachey (Ed. & Trans.), *The standard edition of the complete psychological works of Sigmund Freud* (Vol. 22, pp. 1–184). London: Hogarth Press.

Freud, S. (1940). *An outline of psycho-analysis.* In J. Strachey (Ed. & Trans.), *The standard edition of the complete psychological works of Sigmund Freud* (Vol. 23, pp. 144–207). London: Hogarth Press.

Frie, R. (1997). *Subjectivity and intersubjectivity in modern philosophy and psychoanalysis: A study of Sartre, Binswanger, Lacan, and Habermas.* Lanham, MD: Rowman & Littlefield.

Frie, R. (Ed.). (2003). *Understanding experience: Psychotherapy and postmodernism.* London: Brunner-Routledge.

Frie, R. (2007). Letter to the Editor. *Psychologist-Psychoanalyst,* vol. 27(no. 3 summer), p. 5.

Friedman, H. J. (2010). Preserving the gap between Freudian and relational psychoanalysis. *Contemporary Psychoanalysis, 46*(1), 142–151.

Furer, M. (1967). Some developmental aspects of the superego. *International Journal of Psychoanalysis, 48,* 277–280.

Gadamer, H.-G. (1960). *Truth and method* (2nd ed.). New York: Crossroad, 1989.

Gargiulo, G. J. (2004). *Psyche, self and soul.* London: Whurr.

Gargiulo, G. J. (2006). Ontology and metaphor: Reflections on the unconscious and the "I" in the therapeutic setting. *Psychoanalytic Psychology, 23*(3), 461–474.

Gargiulo, G. J. (2010). Mind, meaning, and quantum physics: Models for understanding the dynamic unconscious. *Psychoanalytic Review, 97*(1), 91–106.

Gay, P. (1988). *Freud: A life for our time.* New York: Norton.

Gerson, S. (1996). Neutrality, resistance, and self-disclosure in an inter-subjective psychoanalysis. *Psychoanalytic Dialogues, 6,* 623–645.

Giovacchini, P. (1999). *Impact of narcissism: The errant therapist on a chaotic quest.* Northvale, NJ: Jason Aronson.

Giovacchini, P. (2005). Subjectivity and the ephemeral mind. In J. Mills (Ed.), *Relational and intersubjective perspectives in psychoanalysis: A critique.* Northvale, NJ: Jason Aronson.

Glover, E. (1933). Review of Klein's *The psychoanalysis of children. International Journal of Psychoanalysis, 14,* 119.

Greenberg, J. (1991). *Oedipus and beyond: A clinical theory.* Cambridge, MA: Harvard University Press.

Greenberg, J. (2001). The analyst's participation: A new look. *Journal of the American Psychoanalytic Association, 49*(2), 359–381.

Greenberg, J. (2011, April). *Roundtable discussion: The future of psychoanalytic publishing.* Paper presented at the 31st Annual Spring Meeting of the Division of Psychoanalysis (39) of the American Psychological Association, New York.

Greenberg, J., & Mitchell, S. (1983). *Object relations in psychoanalytic theory.* Cambridge, MA: Harvard University Press.

Grosskurth, P. (1986). *Melanie Klein: Her world and her work.* Cambridge, MA: Harvard University Press.

Grosskurth, P. (1991). *The secret ring.* Toronto: MacFarlane, Walter, & Ross.

Grünbaum, A. (1984). *The foundations of psychoanalysis.* Berkeley: University of California Press.

Grünbaum, A. (2006). Is Sigmund Freud's psychoanalytic edifice relevant to the 21st century? *Psychoanalytic Psychology, 23*(2), 257–284.

Grunbaum, A. (2004). The hermeneutic versus the scientific conception of psychoanalysis. In J. Mills (Ed), *Psychoanalysis at the limit: Epistemology, mind, and the question of science.* Albany: SUNY Press, pp. 139–160.

Haddad, G. (1981, September 20). Une pratique [A practice]. *L'Ane, 3.*

Harris, A. (1996). The conceptual power of multiplicity. *Contemporary Psychoanalysis, 32,* 537–552.

Hartman, S. (2005). Book review of Roger Frie's *Understanding experience: Psychotherapy and postmodernism*. *Contemporary Psychoanalysis, 41*(3), 535–544.

Hegel, G. F. W. (1807). *Phenomenology of spirit* (A. V. Miller, Trans.). Oxford: Oxford University Press, 1977.

Hegel, G. F. W. (1812). *Science of logic* (A. V. Miller, Trans.). London: George Allen & Unwin, 1831/1969.

Hegel, G. F. W. (1817a). *The encyclopaedia logic* (T. F. Geraets, W. A. Suchting, & H. S. Harris, Trans.). Indianapolis: Hackett, 1991.

Hegel, G. F. W. (1817b). *Philosophy of mind* (W. Wallace & A. V. Miller, Trans.). Oxford: Clarendon Press, 1827/1830/1971.

Heidegger, M. (1927). *Being and time* (J. Macquarrie & E. Robinson, Trans.). San Francisco: Harper Collins, 1962.

Hesse, E., & Main, M. (2000). Disorganized infant, child, and adult attachment: Collapse in behavioral and attentional strategies. *Journal of the American Psychoanalytic Association, 48*(4), 1097–1127.

Hirsch, I. (2008). *Coasting in the countertransference: Conflicts of self-interest between analyst and patient*. New York: Analytic Press.

Hoffman, I. Z. (1994). Dialectical thinking and therapeutic action in the psychoanalytic process. *Psychoanalytic Quarterly, 63*, 187–218.

Hoffman, I. Z. (1998). *Ritual and spontaneity in the psychoanalytic process: A dialectical-constructivist view*. Hillsdale, NJ: Analytic Press.

Hoffman, I. Z. (2007). Reply to Jon Mills (2006): An open letter to the members of Division 39. *Psychoanalytic Psychology, 24*(2), 401–405.

Howell, E. F. (2005). *The dissociative mind*. Hillsdale, NJ: Analytic Press.

Hughes, J. (1989). *Reshaping the psychoanalytic domain*. Berkeley: University of California Press.

Husserl, E. (1950). *Cartesian meditations: An introduction to phenomenology* (D. Cairns, Trans.). Dordrecht: Kluwer.

Iannuzzi, V. P. (2006). *Is the unconscious necessary?* Retrieved from www.sectionfive.org.

Jacobs, M. S. (2006). Assertions of therapeutic excess: A reply to Mills (2005). *Psychoanalytic Psychology, 23*(1), 189–192.

James, W. (1890). *The principles of psychology*. New York: Dover, 1890/1950.

James, W. (1902). *The varieties of religious experience*. New York: Modern Library.

Jones, E. (1955). *The life and work of Sigmund Freud* (Vol. 2). New York: Basic Books.

Jones, E. (1957). *The life and work of Sigmund Freud* (Vol. 3). New York: Basic Books.

Josephs, L. (2001). The relational values of scientific practice: A response to commentaries by Silverman (2000) and Mitchell (2000). *Psychoanalytic Psychology, 18*(1), 157–160.

Jung, C. G. (1961/1963). *Memories, dreams, reflections.* New York: Vintage.

Kant, I. (1781). *Critique of pure reason* (N. K. Smith, Trans.). New York: St. Martin's Press, 1965.

King, P., & Steiner, R. (Eds.). (1991). *The Freud-Klein controversies.* London: Routledge.

Klein, M. (1961). *Narrative of a child analysis.* London: Hogarth Press/ Delacorte Press.

Klein, M., Heimann, P., & Money-Kyrle, R.E. (Eds.). (1957). *New directions in psychoanalysis.* New York: Basic Books.

Kristeva, J. (1990). Psychoanalysis and the polis. In G. L. Ormiston & A. D. Schrift (Eds.), *Transforming the hermeneutic context: From Nietzsche to Nancy.* Albany: SUNY Press.

Kristeva, J. (2001). *Melanie Klein.* New York: Columbia University Press.

Lacan, J. (1964). Excommunication. In *The four fundamental concepts of psycho-analysis* (A. Sheridan, Trans). New York: Norton, 1978.

Lacan, J. (1973). *Le seminaire, Vol. XI.* Paris: Seuil.

Lacan, J. (1977). *Écrits: A selection* (A. Sheridan, Trans). New York: Norton.

Lear, J. (1990). *Love and its place in nature: A philosophical interpretation of Freudian psychoanalysis.* New York: Noonday Press.

Levenson, E. A. (2010). The schism between "drive" and "relational" analysis: A brief historical overview. *Contemporary Psychoanalysis, 46*(1), 7–9.

Levy, D. (1996). *Freud among the philosophers.* New Haven, CT: Yale University Press.

Lichtenberg, J. D., Lachmann, F. M., & Fosshage, J. (2002). *A spirit of inquiry: Communication in psychoanalysis.* Hillsdale, NJ: Analytic Press.

Loewald, H. (1970). Psychoanalytic theory and the psychoanalytic process. In *Papers on psychoanalysis* (pp. 277–301). New Haven, CT: Yale University Press, 1980.

Lohser, B., & Newton, P. (1996). *Unorthodox Freud: A view from the couch.* New York: Guilford Press.

Lothane, Z. (2003). What did Freud say about persons and relations? *Psychoanalytic Psychology, 20*(4), 609–617.

MacIntyre, A. (1958). *The unconscious: A conceptual study.* London: Routledge.

Main, M. (2000). The organized categories of infant, child, and adult attachment: Flexible vs. inflexible attention under attachment-related stress. *Journal of the American Psychoanalytic Association*, *48*(4), 1055–1096.

Masling, J. (2003). Stephen A. Mitchell, relational psychoanalysis, and empirical data. *Psychoanalytic Psychology*, *20*(4), 587–608.

McGuire, W. (Ed.). (1974). *The Freud/Jung letters: The correspondence between Sigmund Freud and C. G. Jung* (R. Manheim & R. F. C. Hull, Trans.). Princeton, NJ: Princeton University Press.

Meisel, P., & Kendrick, W. (Eds.). (1985). *Bloomsbury/Freud: The letters of James and Alix Strachey, 1924–1925*. New York: Basic Books.

Meissner, W. W. (1998). Review of *Influence and autonomy in psychoanalysis. Psychoanalytic Books*, *9*, 419–423.

Miles, T. R. (1966). *Eliminating the unconscious*. Oxford: Pergamon Press.

Mill, J. S. (1859). *On liberty*. London: Penguin.

Mills, J. (1996). Hegel on the unconscious abyss: Implications for psychoanalysis. *The Owl of Minerva*, *28*(1), 59–75.

Mills, J. (2000a). Dialectical psychoanalysis: Toward process psychology. *Psychoanalysis and Contemporary Thought*, *23*(3), 20–54.

Mills, J. (2000b). Hegel on projective identification: Implications for Klein, Bion, and beyond. *Psychoanalytic Review*, *87*(6), 841–874.

Mills, J. (2002a). Deciphering the "genesis problem": On the dialectical origins of psychic reality. *Psychoanalytic Review*, *89*(6), 763–809.

Mills, J. (2002b). *The unconscious abyss: Hegel's anticipation of psychoanalysis*. Albany: SUNY Press.

Mills, J. (2002c). Whitehead idealized: A naturalized process metaphysics. *Process Studies*, *31*(1), 32–48.

Mills, J. (2003a). Lacan on paranoiac knowledge. *Psychoanalytic Psychology*, *20*(1), 30–51.

Mills, J. (2003b). Whitehead's unconscious ontology. *Theory and Psychology*, *13*(2), 209–238.

Mills, J. (2005a). A critique of relational psychoanalysis. *Psychoanalytic Psychology*, *22*(2), 155–188.

Mills, J. (Ed.). (2005b). *Relational and intersubjective perspectives in psychoanalysis: A critique*. Lanham, MD: Jason Aronson/Rowman & Littlefield.

Mills, J. (2005c). *Treating attachment pathology*. Northvale, NJ: Jason Aronson.

Mills, J. (2006). A response to my critics. *Psychoanalytic Psychology*, *23*(1), 197–209.

Mills, J. (2010). *Origins: On the genesis of psychic reality*. Montreal: McGill-Queens University Press.

Mills, J., & Polanowski, J. (1997). *The ontology of prejudice.* Amsterdam/ New York: Rodopi.

Mitchell, S. A. (1986). Roots and status. *Contemporary Psychoanalysis, 22,* 458–466.

Mitchell, S. A. (1988). *Relational concepts in psychoanalysis: An integration.* Cambridge, MA: Harvard University Press.

Mitchell, S. A. (1992). True selves, false selves, and the ambiguity of authenticity. In N. J. Skolnick & S. C. Warshaw (Eds.), *Relational perspectives in psychoanalysis* (pp. 1–20). Hillsdale, NJ: Analytic Press.

Mitchell, S. A. (1993). *Hope and dread in psychoanalysis.* New York: Basic Books.

Mitchell, S. A. (2000). *Relationality: From attachment to intersubjectivity.* Hillsdale, NJ: Analytic Press.

Mitchell, S. A., & Aron, L. (Eds.). (1999). *Relational psychoanalysis: The emergence of a tradition.* Hillsdale, NJ: Analytic Press.

Modell, A. H. (1991). The therapeutic relationship as a paradoxical experience. *Psychoanalytic Dialogues, 1,* 13–28.

Naso, R. C. (2007). In the "I"s of the beholder: Dissociation and multiplicity in contemporary psychoanalytic thought. *Psychoanalytic Psychology, 24*(1), 97–112.

Naso, R. C. (2010). *Hypocrisy unmasked: Dissociation, shame, and the ethics of inauthenticity.* Lanham, MD: Jason Aronson.

Nersessian, E. (2010). Is there value in "minding the gap"? *Contemporary Psychoanalysis, 46*(1), 10–18.

Nissim-Sabat, M. (2009). *Neither victim nor survivor: Thinking toward a new humanity.* Lanham, MD: Lexington Books/Rowman & Littlefield.

Ogden, T. H. (1986). *The matrix of the mind.* Northvale, NJ: Jason Aronson.

Ogden, T. H. (1994). The analytic third: Working with intersubjective clinical facts. *International Journal of Psychoanalysis, 75,* 3–19.

Ogden, T. H. (1995). Analyzing forms of aliveness and deadness of the transference-countertransference. *International Journal of Psychoanalysis, 76,* 695–709.

Orange, D. M. (1995). *Emotional understanding.* New York: Guilford Press.

Orange, D. M., Atwood, G., & Stolorow, R. D. (1997). *Working intersubjectively: Contextualism in psychoanalytic practice.* Hillsdale, NJ: Analytic Press.

Ormiston, G. L., & Schrift, A. D. (Eds.). (1990). *The hermeneutic tradition: From Ast to Ricoeur.* Albany: SUNY Press.

Phillips, A. (1996). *Terrors and experts.* London: Faber.

Pizer, B. (2003, April). *Risk and potential in analytic disclosure: Can the analyst make "the wrong thing" right?* Paper presented at the 23rd Annual Spring Meeting of the Division of Psychoanalysis (39) of the American Psychological Association, Minneapolis, MN.

Pizer, S. (2006). "Neither fish nor flesh": Commentary on Jon Mills (2005). *Psychoanalytic Psychology, 23*(1), 193–196.

Plato. (1961). *Cratylus.* In *The collected dialogues of Plato* (E. Hamilton & H. Cairns, Eds.). Princeton, NJ: Princeton University Press.

Popper, K. (1972). *Conjectures and refutation.* London: Routledge.

Rangell, L. (1980). *The mind of Watergate.* New York: Norton.

Rangell, L. (1982). Transference to theory: The relationship of psychoanalytic education to the analyst's relationship to psychoanalysis. *Annals of Psychoanalysis, 10,* 29–56.

Rangell, L. (2004). *My life in theory.* New York: Other Press.

Rangell, L. (2007). *The road to unity in psychoanalytic theory.* Lanham, MD: Jason Aronson.

Raubolt, R. (2006). *Power games: Influence, persuasion, and indoctrination in psychotherapy training.* New York: Other Press.

Reeder, J. (2004). *Hate and love in psychoanalytical institutions: The dilemma of a profession.* New York: Other Press.

Regulated Health Professions Act, Ministry of Ontario, Section 4 (Subsection 3), Sexual Abuse of a Patient (1991). (Last amended 2009)

Reisner, S. (1992). Eros reclaimed: Recovering Freud's relational theory. In N. J. Skolnick & S. C. Warshaw (Eds.), *Relational perspectives in psychoanalysis* (pp. 281–312). Hillsdale, NJ: Analytic Press.

Renik, O. (1993). Analytic interaction: Conceptualizing technique in light of the analyst's irreducible subjectivity. *Psychoanalytic Quarterly, 62,* 553–571.

Reppen, J. (2007). Editor's note. *Psychoanalytic Psychology, 24*(2), 406.

Richards, A. D. (1999a). Book review of *Ritual and spontaneity in the psychoanalytic process: A dialectical-constructivist view. Psychoanalytic Psychology, 16*(2), 288–302.

Richards, A. D. (1999b). Squeaky chairs and straw persons: An intervention in the contemporary psychoanalytic debate. *The Round Robin, 14*(1), 6–9.

Ricoeur, P. (1970). *Freud and philosophy.* New Haven, CT: Yale University Press.

Roazen, P. (1995). *How Freud worked.* Northvale, NJ: Jason Aronson.

Roustang, F. (1990). *The Lacanian delusion.* New York: Oxford University Press.

Rudnytsky, P. L. (2002). *Reading psychoanalysis.* Ithaca, NY: Cornell University Press.

Safran, J. D. (2003). The relational turn, the therapeutic alliance, and psychotherapy research. *Contemporary Psychoanalysis, 39*(3), 449–475.

Sartre, J. P. (1943/1956). *Being and nothingness* (H. Barnes, Trans.). New York: Washington Square Press.

Sartre, J. P. (1957). *The transcendence of the ego* (F. Williams & R. Kirkpatrick, Trans.). New York: Noonday Press.

Schafer, R. (1976). *A new language for psychoanalysis.* New Haven, CT: Yale University Press.

Schelling, F. W. J. (1800). *System of transcendental idealism* (P. Heath, Trans.). Charlottesville: University Press of Virginia, 1978.

Searle, J. (1992). *The rediscovery of mind.* Cambridge, MA: MIT Press.

Seligman, S. (2003). The developmental perspective in relational psychoanalysis. *Contemporary Psychoanalysis, 39*(3), 477–508.

Shaw, D. (2006). Narcissistic authoritarianism in psychoanalysis. In R. Raubolt (Ed.), *Power games: Influence, persuasion, and indoctrination in psychotherapy training* (pp. 65–82). New York: Other Press.

Silverman, D. K. (2000). An interrogation of the relational turn: A discussion with Stephen Mitchell. *Psychoanalytic Psychology, 17*(1), 146–152.

Sokal, A. D. (1996a). Transgressing the boundaries: An afterword. *Dissent, 43*(4), 93–99.

Sokal, A. D. (1996b). Transgressing the boundaries: An afterword. *Philosophy and Literature, 20*(2), 338–346.

Sokal, A. D. (1996c). Transgressing the boundaries: Towards a transformative hermeneutics of quantum gravity. *Social Text, 46/47,* 217–252.

Solomon, J., & George, C. (Eds.). (1999). *Attachment disorganization.* New York: Guilford Press.

Sound Images, Inc. (2005, April 13–17). *Being and becoming: 25th Annual Spring Meeting of the Division of Psychoanalysis (39) of the American Psychological Association, New York* [Tape No. D3905-CDROM]. www.soundimages.net.

Spence, D. (1982). *Narrative truth and historical truth.* New York: Norton.

Spezzano, C. (1997). The emergence of an American middle school of psychoanalysis. *Psychoanalytic Dialogues, 7,* 603–618.

Stepansky, P. E. (2009). *Psychoanalysis at the margins.* New York: Other Press.

Stern, D. B. (1997). *Unformulated experience: From dissociation to imagination in psychoanalysis.* Hillsdale, NJ: Analytic Press.

Stern, D. B. (2010). Unconscious fantasy versus unconscious relatedness. *Contemporary Psychoanalysis, 46*(1), 101–111.

Stern, D. N. (1985). *The interpersonal world of the infant.* New York: Basic Books.

Stolorow, R. D. (1998). Clarifying the intersubjective perspective: A reply to George Frank. *Psychoanalytic Psychology, 15*(3), 424–427.

Stolorow, R. D. (2001a). Foreword. In P. Buirski & P. Haglund, *Making sense together: The intersubjective approach to psychotherapy.* Northvale, NJ: Jason Aronson.

Stolorow, R. D. (2001b). World horizons: A post-Cartesian alternative to the Freudian unconscious. *Contemporary Psychoanalysis, 37,* 43–61.

Stolorow, R. D. (2004a). Phenomenology, hermeneutics, and contextualism: Summer reading notes. *Psychologist-Psychoanalyst, 23*(4), 28–29.

Stolorow, R. D. (2004b). The relevance of early Lacan for psychoanalytic phenomenology and contextualism: Preliminary communication. *Psychoanalytic Psychology, 21*(4), 668–672.

Stolorow, R. D. (2007). *Trauma and human existence: Autobiographical, psychoanalytic, and philosophical reflections.* New York: Analytic Press.

Stolorow, R. D. (2010). A phenomenological-contextual psychoanalyst: Intersubjective-systems theory and clinical practice. Interviewed by A. Sassenfeld. *Psychologist-Psychoanalyst, 30*(3), 6–10.

Stolorow, R. D. (2011). *World, affectivity, trauma: Heidegger and post-Cartesian psychoanalysis.* New York: Routledge.

Stolorow, R. D., & Atwood, G. (1992). *Contexts of being: The intersubjective foundations of psychological life.* Hillsdale, NJ: Analytic Press.

Stolorow, R. D., Atwood, G., & Orange, D. M. (2002). *Worlds of experience.* New York: Basic Books.

Stolorow, Atwood, & Orange (2006). Contextualizing is not nullifying: Reply to Mills (2005). *Psychoanalytic Psychology, 23*(1), 184–188.

Stolorow, R. D., Brandchaft, B., & Atwood, G. (1987). *Psychoanalytic treatment: An intersubjective approach.* Hillsdale, NJ: Analytic Press.

Strenger, C. (2010). Review of psychoanalysis at the margins. *Psychoanalytic Psychology, 27*(3), 376–388.

Sulloway, F. (1979). *Freud: Biologist of the mind.* London: HarperCollins.

Summers, F. (2004). The epistemological basis for psychoanalytic knowledge: A third way. In J. Reppen, J. Tucker, & M. A. Schulman (Eds.), *Way beyond Freud: Postmodern psychoanalysis observed* (pp. 113–131). London: Open Gate.

Summers, F. (2008). Theoretical insularity and the crisis of psychoanalysis. *Psychoanalytic Psychology, 25*(3), 413–424.

Teicholz, J. (1999). *Kohut, Loewald, and the postmoderns*. Hillsdale, NJ: Analytic Press.

Thompson, M. G. (2004). *The ethic of honesty: The fundamental rule of psychoanalysis*. Amsterdam/New York: Rodopi.

Valone, K. (2005). Consilient psychoanalysis. *Psychoanalytic Psychology*, *22*(2), 189–206.

Verhaeghe, P. (2004). *On being normal and other disorders*. New York: Other Press.

Webster, R. (1995). *Why Freud was wrong: Sin, science, and psychoanalysis*. New York: Basic Books.

Whitehead, A. N. (1925). *Science and the modern world*. New York: Free Press.

Whitehead, A. N. (1929). *Process and reality* (D. R. Griffin & D. W. Sherburne, Eds.). New York: Free Press, 1978.

Wilber, W. (2003, April). *Hope, play and emergent unconscious experience*. Paper presented at the 23rd Annual Spring Meeting of the Division of Psychoanalysis (39) of the American Psychological Association, Minneapolis, MN.

Willock, B. (2007). *Comparative-integrative psychoanalysis: A relational perspective for the discipline's second century*. New York: Analytic Press.

Wilson, E. O. (1998). *Consilience: The unity of knowledge*. New York: Knopf.

Wisdom, J. (1969). *Philosophy and psychoanalysis*. Berkeley: University of California Press.

Wittels, F. (1924). *Sigmund Freud*. London: George Allen & Unwin.

Wittgenstein, L. (1958). *The blue and brown books*. Oxford: Blackwell.

Wittgenstein, L. (1966). Conversations on Freud. In C. Barrett (Ed.), *Lectures and conversations on aesthetics, psychology and religious belief*. Berkeley: University of California Press.

Wollheim, R. (1971/1990). *Sigmund Freud*. Cambridge: Cambridge University Press.

Young-Bruehl, E. (1996). *The anatomy of prejudices*. Cambridge, MA: Harvard University Press.

Index